BLACK
FLIGHT

BREAKING BARRIERS TO BLACKS IN AVIATION

Roger Albert Forsyth, M.D.

First Edition

AllCourt Publishing·Los Angeles, California

BLACK FLIGHT
BREAKING BARRIERS TO BLACKS IN AVIATION
By Roger A. Forsyth, M.D.

Published by:
AllCourt Publishing
P.O. Box 491122
Los Angeles CA 90049
Website www.blackflight.org
Email: allcourtpublishing@yahoo.com

ISBN, print ed.   0-9715414-1-8
First Printing 2002
Printed in the United States of America

Publisher's Cataloging-in-Publication

Forsyth, Roger A.
    Black flight : breaking barriers to blacks in
aviation / Roger Albert Forsyth. -- 1st ed.
    p. cm.
    LCCN 2001127022
    ISBN 0-9715414-1-8

    1. Forsythe, Albert. 2. African American air pilots
--Biography. 3. African American physicians—Biography.
4. African Americans in aeronautics—History. 5. United
States—Race relations. 6. Caribbean Area--Race
Relations.   I. Title.

TL540.F67F67 2002   629.13092
                             QBI01-201475

CONTENTS

About the Author
Foreword
Acknowledgments

About the Author

Roger Forsyth is the nephew of Albert Forsythe, the subject of this book. Like his uncle, he spent his early life in Jamaica, left before adulthood, lived in the Midwest, became a physician, and spent about a year in Jamaica as a young adult. Additional understanding of his uncle's life experiences was provided by retracing part of the route of Albert's pioneering Goodwill flight and being involved in the 1999 re-creation of his coast-to-coast and return flight. These exposures provided him with further insight into one of the themes of this biography—that the factors to which we are exposed interact to determine the path that we take and the goals that we accomplish.

Roger has written on diverse subjects such as travel, finance, and health care administration, has published medical research, and has co-authored three editions of a book for family practitioners. In addition to his office practice, he has spent 18 years as a medical administrator and is a clinical professor of family practice.

FOREWORD

In the 1930's, blatant racial discrimination against blacks by government and by individuals, both in the North and in the South, was rampant. Albert Forsythe, a physician brought up in the West Indies where discrimination was less severe, born into a middle class family that was accustomed to respect, a student of Booker T. Washington who advocated racial advancement through example rather than confrontation, and sobered by the rigors of the menial jobs that he had to take because of discrimination, was drawn by these life experiences to undertake a series of dangerous airplane flights in order to demonstrate to the country that blacks were fully capable of participating in the upcoming age of aviation.

Blacks had flown previously, but none had exhibited the vision, the planning, and the selfless approach that he employed. Albert fostered black pride by getting the community involved. He underwrote the major expense--the planes that were used in the flights--and overcame gales, an electrical storm, heat, hail, fog, tropical storms, mechanical failure, primitive landing sites, and emergency landings to dispel the myth of black inferiority. During this time he met Charles Lindberg, the Cuban dictator Batista, the Jamaican Marcus Garvey, and the Dominican dictator Trujillo. He was aided by President Roosevelt, and was feted by many mayors and governors in the United States and abroad.

Black Flight is more than a biography--it is a reminder of the destructive forces of discrimination and prejudice that existed 80 years ago and are still at work. It is as an analysis of the role of the factors such as family background, cultural heritage, social standing, educational experience, and social milieu that combine to make each one of us the person that we are.

ACKNOWLEDGEMENTS

Albert. Forsythe's widow, Frances Forsythe, provided invaluable personal information, photographs, and newspaper
articles. Additional family members who contributed were
his sister-in-law Ruth Forsyth, his nieces June Forsyth, Mary
Ann Forbes, and Toni Forsyth, and his nephews, Owen and
George Munro. The majority of information came from the
writings and statements of Dr. Forsythe and contemporary
documents or newspaper articles. The conversations of the
individuals depicted are representations based on the data
gathered but the excerpts of speeches or letters are actual
quotations and not dialogue.

I

THE FAMILY TREE

Fear was not a stranger. Although familiar, it never failed to provoke an uncomfortable response with an arrival that was irregularly periodical, yet always unexpected and unwanted. It's presence evoked memories of a disreputable second cousin who traveled with an aura of potential misfortune in constant attendance—a misfortune that was all too likely to involve those nearby.

His fear, on this occasion, was not the fear of a man who seriously believes that his life is at risk. He had experienced that type of fear two days ago in the storm. Nor was it the fear that causes a young child to cower under the covers on a night when all of the house lights have been extinguished, the moon is dark, everyone else is asleep, and strange noises conjure up images of monsters who are feared because they and what they might do, are unknown.

True, there was some physical risk at this time, some element of the unknown, but more than anything, at this moment, he experienced the fear that comes from the knowledge that failure is not simply an unlikely alternative but is, in fact, a tangible possibility. However, while fear can paralyze you and can even kill you if you succumb to it, fear can also stimulate achievement in those who understand it, channel it, and surmount it.

All aviators can master fear because they possess a sense of invincibility. Without such a conviction, they could not be aviators. They have an inherent love of flying, an appreciation for the thrill of overcoming gravity, achieving the freedom of the birds, seeing the world from above, traversing in minutes the miles that had taken days on horseback. However, unusually hazardous flights such as their current one were not undertaken simply because of a love of flying or a feeling of invincibility, but because of other factors.

For some, the factor was financial. For example, cash prizes had been offered for 'firsts' such as the first flight across the Atlantic. Other financial rewards followed in the form of enhanced individual job opportunities. Then there was the glory, the frosting on the financial cake. Individual praise was heaped on anyone who accomplished a significant first. However these two aviators had not undertaken a hazardous flight in an under equipped plane for any of those reasons. They had done so for a cause, a cause that would not receive any tangible financial prize, a cause that would receive much of the publicity that was normally accorded to the participants.

As fear made its arrival known, he felt the cadence of his heart accelerate until he was unaccustomedly aware of its presence in his chest. The palms of his hands moistened ever so slightly causing his grip on the plane's controls to be less secure. Accelerated by the desert heat, beads of moisture formed on his forehead and threatened to join into rivulets that could obscure his vision. Conversely, his mouth became parched and swallowing was difficult. An instantaneous message was relayed to his internal glands causing adrenalin to discharge into the circulation and then diffuse into every muscle as his body prepared for a heightened response to a perceived emergency. The old adage was true; flying is hours of boredom interspersed with moments of terror or fear. This was such a moment.

....

Even if airplanes had been in service on February 25, 1897, Horatio Alexander Forsyth could never has envisioned that Albert Ernest, his newborn son on the island of New Providence in the Bahamas, would be risking death in one thirty-six years later. Had airplanes been present, it would have been assumed that they would be used by the few whites that controlled the islands and not by the majority of Bahamians, people whose ancestry was almost pure African, pure East Indian, or a mixture that included Caucasian.

While there were more opportunities for a Bahamian of color in the late 1890's than for a American of color in the post civil war United States, prejudice still created some limitations for Bahamians when choosing a career or engaging in recreational activities. However the social, economic, and political dominance of the white population was not absolute and had, for decades, been in a decline that was imperceptible unless one generation was compared to another. The centuries long intermingling of the different ethnic groups that had come to the islands had created a culture that was shared by all of the groups, was unique to the area, and was a source of pride to the inhabitants.

That pride, through an interaction with many different influences over his lifetime, would shape the character of Albert in the years to come. His heredity, cultural influences, education, and individual experiences, plus the events that were transpiring in the world that he lived in, combined to make Albert one of those rare individuals who are willing to risk their lives in an endeavor that benefits society rather than in one intended to achieve fame or riches. In considering the factors that affected Albert Forsythe, each one of us may better understand the forces that shape our own decisions.

Albert's father, Horatio, typified the amalgamation of races that was characteristic of the Bahamas and the other Caribbean islands. He was the son of a father whose ancestry was Scottish and a mother who was referred to in family history as being East Indian but whose surname, Strachan, suggests that she had some European ancestry on her father's side. In addition, she, like most Bahamians, may have had an African component to her heritage. The paternal family of Albert's mother, Byndloss, was Jamaican, a heritage that was primarily African and European.

In keeping with the Forsyth tradition of fostering family pride, Horatio had been given his paternal grandfather's first name as his middle name. Although his parents separated before he was four years old, he maintained a close relationship with his father and took pride in his heritage as evidenced by the fact that he gave his fathers first name to his firstborn child, a boy who died in infancy. Because Horatio's second child was a girl, Albert, his third born, was raised with the mantle of expectations that was commonly conferred upon a firstborn son. This mantle was woven from threads of DNA that were drawn not only from his immediate parents but also from the multiple combinations of chromosomes and genes that preceded them.

Horatio's children would be most aware of their father's paternal ancestry—partially because this is where western society traditionally places its emphasis, partially because keeping up with the paternal side required information on only one name, Forsyth, rather than the many maternal names such as Byndloss, Strachan, Jones, Evans, Nairn, Taylor, and McQueen, and partially because their most famous relative at the time was a Forsyth, Horatio's uncle, James McQueen Forsyth, an admiral in the United States Navy. However they were also aware of their East Indian heritage on their maternal side and the fact that their grandmother had a reputation of being very independent and had been held in such esteem that she had been referred to as the "Queen of Rum Cay".

While they were had not developed any knowledge about their African lineage because of the disruptive effect of slavery on the African families, they also had not developed the feeling that the slavery that had brought these ancestors to the islands in the past was in any way a negative reflection on them in the present. In fact, they, like all Bahamians, took pride in many of the remnants of the African culture such as the calypso music of the West Indies that was famous throughout the world, and the spicy dishes that were the staple of their diets.

Although some of the Forsyth family history was temporarily lost after the family moved from the Bahamas, Horatio instilled in his children a sense of pride in the family name and heritage. In later years Albert developed an interest in his family's genealogy and was able to assemble a fairly complete Forsyth family tree that covered almost two hundred years. This eventually allowed his nephew to trace the family back over 1,500 years.

For those who have an interest in tracing their genealogy, obituaries are often a very fertile source of information. In this instance, the key to linking the generations was found after a friend sent Albert the obituary, published in Nassau, of an uncle who was named Elgin. This obituary revealed that the first Forsyth to settle in the Bahamas, Alexander, had come there from North Carolina but was originally from Scotland where the family had supported Bonnie Prince Charles in his defeat at Culloden in 1746. Their exodus was said to be a result of that support.

He must have been a person of means since his intent when he arrived in 1786 was to start a plantation. The obituary also stated that Alexander had a son who he named James and that James had married the daughter of a prominent Major, another indication of their high social standing. It was one of James' sons who became the admiral that Albert had heard about as a child.

In trying to link the Bahamian Forsyth to the Scottish Forsyths, books on genealogy were consulted. The earliest definite ancestor of the Forsyth lineage was Roderic, Lord and Prince of Denmark in 400 A.D. In France, 350 years later, DNA from descendants of Roderick, now members of the French aristocracy, and DNA from a member of the Scottish aristocracy, combined to create a boy who was given the name Forsaith. The family was very prominent—his paternal grandfather was Charles Martel, a famous administrator who lived from 688 to 741 A.D., his paternal cousin was the Emperor Charlemagne, and his maternal grandfather was a Scottish chieftain.

In 768 A.D. Charlemagne built a strategic castle that he located twenty miles northeast of Bordeaux in France. His cousin Forsaith, who he had adopted as his son after Forsaith's father was killed, was put in charge of that castle and given the title of Vicomte de Fronsac. The family held that title until 924 A.D. After Forsaith's death, members of the family continued to use the name Forsaith to identify their origin; for example, David of Forsaith Castle came to be referred to as David de Forsyth. The 'de' was dropped from the name around 1540 A.D. by John Forsyth, Lord of Dykes in Scotland.

A branch of the family had settled in Scotland around 1236 A.D. when one of Forsaith's descendants, Osbert de Forsyth, decided to remain there after he had escorted a French noblewoman to Scotland to be married. In Scotland the name Forsyth means "descendant of Fearsithe" (man of peace). The family prospered and in 1488 A.D. acquired a Coat of Arms that has a Motto "Instaurator Ruinae" or repairer of ruins. The Forsyths held various titles over the generations: Lord of County Peebles, Governor of Sterling Castle, Baron of Nydie, and Lord of Dykes.

There was a prior historical reference to the name Forsyth--around the time of the birth of Christ. Forsite was the grandson of Odin, the ruler of a Scythian tribe in Turkestan in 70 B.C. who moved his tribe to an area in Germany now known as Westphalia and Hanover. There he made an alliance with the King of Sweden. When Forsite assumed leadership from Odin's son Balder, he came to be referred to as Forsite the Good because his reign was noted for peace and prosperity. However there is no evidence that Forsite the Good was an ancestor of the current bloodline.

Because of the prominence of the family, their history has been chronicled in detail. Between these chronicles, the excellent records that are kept in Scotland, the availability of data on computers, and the information from family obituaries, a likely link was found between the Forsyths of Scotland, chronicled since 400 A.D., and the data available on the Bahamian Forsyths since 1786.

We know from Elgin's obituary that Alexander came to the Bahamas sometime after 1746. Historical texts indicate that after the defeat of Bonnie Prince Charles at Culloden in April of 1746, tens of thousands of Scots immigrated to the United States over a thirty-year period-- either because of the political pressures placed on them because they supported the losing side or because of the economic upheavals that resulted from that war. Many of these Scots went to North Carolina, especially in the early 1770's, where they again demonstrated a willingness to resist authority by successfully opposing a Stamp Act, then again by becoming involved in the Revolutionary War—this time with unsuccessful results. Once again they were on the losing side and once again they were forced to migrate, many to East Florida and thereafter to the Bahamas.

Alexander must have left Scotland sometime between the 1746 and the 1776 wars. He must have been an adult at that time since he was a person of means; moreover it is unlikely that a child would have been able to survive the rigors of the voyage from Scotland to the United States. While there is no record of Alexander's date of birth, his obituary states that was at "an advanced age" when he died in 1826. An "advanced age" suggests that he was in his seventies or eighties. Taken together, these facts suggest that he was born between 1730 and 1750.

A review of the chronicles of Forsyth history did not reveal such an individual. However they did show an Alexander who was born in Elgin Scotland on November 9, 1707 to James, the third son of the Lord of Dykes. This Alexander, a very successful merchant who had two wives and twenty-one children, would have had children born between 1730 and 1750, would have been very likely to have named one of his twenty-one children Alexander, and would have been able to help finance emigration to America and the establishment of a plantation. Moreover, he had several things in common with the Bahamian Alexander. First, his father was named James and James was the name given to the son of the Bahamian Alexander. Second, he was born in Elgin and Elgin was the middle name given to one of the descendants of the Bahamian Alexander. In fact, a sibling of Elgin was given Ferres as a middle name and Ferres is a town near Elgin.

In genealogy, similarities such as these are usually a reflection of design rather than coincidence. Maiden names, frequently only available from a marriage license or an obituary, are often the source of a first or middle name in a subsequent generation and can be the key to making a crucial connection. Meticulous detective work and the application of puzzle solving skills are required if a family tree is to be delineated. Clues have to be ferreted out and the pieces of the puzzle must be rotated to see if a fit can be found. When working forwards fails, one must try working backwards-- and vice versa.

In this case, although there was no reference in the family chronicles to an Alexander who was born between 1730 and 1750, a computer search of the Scottish archives using the resources of the Mormon Church found that such an individual was born on November 8, 1741 to Margaret Ross. The Forsyth chronicles revealed that Margaret Ross was the name of the first wife of the merchant Alexander. This second Alexander, not a potential heir to the family title, born in a time of economic upheaval to a very large but well-to-do family, perhaps under pressure from his father's second wife, would have been very likely to migrate in an effort to make his fortune, and as a consequence of migrating, disappear from the Scottish records.

These links are of interest because they demonstrate the potential that Albert's genealogy had to affect his character. It is possible that the leadership, tendency to resist authority, and willingness to migrate that were in evidence in many generations of the Forsyth family were inherited traits that were passed on to Albert. It is definite that for centuries the Forsyth's had taken pride in their heritage and passed that pride to succeeding generations. The sense of self-worth that existed in Albert's branch of the Forsyth family was not limited to any one racial component of their lineage and certainly was not despite the presence of any of their many racial components. In the paternalistic society that existed in the 1900's, they knew more about the Scottish side of their family than the maternal side that contained their African and East Indian ancestry, but they cherished their entire heritage. Their pride and their intrinsic certainty in the worthiness of the members of the family undoubtedly were factors in the self-confidence that Albert had and in his unwillingness to allow others to denigrate his value, and that of others, as human beings.

....

In 1900 a search for opportunities led Horatio to decide to move his family from the city of Nassau on the small island of New Providence in the island group known as the Bahamas, to the larger island of Jamaica. In the eighteenth and nineteenth century, migration between the different islands of the Caribbean and between the islands and the United States was fairly common both because of the proximity of the islands to each other and to the United States, and because ownership of the islands often shifted.

British settlements were begun in the Bahamas in the mid -1600's. This led to the islands becoming a British colony in 1717. After the American Revolutionary War ended in 1783, many British loyalists came to the Bahamas with their slaves and established plantations there. This tie to the United States plus their proximity to Florida made movement between the Bahamian islands and the mainland fairly common. The ties to the British Empire made the movement to other British possessions permissible. These historical quirks facilitated back and forth migrations by the Forsyth family.

Jamaica was somewhat unique among the islands of the West Indies with respect to the relationship that developed between the colonizers, the slaves, and the descendants of those two groups or of unions between the two groups. Prior to colonization, the island was occupied by an estimated 100,000 Arawak Indians, a tribe that had migrated to the island around A.D 650. These settlers found an island on which fish, fresh water, and fruits were in plentiful supply. They prospered without resorting to the savagery of their neighbors, the Caribs. Because they were peaceful, they were unable to offer much resistance to the Spanish when they arrived in 1510 and were soon enslaved. The Spanish decimated the Indians to such an extent that by 1517 they began to import slaves from Africa in order to replace the Indian labor. After a century of Spanish rule, the Arawak population had been reduced to 70.

With time, the idyllic climate of the island seems to have had the same tranquilizing effect on the Spanish as it had had on the Arawaks. The tropical location, the currents, and the breezes result in very little variation from night to day and from winter to summer in the temperature and the humidity. Both only vary slightly from an average of 80.

The breeze that comes from the ocean in the daytime is popularly known today as the 'Doctor Breeze' while an evening respite is obtained through the cooling currents from the mountains that some have given the colorful name of the 'Undertaker's Breeze'. Whether it was due to the climate or was a result of their natural proclivities, the Spaniards made no effort to develop the island

As a result of their relaxed attitudes, the separation between slaves and masters was not very rigid. Since very few European women were available, sexual alliances between masters and female slaves were quite common. Consequently the percentage of the population that was identified as being colored or mulatto, i.e. of mixed European and African parentage, grew over the decades.

When on May 10, 1655 the English attacked the Spanish in Jamaica, the population that had numbered 100,000 Arawaks stood at a total of about 2,600 Spaniards and 1,400 slaves of both pure African and mixed heritage. The lethargic Spaniards were poorly organized, put up very limited resistance to the English, and capitulated within one week. In that week, they freed their slaves and encouraged them to flee to the mountains instead of submitting to the English.

The freed slaves became known as Maroons, a name that may have come from the French word *marron* that means "runaway slave." The island was mountainous and contained forests made dense by the combination of an abundant rainfall and a temperature that had a catalytic effect on the growth of vegetation. This topography made the efforts of the British to find and subdue the Maroons unsuccessful. Consequently it was not until Horatio Nelson came to the island in 1739, 83 years after the onset of the rebellion, that a peace treaty was concluded. The Maroons were given a level of independence that was not achieved anywhere else in the Caribbean.

While relatively small in number, the Maroons symbolized a spirit of resistance to unjust authority that was transferred to those who were brought to the island as slaves, embraced by those born into slavery over the following centuries, and transmitted to their descendants. This spirit is integral to the character of the Jamaican; it is a spirit that gave the islanders an international reputation that is disproportionate to their numbers; it is a spirit that has served them well as they migrated to other countries; it was a spirit that was being imparted to Albert as he grew up in that country and adsorbed its historical traditions.

The British showed more ambition than the Spanish with regard to developing the island agriculturally. Sugar became an extremely important crop—so much so that many wars were fought over it and many Europeans became wealthy because of it. This resulted in a great deal of land speculation and development in Jamaica between 1660 and 1820 and the importation of over 800,000 slaves from Africa to Jamaica to provide cheap labor for the plantations. While almost half of these slaves died in transit or shortly after arrival, their numbers were so plentiful that the slaves soon outnumbered the Europeans who had immigrated to the island in the hope of establishing their fortune.

The scarcity of white females meant that the children of a liaison between a white male and an African or a mixed race female were often the only children that the man could expect to have. For this reason, such children were often educated, granted freedom, and allowed to inherit their father's wealth. However some legal restrictions limited the potential of these children in that they often could not inherit his lands.

Unlike the circumstances in the southern United States where slaves were a minority and were rarely freed, the Jamaican slaves were such a significant majority that some had to be freed in order to make the system workable. Hence a Jamaican who was of purely African heritage, commonly referred to as blacks, could still aspire to freedom if they were able to distinguish themselves by learning a trade that was in short supply. A complex social structure developed between whites, coloreds, and blacks that differed not only from the social structures in the United States, but also from those in the rest of the Caribbean.

The different populations grew at very different rates. To illustrate, in 1734 the population was listed as being composed of 9,000 whites and 87,000 Negroes—a non-white to white ratio of less than ten to one. In 1791 the makeup was described as 30,000 whites, 10,000 free people (who consisted of both coloreds and blacks), and 250,000 slaves; by 1844, after the abolition of slavery, whites had dropped to 16,000 and the balance of the population was described as being composed of 69,000 coloreds and 293,000 blacks, a non- white to white ratio of over twenty to one. In only fifty years, whites had decreased by almost fifty percent, coloreds had increased by seven hundred percent, and blacks had increased by over fifteen percent.

The significant change in demographics that occurred after the abolition of slavery is a large part of the explanation as to why the psychology of the slaves in Jamaica, repressed but in the majority, was usually quite different from the psychology of the slaves in the United States who were both repressed and in the minority. Eventually Jamaica would adopt a motto that expressed the national ethos—"Out of many people, one".

Since slaves were not plentiful in England, they were not a matter of major concern and were accorded a more relaxed legal status than in the United States. By British law, mulatto's who were of one-sixteenth or less African ancestry could own property, vote, and be legally considered white. Those who had more than one-sixteenth African ancestry could attain freedom, could be wealthy and maintain slaves of their own, but could not vote or own property. In the southern United States, there were some freed slaves but any amount of African ancestry classified the individual as being black and ineligible to vote or enjoy most of the other rights of citizens.

By offering these tiers based on a class system that involved color but permitted some mobility, and not on a rigid system that relied solely on race, the British were able to maintain their slave society with a modicum of discontent even though masters were greatly outnumbered by the slaves. However the rapid growth in the number of people who were free yet unable to own property and have a say in their government promoted discontent and pressures that eventually led to change.

The economic changes that occurred in the eighteenth and nineteenth centuries were another significant factor that contributed to the elimination of slavery. As the importance of sugar in the world economy diminished, the price of land fell in Jamaica, the white population became smaller, and it became impossible to continue to maintain the status quo. In 1830 the Jamaican assembly, although controlled by whites, yielded to the repeated demands of the freed slaves and granted them property and voting rights. Then, in 1834, the British Parliament voted to emancipate the remaining slaves.

The slaves left the sugar cane plantations where the work was extremely grueling and began to farm their own small plots of land. This led to severe economic upheavals on the plantations and friction between the owners and the former slaves. In 1865 these frictions led to uprisings that were termed the Morant Bay Rebellion. After British troops put down the rebellion, Jamaica's assembly, the institution that had governed for 200 years, was disbanded and Jamaica became a crown colony that was governed by England.

Despite the loss of self-rule, Jamaica had several advantages. It had a history of a successful rebellion by slaves and a resultant self pride, it had a large group of slaves who had been freed prior to abolition and allowed to achieve some education, status, and wealth, and it had achieved total freedom for its remaining slaves without the acrimony of the Civil War that the United States had to endure in order to free their slaves. Color mattered, but it was not the sole factor. Moreover Jamaica had a 30-year head start over the United States in adapting to the freeing of the slaves. By the twentieth century, while there was animosity between the former masters and slaves in Jamaica, it was at a relatively low level when compared to the level in America.

....

By 1900 when Horatio immigrated to Jamaica, the full meaning of slavery had been erased from the minds of the young but the strong class system that permeated the society was firmly in place. Upward mobility was available for those of any color if they possessed desirable skills, but was especially easy if one was in the right class and easier yet if one was of the right complexion. Three-year-old Albert would now be shaped by a cultural heritage as well as a family heritage.

Horatio's education qualified him for the middle class and his appearance advertised his status. His features were a combination of his father's Scottish origins, his mother's partial East Indian ancestry, and their African heritage. At six feet four inches, he towered above the average Jamaican. He was obviously a mixture of races with straight black hair and a complexion that was unquestionably darker than that of a European, but significantly lighter than a pure African or an East Indian. He displayed a handsome countenance, a luxuriant moustache, and an air of authority.

His education had been achieved while working in shipbuilding for the Designing Department in Nassau over a period of three years. He demonstrated an ambition that seemed characteristic of many of the Forsyths in that he taught himself calculus and took several correspondence courses in order to further his education. On completion of his studies, he was granted certificates as a mechanical engineer and as an architectural draftsman. Shortly after this, in a ceremony by a Wesleyan Minister in 1892, he married Lillian Maud Byndloss, a young lady of Jamaican heritage and European and African ancestry. Leon Dupuch, later a founder of the Nassau *Tribune*, was the witness.

Horatio's marriage certificate showed his name spelt with an 'e' that was crossed out. Since the Forsyths of the Bahamas did not use an 'e' it is likely that this was an error by the recording clerk. This may be the reason why part of the family, including Bert, spelled the name as Forsythe, while others spelled it as Forsyth. In any event, Horatio then took a job with the Boston Fruit Company, an organization that later became part of the United Fruit Company.

After working for the Boston Fruit Company in Nassau for several years, Horatio was transferred to the town of Port Antonio on the north coast of Jamaica where the company was headquartered. He was the chief engineer for their electric light and ice companies for many years. He also went into the construction business where he developed a reputation as an excellent builder but more importantly as being a man whose word was his bond. He prospered and was commonly addressed by his title of 'Chief'.

In 1900, Bert, as he was now known, and his older sister May, learned that the sibling who had just been delivered at home by the midwife would be named Roger Alexander. In appearance, Bert and Roger had features that represented the partially East Indian heritage of Horatio's mother more than the European ancestry of Horatio's father—complexions that were darker than those of Horatio and Lillian and straight black hair. May had a coffee with extra cream complexion and fine hair with a hint of curl. Sadly, a few years after Roger's birth, Lillian died of a pneumonia that she contracted after a hurricane.

An early death from infection was not an uncommon occurrence at the turn of the century when there were no antibiotics available. This was especially true for women in the childbearing ages and for infants. In fact, Horatio and Lillian had had a fourth child while they were living in the Bahamas, a girl named Grace, who had died in infancy.

As a result of the high mortality for women, remarriages and large families were common. As previously mentioned, the Alexander Forsyth born in 1707 had two wives and 21 children. The Alexander born in 1829 had two wives and 10 children. Horatio Alexander would eventually have 13 children by two wives as well as having a third wife who did not have any children.

Roger, May, Albert (left to right) with Horatio

For a short time the sole responsibility for raising the three motherless children was assumed by a relative of their mother who had accompanied the family to Jamaica when it left Nassau. Her real name was Mary Ann Jones but everyone, including the maids, called her Baa. Her frequent recitations of the nursery rhyme 'Baa Baa Black Sheep' caused the children to give her that name and it somehow seemed to fit her. Baa was a bit of a character in that no matter how warm it was, she always wore a woolen shawl. She would complete her highly individual ensemble with a cork-lined helmet. On Sundays she could be found in this outfit giving Sunday school lessons to children at the local church. At night, she invariably had a sip of brandy from a small flask. All who knew her remembered her repetition of the phrase "The world is in a turmoil."

As a widower in his early thirties with three children under the age of nine, remarriage by Horatio was to be expected. After a respectful interval as a widower, he took Juanita Bertola, the daughter of a Cuban revolutionary, as his second wife. With almost biannual precision, this union produced a second set of children who filled the large six bedroom house that he later built on the hill near the center of town where it overlooked Port Antonio harbor.

In typical Jamaican fashion, Baa remained in the household to assist with the rearing of the children until her death at age 98. Jamaicans who were financially able were expected to care for their less fortunate relatives, even when it was not a blood relationship, and especially if the individual was female. Often times the individual was relegated to a small room at the rear of the house where guests never saw them. No cruelty was intended, this was just the prevailing custom. This informal type of social security was at times extended to servants who had been with the family for a significant period.

Port Antonio at the turn of the century was a bustling place. Its natural harbor has been described as the most beautiful in the West Indies, an area known for beauty. A large promontory of land divided the harbor into sections that were appropriately named East Harbour and West Harbour. At the very tip of the promontory was Tichfield School where boys of Bert's station were expected to attend. Nearby was the luxurious Tichfield Hotel. It sat on a low hill that afforded spectacular views of the harbor and was renowned as a destination for the well to do ship passengers who came to experience the charm of the scenery and the warmth of the climate.

Across from these landmarks was Navy Island, an island of over 60 acres that would be purchased in the mid 1940's by the roguish movie actor Errol Flynn who fell in love with the area after being forced to take refuge in the harbor during a storm. He, along with luminaries such as Noel Coward, Ian Flemming, and Robin Cook, made the beauty of the area famous in the period after World War II.

The east end of the East Harbour was demarcated by a promontory that housed the Folly Point Lighthouse. The title of Folly was bestowed after an American, Albert Mitchell of New London Connecticut, built a large mansion there in 1905. Local legend states that he ignored the admonitions of the Jamaicans that he should use river bottom sand rather than the nearby sea sand to build. Convinced that the locals were trying to trick him into spending more by importing the river sand, he built a house that crumbled as the salt from the sea sand destroyed the metal reinforcements in the concrete. Almost one hundred years later, the ruins still stand as testament to what the native Jamaicans of all classes *knew* and were willing to verbalize—that whites were no more intelligent than coloreds or blacks.

It was commonly believed in Jamaica that coloreds and blacks in America often lacked this same certainty in their equality of ability. If there were some self-doubts in colored Americans, especially those of minimal education and income, they should have been attributed to the effect of the abuse that white Americans continued to display to the ex-slaves long after the abolition of slavery. Having lost the benefits of slavery by abrupt force rather than by gradual negotiation, Southerners seemed to wreak their vengeance by making daily efforts to prove that the ex-slaves were inferior. In any event, these doubts were not part of the Jamaican ethos for any class or color and certainly were not part of the psychological make up of the members of the Forsyth family—a family raised to be proud of their entire heritage.

To the west of Folly was a deep cove known as Blue Hole because of the deep blue color of its crystal clear water. The cove was surrounded by a plethora of brilliant green banana leaves that were interspersed with aging yellow and beige ones, stately coconut trees with curved tan trunks and green tufted tops garlanded with drooping brown fronds, red-flowered flame of the forest trees, poinsettias drenched with corollas of bright red flowers with central tufts of a white lace, and spectacularly kaleidoscopic croton leaves of pure gold interspersed with some speckled with green or leaves of various colors. Further along was Anchovy Valley where members of his family would later purchase a small banana grove on a plot that extended down to the ocean.

In the West Harbour, one half mile to the west of the center of the town near the promontory, was the Boundbrook Wharf where the bananas and other produce were brought to be loaded onto the ships which sailed into this visual paradise. The bananas grew in bunches whose size was measured in hand widths and were picked while still green so that they could be shipped by sea without spoiling. With the decline in the value of sugar, bananas were now the life's blood of the Jamaican economy. Sugar was still a major crop but it was facing severe competition as other islands and the South American countries put more and more land into cultivation. Being a crown colony in the British Empire guaranteed Jamaica a market for its produce. While a disproportionate share of the proceeds went abroad and to the local Englishmen who came to the colonies to make their fortune, the traffic presented an opportunity for enrichment for the middle class locals with ambition. In the years that followed his marriage to Juanita and the birth of eight more children, Horatio prospered.

....

This then was the ancestral and cultural background of the aviator who now faced one of the many perils encountered by the pioneers of aviation. The paternal genes that he had inherited came from progenitors who had resisted the status quo from the battles of Charlemagne in Europe to the battle of Culloden in Scotland, the Stamp Act in North Carolina, and then the Revolutionary War. The lineage had a history of achievement and respect as members of the aristocracy and as businessmen. His immediate maternal ancestors were similarly admirable individuals.

The culture that he had grown up in had a minority, the Maroons, that had successfully resisted slavery for over 80 years, and a majority that had achieved universal freedom in an evolutionary and mostly bloodless manner rather than by a polarizing civil war. In this society, class rather than race was the primary factor used to determine an individual's status.

The immediate family that nurtured him enjoyed comfortable surroundings, was accustomed to respect because of its middle class status, yet was aware that their mixed racial heritage created some limitations in the racially stratified society in which they lived.

It is understandable that some-one of this pedigree would, as an adult, be resistant to limitations that were imposed solely on the basis of the fact that the color of his skin was dark, and with complete disregard for the intelligence of his mind or the content of his character. Yet there were many others of similar family and cultural histories that were content to accept the status quo. What made the difference?

Instaurator-Ruinae

Forsyth

FORSYTH COAT OF ARMS AND MOTTO

2

PORT ANTONIO

At times of stress, odors, visions, or words from experiences that are almost lost from the conscious memories can instantaneously make their way through the convolutions of the brain and flash vividly at the surface. Like a firefly zigzagging through an evening sky, they briefly illuminate one subject, disappear, and then reappear in a seemingly random pattern. Perhaps a tingling in the spine will recreate the picture that the optic camera recorded when it last experienced that sensation; then again it may be the odor of a perfume that precipitates the sadness of a love long lost. Whatever the stimulus, once the cascade has begun, it has to run its course.

So it was that as Bert and his co-pilot Al Anderson fought the effects of the heat that arose from the Mojave Desert on his 95 horsepower Fairchild 24 monocoupe, the Pride of Atlantic City, the heat triggered a memory of another hot day, a memory that had been stored decades ago in the primitive areas of his brain where long term memories slept peacefully as they awaited an opportunity to reappear. In nanoseconds, the stimulated areas relayed images that undulated along the sulci of his brain to the white matter of his cortex where conscious thoughts appeared in rapid succession.

As the cascade began, Bert visualized himself standing in the heat on Boundbrook Wharf in the West Harbour of Port Antonio while awaiting transportation to the boat that would provide the means for his departure to school in the United States. He clearly recalled the thoughts that danced through his mind that day as he thought about his life up to that point in time.

....

At the turn of the century, the eldest son in a family was expected to follow in his father's footsteps. Since Horatio was a civil engineer, he had decided that it would be appropriate that his son study architecture and engineering. Besides being very gifted in mathematics, Bert had a very steady hand that would be an asset when it came to rendering sketches of proposed buildings.

With a soft pencil, Horatio's eldest son could transform an ordinary sheet of paper into a forest where shadows gently spilled from perfectly proportioned trees or into a countryside where farmers trudged down an unpaved country road to market while cows grazed in adjacent fields. At other times he constructed landscapes that consisted of sparse, broad-leaved grasses that protruded through the darkened swatch on the paper canvas that represented the earth made cordovan red by the bauxite ore within.

Then again Bert would prop up a reproduction of an old master and try to perfect his techniques by rendering and exact copy or inveigle a sibling to sit still while he captured amazing likenesses on a sheet of plain paper. Everyone who saw his work expressed their admiration for his skill and encouraged him to develop his talent.

Bert, like his older sister May and his younger brother Roger, was a very good student. In general, this saved them from the canings which headmasters often dispensed under the British system of education that prevailed at the beginning of the century. When a student did poorly on an exam or engaged in some infraction, it was unquestioned that the teacher had the authority to administer some corporal punishment.

However, when a teacher attempted to administer an undeserved caning to his brother, Roger refused to accept it. This type of action, unthinkable for anyone of a lesser social standing and unheard of in any event, became famous in Port Antonio. Of course the teacher reported this to Horatio but after listening carefully to the teacher's complaint and to Roger's explanation, Horatio refused to punish his son. The refusal to submit to unjust authority would manifest itself again and again in the family.

In 1911 when the 14-year-old Albert had finished his secondary schooling, the headmaster of Titchfield School, Major Plant, asked to meet with Horatio. "Bert has a fine mind, Mr. Forsythe," said the major as he sipped from the ubiquitous cup of tea that was routinely offered at all social occasions and at many business meetings. "It is my opinion that he should pursue his studies further. I would recommend to you that you send him to England where he can get a first class English education."

To a subject of the British Empire, no education could compare to that provided in England. The educational process at Titchfield was molded after the British system and was, in fact, quite good. At age 14, Bert had studied Latin and Spanish. He had had shown himself to be exceptionally capable in mathematics and as a result had been allowed to begin studying calculus. However with six children, a seventh on the way, and no way of knowing how many would follow, Horatio could not afford to send him to England for further studies. Instead, Tuskegee Institute in Alabama was chosen as the place for young Bert to attend in order to study architecture. This was a decided disappointment to Major Plant.

Three decades after being founded for the purpose of educating the recently freed slaves, Tuskegee had developed a good reputation due to the diligence of its founder, Booker

T. Washington. However it did not have the tradition, the resources, or the caliber of students that would have been found at an English school. The entrance fee at Tuskegee was reasonable at ten dollars, tuition was free, and the charge for room and board was only ten dollars a month for a school year that lasted from September to May.

Although Bert had harbored thoughts of becoming a physician, disagreement with his father about his vocation would have been unthinkable. Nevertheless, he and his brother Roger often talked about becoming physicians. A large part of their attraction to medicine was their impression that in the new century in which they found themselves, science would be much more interesting than architecture. Another attraction was the level of respect that the local physician enjoyed. To be held in respect was very important in the small town of Port Antonio, a product of over 200 years of the British class system.

These reservations about his future profession were never verbalized to his father however. One did not disagree with their father in matters such as this. Besides, although he got along well with his stepmother, the fact that she now had three children of her own made Bert feel that he should leave his home and begin to make his way in the world.

As is almost universal with teenagers, he was experiencing a strong urge to become independent, to make his own decisions, and to earn his own income so that he could be master of his own destiny. He looked forward to leaving home and felt very little trepidation about being in a strange new country. Had he been more astute about life in the United States, he might have thought about how his clothes would be cleaned and ironed, whether boarding school would provide him with opportunities to satisfy an in-between-meal craving for fruits or sweets, and the effect of a different social system on his quality of life. In truth, these considerations never entered his mind.

It was a very comfortable upper middle class exist-ence that Bert was leaving. As a man of property, Horatio had a maid, a nanny, and a man who spent a full day on the yard each week. As a result, Bert never had to be concerned with such mundane personal chores as shining his own shoes and never had any responsibilities such as mowing the lawn. His primary responsibilities were to study hard in school, earn good grades, and to spend some time in apprenticeship to his father as an engineer.

Free time was most often spent bathing in the ocean, fishing, or taking advantage of the ability of the prevailing breeze to propel his brightly colored kites high into the clear blue skies. He enjoyed making these kites out of tissue paper that he purchased from one of the town's small stores, and bamboo that he himself cut from one of the many plants that were abundant throughout the area.

The kite that was usually constructed consisted of three equal slivers of green bamboo that crossed at their centers where they were fastened by a figure of eight wrapping of string. The shape was maintained by notching the outer tips of the bamboo then running some additional string through the notches to form a hexagon. Triangles of differently colored paper were glued to the sectors formed by the bamboo within the hexagon from glue that was made out of flour and water. The maid could always be counted on to find some rags that could be torn into strips then knotted together, made into a tail, and attached to the lower corners of the hexagon. A fourth piece of string was used to bow the transverse slat of bamboo while a fifth was attached to the upper corners to form a vee which was then anchored to the center of the kite.

The mortality on these kites was quite high. At times they attached blades to the kites and engaged in kite fights. Even without these fights, the kites had a penchant for receiving fatal punctures after diving into one of the many coconut, mango, or breadfruit trees that adjoined his kite flying area or else simply snapping their lines and floating away. This was never discouraging because the making of the kite was as important as the flying. First you had to wheedle sixpence from father in order to buy the tissue papers that you needed. Of course, one would also ask for a tuppence to buy guava cheese, the molasses laden, thick doughy pastries known as bullas, or the coconut candy concoctions known as grater cakes to take along as a snack.

One of his father's businesses was a factory that made the carbonated beverages called aerated water. Hence there was never a problem getting a drink with flavors such as Champaign cola, pineapple, ginger beer, or cream soda to add to his snack. In his pre-teen opinion, these drinks were far superior to the rum that adults took with coconut water or cola or made into a 'planters punch' with limejuice.

He never got to taste rum unless he had a fever in which case Juanita or Baa would give him a dilute mixture of rum, water, cane sugar, and limejuice and then put him to bed. The medicinal properties of rum seemed quite remarkable to him in that he never failed to sleep soundly after this treatment and then awaken feeling completely refreshed the next day.

To complete his kite-flying feast, he would stop into the Chinese grocery store and buy an early version of fast food that was known as a patty. This was composed of a spicy ground beef enclosed in a greasy, flaky thin pastry and kept warm by proximity to a light bulb. Jamaicans had an affinity for spicy food that was attributed to the African heritage of the majority of the islanders. A distinctive cuisine developed on the island as many different cultures— the Tainos, the Arawaks, the Spanish, the English, the Scotch, the East Indians, and the Chinese—blended into one.

When he was not in the mood for a patty, he often stopped by a roadside stand where pork, often covered by a green pimento wood, was roasted slowly over a period of hours while herbs and spices were repeatedly applied. All over the island pork and chicken were cooked in this style that came to be known as 'jerk' but Port Antonio was especially famous for the tender, succulent morsels that were prepared with professional care by country people who earned their living by raisings pigs then converting them into this culinary treat. This preeminence in Port Antonio was attributed to the fact that the Cormantee warriors of West Africa, the group to whom this process is attributed, had been settled in large numbers in the Port Antonio area after being captured and sold into slavery.

At other times he favored curried goat from a small restaurant that sat back from the main road that ran through the center of town. The use of curry had been popularized by the East Indians who had been recruited to come to the island to work in the fields as indentured servants between 1838 and 1917, after slavery had ceased to be an acceptable method of providing labor. These new arrivals represented a competition for jobs that lead to a low level of resentment that persisted long after they were assimilated into the population. As a result, low income East Indians were at times referred to in a derogatory way as 'coolies' a word that originally was simply a descriptive Asian term for an unskilled laborer.

The culinary impact of the East Indians had been greater than that of the Chinese who were brought to Jamaica to provide cheap labor for the construction of the railroad. At the turn of the century the Chinese had not yet had a significant impact on the diet of the island and were not represented in the small restaurants that were sporadically found along the roadsides. Instead those Chinese who remained on the island after the railroad was completed demonstrated their entrepreneurial proclivities by opening small grocery stores. They tended to save their money so that they could bring brides and relatives to the island. There was intermarrying, but at this point in time there was less than had occurred with the other nationalities that made up this island potpourri of people.

The economically dominant group on the island was the white population, primarily people of English, Irish, and Scottish ancestry. Some could trace their ancestry on the island back hundreds of years. Others were fairly recent arrivals, part of the group of ex-patriates who left their homeland with the expectation that they would make their fortune in the colonies. With every new generation, newcomers were drawn to the island by its romantic history and the dream of establishing a new dynasty.

The final prominent minority group in Jamaica was commonly referred to as the Syrians. In fact, many of them were Lebanese Christians. They were small in number but economically influential. They had a tradition of being excellent merchants who thrived financially by opening small retail stores in many types of businesses then adding to their holdings through purchases of land and other businesses. The success of these recent arrivals caused some muttering by the native Jamaicans but rarely resulted in open hostility. In the decade of 1910, Jamaicans at the lower end of the economic ladder showed a great deal of tolerance for the disparities in income and class that were prevalent. This would change in the decades that followed.

While he had occasion to come into contact with these different groups, their existence was a matter of fact rather than a matter of concern. At this age he worried only about whether or not his preparations for a day of kite flying would fit into his hours of idle time. When he had assembled his kite, complete with string and tail, he would make his way down the 30 steps that led from his large home on the hill to a street near the center of town. A stop here and a visit there would allow him to gather the provisions necessary to satisfy the quickly recurrent hunger that was characteristic of active growing boys. Then it was off to Old Church Hill where a mountain breeze could always be found, the yard behind Titchfield School, or down to the beach where the breezes were always kite-friendly and a boy could escape from the world of sisters and dolls. These sojourns were usually not made alone. His most frequent companion was Roger, the brother who was three years younger. There was an especially strong bond between the boys, a bond strengthened by the fact that they shared the same mother in a family that was now guided by a woman who understandably spent more time with the three children who were her own than with the three which she had inherited on her marriage to Horatio. Roger idolized his older brother and Bert reciprocated by protecting him from bullies and including him in his activities.

Various other boys would join in on these kite excursions to the beach. Middle class Jamaica consisted of some very eclectic groups. The pure English were not a significant presence in a small country town such as Port Antonio. They tended to live in great houses in the countryside where their primary social contacts were with each other, and often sent their children away to school. They were primarily seen on Sunday when they came into town for their ritual appearance at the Anglican Church.

In and around the town there were several families that were termed 'Jamaica whites". These were people who for several generations had married either Europeans or other Jamaicans of mixed parentage with the result that their complexions were quite light. They often went into a profession and usually had some property of modest to moderate size. A light skin was usually, but not always, an indication of membership in the middle class. In general, the lighter ones color, the higher the presumed social standing. Actual standing depended on many factors.

Middle class Jamaicans of medium to dark complexions were more common than the Europeans or Jamaican whites. This group consisted of people who had some skills and some property and considered themselves to be the backbone of the country. Depending on their social rank, they could be clerks, managers, or professionals. At the bottom of the social structure were the Jamaicans of limited means. The upper tier of this group ran small businesses and owned small properties; the lower ranks worked as laborers and often lacked steady employment. They were most frequently of pure African decent and very dark in color. They could however be any color from near white to coal black. A patois dialect was a clearer determinant of a low social standing than was color, and class more than color determined who played with whom. Bert was darker than many of his playmates but he was the unquestioned leader both by virtue of his social standing and by virtue of his intelligence.

Bert and his friends usually engaged in their kite flying during the middle of the day when the prevailing wind was the Doctor Breeze from the ocean. One boy held the kite high overhead while the others positioned themselves about twenty feet down the beach before beginning a barefoot dash over the hot sand in an effort to coax the kite up to a level where it could catch the tropical breeze. An accomplished kite flyer knew how far to run before jerking on the line to create lift, then releasing just enough string to send the kite soaring and not so little that it hesitated and fell. Meanwhile they had to avoid the tall coconut trees that demarcated the edge of the white sandy beach. After everyone had their turn, it was time to take off all clothes and luxuriate in the Caribbean.

In later years as Bert traveled the world, he would learn that there was no place to compare to this paradise in which he spent his childhood. As a country that is close to the equator, Jamaica could potentially be very hot. In fact, the sun's proximity to the earth in this area causes the sea near the shore to maintain a very comfortable year around temperature of over 80 degrees. The buoyancy of the salt water combined with its delightful temperature produced a torpor that relaxed every muscle in ones body.

Meanwhile the trade winds that cross the Atlantic Ocean from Africa provided a respite from the midday heat of the near equatorial sun. To add to this perfection, the presence of Navy Island protected the harbor and minimized the incoming waves so that they gently rocked the floating boys rather than tossing them about and depositing them rudely on the beach.

The promontory that divided the harbor in half had two salutary effects. It isolated the East Harbour from the modest pollution caused by the banana boats that came in and out of the West Harbour, and it contributed to the deposition of a white sand that was neither so fine that one sank into it nor so gritty that it irritated your feet as you ran along the beach. There was very little to concern a pre-pubertal boy as he floated in the ocean, contemplated the horizon, and dreamed about the wonders that lay across the sea.

When he reached his teens, a favorite pastime on Saturday mornings was to rise around 5 A.M., gather a hand held fishing line complete with hooks and sinkers, rendezvous with one or two friends, then go down to the beach where a small flat bottomed rowboat was available. With long deep strokes the boys would overcome the gentle incoming waves in the harbor and make their way to a favorite fishing spot near Navy Island.

As it had for the Arawak Indians, the sea yielded a myriad of fish. Yellowtail, snapper, bass, bonita, barracuda, and many others provided an exciting and fatiguing battle for the boys with their hand held lines. A sudden tug on the line when the fish took the bait would be quickly answered by a yank that set the hook, then a steady and unhurried hand over hand effort to bring the fish in. With expert care they would deposit the line in the bottom of the boat using a circular pattern that was designed to preclude any snagging of the line when it was cast out again. Once the fish was safely landed and secured in the bow of the boat, the line was recast in anticipation of quickly repeating the process.

At times the boys were occasionally rewarded with the sight of large marlins in the distance as they unexpectedly erupted through the waves with a graceful leap that accentuated their arched back and sword like beak. At other times they watched as a sea turtle lazily made its way through the ocean. When the sun began to be oppressive and the incoming breezes gathered strength and provided propulsion to the shore, the boys would head home, always with a reasonable catch. Then they would strip naked on the beach and swim and splash in the ocean's waters before heading for home.

As chief engineer for the United Fruit Company, his father was in charge of the ice factory so there was never a shortage of the ice needed to preserve the fish. Vie, the maid, would clean and gut the fish, add a little salt and lime, then lay them on the ice until it was time to cook them for supper. Somehow the fish always tasted much better when he caught them than when Vie bought them from the fishermen. Probably because the fish he caught were fresher he reasoned. In any event, he never tired of his cycle of ocean fishing followed by a sea bath and a meal of fresh fish.

The relationship that he had with Vie and the other employees of his father in the home and at his father's work was well defined although there were no written rules and he never received any training on the subject. By an osmotic process that automatically imbued every individual with the appropriate societal behavior patterns, all parties knew that while every human being was deserving of respect, your station in life made a difference. Bert was treated with some deference, but had he ever tried to be rude to someone of a lower station, he would have received swift punishment from his father and less respect from his father's employees. At this point in Jamaican history, the understandable resentment of the 'have-nots' towards the 'haves' existed, but at a relatively latent level.

There were other waters to be enjoyed near Port Antonio. To the west was the Rio Grande River where rafters often were seen, and Somerset Falls where the family might go for a Sunday picnic. Occasionally, his parents would decide that their bodies were in need of the relaxation provided by the mineral springs at the city of Bath to the east. On the way they would pass by signs to colorful destinations such as Moore Town where the descendants of the Maroons might be found or Corn Puss Gap, a place that the family never traveled to but a place that always fascinated him because of its name

His favorite area was a deep horseshoe bend in the coast road to the east called 'See Me No More'. It was said that a century ago highwaymen used to lay in wait there for victims who were never again seen after entering the area. His younger siblings always seemed to sit a little closer to him or their parents as they made their way through the dense foliage that occupied this narrow, sunken, winding stretch of road. He of course was never afraid, but he was not averse to watching the roadside for any sign that someone might be lurking there.

Of course it was not always fun and games. The heat, the nearby ocean, the trade winds, and the mountainous topography combined to explain why the original Arawak Indians named the island Xaymaca which means "Land of Wood and Water". The heat sucked immeasurable amounts of water up into the skies from the ocean. The winds then transported these moisture-laden volumes of air towards wooded mountainous humps.

Most mountains were rounded in the manner of giant prostate glands and were unnamed. Some were given descriptive names such as Sugar Loaf. As the air encountered the mountains that had been made cool by the forests, it would suddenly relieve itself of its liquid burden just as a bladder might when it precipitously overwhelmed the bulge of an enlarged prostate. The resultant rain often forced cancellation of his afternoon plans.

The average yearly rainfall on the island was 77 inches with Port Antonio's parish of Portland recording up to 200 inches in one year. The downpours were heaviest in March and again in October, the end of the hurricane season. The rest of the year generally produced a light afternoon shower that quickly evaporated in the tropical sun. This abundant rainfall combined with the bright sunlight to produce thick growths of fine woods such as mahogany, massive stands of bamboo, and ample opportunities for Bert to stay inside and receive training in draftsmanship from his father.

On these afternoons Bert enjoyed an English style afternoon tea at 4 P.M. Besides the tea itself, one would have a choice of dainty triangles of a warm home made bread with the edges cut off and adorned with meats, cheeses, or jellies. A jelly made from the fruit of the guava tree was his favorite. If the sour sop fruit were in season, the maid would mash and strain the fruit, add condensed milk, and create a marvelously satisfying drink.

At these times the kitchen was enveloped with an odor that in later years would flood his mind with pleasant childhood memories whenever he returned home. One sniff and he would instantaneously visualize the kitchen and the large breadbox that housed all of the wonderful breads and pastries that cook always kept on hand. The immediate surroundings and the people would also magically appear as he happily regressed to the age of fourteen. At times he would even recall what he or someone else had been wearing. He never ceased to be amazed by the ability of small things to trigger huge recollections.

The training that he received from his father on these occasions was with the intent of preparing Bert for his future profession as an architect and engineer. Horatio believed that architects would be needed because the banana trade would turn Port Antonio from a sleepy small town into an area of rapid growth and great financial potential.

The boats of the United Fruit Company added to their profitability by maintaining a few staterooms for the wealthy few who traveled for pleasure. The Titchfield Hotel had been built to accommodate the wealthy passengers who came on these boats to experience the charms of the tropical island known far and wide for its seventeenth and eighteenth century legacy as a haven for buccaneers such as Henry Morgan, Calico Jack, and Blackbeard.

A similarly luxurious hotel, the Myrtle Bank, was built on the south coast of the island in the capital town of Kingston. With the construction of suitable hotels, these passengers began to first stay in hotels, and then to purchase land, build houses and order furniture—at times from Horatio's businesses--and to hire maids and gardeners. All levels of the Jamaican society welcomed the infusion of jobs and money.

There was one problem with the tourists however. Although more than two generations had passed since the American civil war and the abolition of slavery, segregation and the inferiority of the ex-slaves was often taken for granted by the wealthy Americans who now traveled to Jamaica. Many expected the locals to accept their prejudices with the same forced acquiescence shown by the ex-slaves in the United States. However, when these tourists displayed an air of arrogance towards a Jamaican servant, they were often surprised to find that despite a desire for the income, the servant was quite willing to walk off the job if they were not shown due respect.

These visitors did not realize that while the ordinary Jamaican recognized and accepted the fact that there were different classes, he did not conclude that one group there-fore had an inherent superiority over another. Even when slavery had been legal, Jamaicans had been taught by their families to remember both the successful rebellion of the Maroons and the unsuccessful uprisings of 1739 and 1831, and to cherish a spirit of independence. Underneath the surface of harmony, there was a resentment of the inequalities that existed.

Most of these facts had not been on Bert's mind as he waited on the wharf to board the boat. As he recalled that day, he did however remember his father's warning that life would be very different for him when he arrived in the southern United States.

"Be careful what you say to the white man in America" his father had admonished. "They are not as civilized as the English and have been known to murder people of color for little or no reason. It makes no difference to them whether or not you are middle class or working class. If you displease them, they can be violent."

The relative incivility of the Americans was an accepted fact in Jamaica. And why not? At the turn of the century, America, late to the national game of imperialism, had become involved militarily in the Caribbean in order to demonstrate its hemispheric dominance. During the time that England had begun to decrease its hegemony in the Caribbean, America had moved in the opposite direction and dispatched troops to Cuba, Puerto Rico, Santo Domingo, and Panama in an effort to increase its influence over others. Moreover, America had not, like England, voluntarily renounced slavery but had been forced to fight an extremely bloody civil war to reach the level of tolerance that the English had shown decades before. And years after the civil war, stories of atrocities being committed against innocent blacks appeared in the Caribbean press at times, a reminder of the countries internal problems.

No, Americans were not civilized. They did not participate in sportsman like activities such as cricket, where rules were scrupulously followed and a pause was taken in the afternoon for a tea break where etiquette and protocol could be practiced. Bert's impression of their concept of sportsmanship had been shaped by a picture in a Miami newspaper of a scene from the American national pastime of baseball. In this photograph, the spikes on the player's shoes were raised in weapon-like fashion as he was hurtling through the air with the obvious intent of injuring his opponent. No, Americans were not as civilized as the English.

To the best of Bert's memory, when a murder occurred in Jamaica, it was invariably because of an altercation between people of low education, and was not perpetrated by the whites. Moreover such deaths were not attributed to such an inconsequential thing as the color of ones skin. Usually there was a woman involved, sometimes a theft, at other times a dispute over property. Overindulgence in the consumption of rum was often the precipitating factor in these crimes.

From its cane sugar Jamaica produced very potent rum that tended to debauch the European missionaries or businessmen who could afford to drink it excessively on a daily basis. They deteriorated during a long-term downwards spiral that ruined their livers, decimated their marriages, and hastened their deaths from so-called natural causes. The Jamaicans of lower class were of course less affluent, could not afford to drink as often, drank a less refined rum, and tended to do their drinking in weekend binges after they received their pay. The sudden suspension of inhibitions caused by the alcohol would then lead to a spontaneous combustion of their emotions with at times fatal results.

Undoubtedly the killing of one person by another just because of their color had occurred in Jamaica during the days of slavery, but this was not in the conscious thoughts of a people who were three generations removed from the last vestiges of a slavery that had developed so differently from that in the United States. Murder was always abhorrent but at least it was understandable when jealousy, money, or revenge was involved. To a Jamaican, it made no sense whatsoever for a white to murder a black simply because of their color.

In Jamaica the use of a color in reference to a person was primarily with the intent of describing them. No conclusion could be drawn about the social status of someone who was said to be black, brown, fair skinned, or white. A light skinned person was likely to be middle class but a physician might be dispassionately referred as being a black man while a maid might be described as being fair skinned. Their occupation gave their class; their color gave their appearance. In the United States on the other hand, color was used to indicate status. You were either white or black and consequently your rights were either equal or unequal. Your shade of black did convey some benefit, but never enough to free you from the possibility of being oppressed.

As he thought about this topic, Bert remembered the constables who maintained order in Jamaica. They were quite dashing in their uniforms of light shirts and black pants with the familiar red stripe down the side and white helmets that protected them from the searing sun. When a disagreement developed, the constable would step in and quickly end it. At this point in time they commanded a lot of respect from the population. They did not carry guns but kept the peace without the use of any weapon other than their stick.

"Of course I will be careful Papa" Bert responded. "If any problems develop, I will look for a constable right away so that they can make sure that nothing bad happens."

"Unfortunately in America the police are often the ones who harm you" said Horatio sadly. "They think differently than the constables here. I cannot understand how they can be that way, but they are. Until you learn their ways, be very careful what you say and do. When you get to Miami I have arranged for friends to meet you and make sure all goes well. They will put you on a train to Tuskegee. Once you are there ask the teachers, students, and other people that you meet what to expect. They have experience and can advise you better than I can."

The thought of going to someone other than his father for advice seemed strange. Papa was the epitome of the rectitude that was usually present in upper middle class Jamaica. He was not what people called overly religious, but he did see to it that the family went to church regularly. He treated his wife with great respect. In later years Bert came to understand what his father had meant when he heard him say to one of his friends that he had never put his shoes under another woman's bed. He realized the pride that his father felt in being an honorable man and was strengthened in his resolve to be equally honorable.

Marriage and fidelity were not always in evidence in Jamaica despite the fact that it is a heavily Christian nation. Some of this was due to the matriarchal nature of the African culture from which most Jamaicans descended. In Africa, mother and children often lived separately from the father. Slavery accentuated this circumstance since slave owners often separated the male slave from the female slave after she had become pregnant. Most unions between the whites and non-whites were never sanctioned by marriage until after slavery was ended. Even then, many of these relationships did not involve the ritual of marriage.

The middle class male in Jamaica adopted the English tradition of marriage, but continued the colonial practice of marrying within ones social sphere then having additional relationships, often with women of a lower social status. To marry and be faithful, as Horatio had done, was to be very middle class.

As Bert prepared to get into the transit boat that would take him out to the ship, the excitement within him grew. His whole family was there to see him off. His older sister May who was so respected because of her piety and gentle manner, his brother Roger who he would sorely miss despite his constant vying for his attention, and his younger half siblings--Iris, who was always called Dottie, Lorenzo, and Irma. Juanita, with a slight arch of her back confirming the early stages of her fourth pregnancy, stood next to Papa, an always imposing figure who dwarfed those around him. Baa, her ever-present helmet protecting her from the tropical sun, was flanked by the maid Vie who had come along to look after the children and say goodbye to the young man who was almost a son to her.

A small group of people stood a short distance away from his family, watching the rituals of departure as if they were a form of entertainment. The countrywomen in this group looked quite colorful with the bandanas that enclosed their short, black, curly hair and the skirts that enclosed ample hips—hips that constantly swayed as they walked and realigned their body's weight in order to balance the goods that they carried on their heads.

Some of these people hoped that one day they too would be able to get on one of the large boats that came to the harbor and travel to America. It was commonly believed that anyone who was willing to work hard could make a large income there and afford luxuries that the average worker in Jamaica would never experience. Although they knew of America's reputation for prejudice, many were willing to trade the possibility of being exposed to prejudice for the certainty of their present situation where opportunities were limited. In the ensuing decades, as the industrial revolution progressed, more and more Jamaicans opted to leave and seek their fortune abroad. Those who remained would exert pressures on the class system that prevailed in 1911 and make it a relic of the Jamaica of Bert's childhood. Most of us expect that the circumstances that prevailed in our childhood will exist forever. But change was inescapable in the past and will be in the future.

'MARKET GIRL' by BARRINGTON WATSON
COLLECTION OF OWEN MUNRO

"Remember Bert", his father admonished, "study hard, get good grades, and always remember that you are a Forsyth. Be sure to write at least once a month so that we know what is happening. Don't forget what I told you about avoiding any problems with the customs of the Americans. It is very different there. Alabama can be a very dangerous place. Get your education, come back home, and don't get involved in their problems in the meantime."

"Don't worry Papa" Bert replied. I wont forget what you told me." Then he turned and said a few words to his well-wishers. "Roger, don't break any of my things while I am gone or you will regret it when I get back. Especially be sure to leave my drawings alone. May, keep reading all those books and make sure that Roger does what I said. I know that you will write often and keep me informed. Vie, make sure that Dottie, Lorenzo, and Irma behave themselves until I get back! Baa, thanks for taking such good care of me. I'll really miss you. Papa says I won't know what to do without you to keep an eye on me but don't worry, I'll get along even though the world *is* in a turmoil. Juanita, the next time I see you, I'll have a new brother or sister. Take good care of yourself and thanks for being such a good mother to all of us."

His siblings each kissed him on the cheek and said a few words of goodbye. The younger ones did not quite understand what this departure meant. They expected to see Bert again in days when in fact it would be ten months before he came home again and many years before he returned for an extended stay. May and Roger had a greater understanding and were consequently sadder than the others. May hugged him a little longer than the others did and Roger showed the depth of his feelings for his older brother by hitting him on the shoulder a little harder than usual.

"Last lick!" cried Roger. This was the ritual used on departure. One sibling would hit the other, cry 'last lick', then dash away in twists and turns in an effort to avoid a retaliatory hit. If you were unable to hit them back, they could then claim the title of having been successful in administering the last lick. Bert made no effort to move but conceded this victory to his brother and smiled as Roger disappeared behind the safety of his father. If you could seek refuge behind an adult, you were pretty well guaranteed of having the adult call an end to the proceedings so that you became the de facto winner.

With all of his goodbyes completed, it was time for Bert to get into the small boat that would take him and two other boys to the ship that awaited them in the harbor. His father would accompany them in the boat to ensure that the three got safely on board. As usual, the swells were minor because of the protection offered by the promontories and Navy Island. The boat rocked gently as it bobbed over the water, past the banana boat that was loading at the dock, and towards the ship that waited a few hundred yards from shore.

After they boarded the ship, his father sought out the captain in order to place the boys in his care. They approached the captain and Horatio made the introductions. "Captain, this is my son Bert. These other two boys are Andrew and Sylvester. They will be with you until Miami where they will be met at the port. Boys, come forward and pay your respects to the captain. Be certain to follow all of his instructions."

The three boys stepped forward, shifted their feet nervously, and spoke their greeting as commanded. "Pleased to meet you sir" they said indistinctly and with no degree of unison.

A stern look came over the captain's face. "Always remove your hat when addressing the captain, boys," he admonished in a voice that commanded respect yet provoked a degree of anxiety. "I'm pleased to have you aboard." The words were said without malice and impressed themselves on young Bert. He was being reminded that a certain respect was always due to those who were in positions of authority.

The class system that Bert grew up in would have an effect on his reaction to the social system that he would encounter in the United States. As a minor, he recognized that respect was due to others such as the captain or the English who were considered representatives of the colonial authority. As a member of the upper middle class, he was accustomed to receiving a certain degree of respect in return. He was also expected to show a certain level of respect to those who were below his station, just as they would show respect to him. Neither his father nor his teachers had even given him any lectures about the responsibilities of the class system, but through encounters such as the one with the captain, every Jamaican learned how to interact with those of another station without either party feeling that they were being treated improperly.

Now his father had warned him that in the United States, his class, his education, and his skills would all be subservient to his color and that he could be subject to disrespect from those below him in class simply because of his color. Had he been of a lower social standing, the discrepancy would not have been as marked and the effect on his psyche not as profound. Hence Bert's class, upbringing, and cultural milieu emerge as additional predisposing factors in his development as a champion of the effort to insure that individuals were judged on the basis of their capabilities rather than their color.

Once on board, Bert found a vantage point that allowed him a view of the dock. He stayed there, waving, until the dock and his family were mere specks in the distance. His eyes glistened with a trace of moisture as he realized the enormity of the change that was about to take place in his life. The adventure had begun.

3

TUSKEGEE

"We have to land the plane or we're going to crash! The temperature of the outside air is so high that the engine is beginning to overheat. When I tried to increase our altitude in order to reach a cooler temperature, the strain on the engine was enough to cause it to get even hotter and start to sputter. This is only going to get worse if we don't do anything. We have to land and jettison everything that we can so that the engine will not have to work so hard. If we do that, I think we should be able to climb above the heat without making things worse"

Bert had spoken these words to his co-pilot, Al Anderson, as they flew in the Pride of Atlantic City over the Mojave Desert after departing on July 17, 1933 from Bader Field in Atlantic City for a trip to Los Angeles and back. Less than half way through their trip the number of near disasters that they had already experienced in their small plane were enough to have convinced a lesser pair to give up their quest. Now they had to come up with a plan that would ensure that this, the latest in a series of challenges, would be surmounted, as all previous problems had been surmounted.

Once the two pilots had talked it over and agreed that the best decision was to land, Bert began to scan the landscape below for an airfield or a site that would be suitable for an emergency landing. Without realizing that it was happening, he bifurcated his thought processes, allowing his conscious mind to focus on the problem at hand while his subconscious resumed the trend of thought that had been previously been triggered by the dry heat of the desert.

....

It had been equally hot that day in 1911 when he arrived in Miami, Florida after leaving Jamaica. He was met at the wharf by the friends of his father who had agreed to look after him and see to it that he was safely on a train to Tuskegee Alabama and this new phase of his life.

He found, to his dismay, that Miami seemed hotter than Jamaica had been. During the day the Doctor Breeze that had lifted his kites was no longer coolly flowing between his loose white shirt and his tobacco brown skin. At night he lay motionless in bed, devoid of the natural air conditioning caused by the Undertaker's Breeze and unwilling to create any movement that might cause his body to generate additional heat. An unaccustomed perspiration created a thin layer of moisture on his torso and aggravated his discomfort. One quarter of an hour passed by, then another. Eventually he succumbed to fatigue and slept.

When he awoke, it felt as if he had not slept at all the previous night. He knew that he must have slept because some of the post midnight hours were unaccounted for when he awoke and tried to reconstruct the previous 24 hours. In the twilight that exists between sleeping and full awareness, he lay in his bed and recalled the goodbyes in Jamaica, the boat trip, the arrival in Miami, and all of the questions that his Jamaican-born hosts had asked him last night about what was going on in Jamaica. He remembered tossing and turning for hours as he wondered about the life that awaited him in Alabama. Then there was a blank—somewhere after 2 A.M. he surmised. He didn't remember the sunrise, so he must have been asleep then. Yes, he must have slept, but it was not a satisfying sleep.

After he arose, he found that the family had prepared a traditional Jamaican breakfast in his honor. A highly salted codfish imparted its flavor and salt to the almost tasteless, springy yellow fruit called ackee that had been boiled to make a favorite Jamaican dish that resembled scrambled eggs. The dough-like fruit of the breadfruit tree was baked, sliced, and served warm with a taste that reminded him of slightly sweetish bread. Green bananas were boiled, mashed and mixed with milk, topped with brown granulated sugar, and served as porridge. Plantains were caressed with a touch of lime, fried, and served as a side dish. Milo, Britain's answer to Ovaltine, was an option, along with fresh orange juice, as a drink. He had been looking forward to an American meal but in retrospect, he truly appreciated the last really Jamaican breakfast he would have for some time to come.

After breakfast, he was taken to the train station. While they were waiting for his departure, his hosts acquainted him with some of the realities that existed for someone with any degree of African heritage in the southern United States. "Here is some food to take with you on the train Bert. No coloreds are allowed in the dining car. Make sure that you don't use any of the bathrooms marked 'whites only' no matter how much you need to go. Sit where the conductor tells you to sit. There will be some colored porters on the train who can help you if you have any questions. The same thing goes when you arrive in Tuskegee; obey all the signs you will see there. Be careful where you eat, drink, sit, or go to the bathroom. If a white man calls you any names, don't answer back and be sure to say 'yes sir' when you talk to them. This isn't Jamaica and the sooner you recognize that, the safer you will be."

He felt his face flush and his stomach spasm as he held back the impulse to ask why people tolerated such indignities. In Jamaica, the white plantation owners and British ex-patriates did command a special position but somehow it did not seem the same. Since ordinary white Englishmen recognized the privileged position of the gentry in England, it did not seem demeaning for native Jamaicans to recognize a special position for the gentry in Jamaica. Furthermore, even though the British were privileged members of the empire and at the top of the social order in Jamaica, they knew that this position did not entitle them to being physically abusive. At times they might be verbally abusive to servants whose performance was deemed unsatisfactory, but this display was based on class more than race. Those whites who were recent arrivals to the island quickly learned to minimize any tendency to arrogance.

The class system in Jamaica had developed in such a way that by and large everyone could accept his or her position without significant rancor. As the son of one of the most prominent men in Port Antonio, Bert was accustomed to showing the whites respect but also to being treated with respect by the whites. Similarly he expected respect from the working classes and never would have considered treating someone of a lower social rank with the type of disrespect that was being ascribed to the whites in the United States. Even within the working class in Jamaica there was a stratification that allowed those of ambition the opportunity to advance and be shown respect. There was nothing in his prior experience that was comparable to what he was being told about America.

The earnest admonitions of his hosts had their intended effect--he resolved to avoid any confrontations in the days to come. After receiving their well wishes he boarded the train that would take him to Tuskegee. His feelings must have paralleled those of the white explorers who were about to embark on a journey that would take them to a strange land occupied by savage and bloodthirsty barbarians who could at any moment launch an unprovoked attack. He felt some fear, the fear of the unknown, but he was able to control it, confident that his father would not have allowed him to make a trip that was not safe.

In Jamaica he had spent over three hours with his father on the train from Port Antonio to Kingston but this journey was nothing like that one. The Jamaican trip was breathtaking as the train wound its way across precipitous mountains past waterfalls and along bamboo-lined gorges that had been forged by mountain streams in the centuries after the island arose from the oceans. Had the train ever derailed on such a mountainside, no one would have survived. All of the scenery was spectacular. The tracks made their way through forests that still contained exotic hardwoods such as mahogany, mahoe, and satinwood. The train strained up the mountains and by palm-thatched huts with corrugated zinc sides that were erected on hillsides that tolerated only small arable plots of land. The people who lived there grew just enough breadfruit, bananas, plantain, and yams that, when supplemented by an occasional pig or one of a small cadre of chickens that ran wild until they were needed, allowed them to survive without fear of starvation.

While the people who lived in these homes were poor by any standard, they had chosen to live under these circumstances, surrounded by the beauty of nature, rather than to migrate to the artificiality of a city with its promise of greater wealth. In this visual paradise, giant flame of the forest trees, easily discernible with their large orange-red flowers, sprouted unattended in the surrounding forests. Hedges of multicolored crotons were planted on the paths to their makeshift home in an effort to add to the beauty of their environment. Clusters of red, white, blue, and orange bougainvillea flowers adorned their doorsteps. It was truly a sight to behold.

His father always paid a shilling more for each ticket so that they could ride in the better coach and avoid the crowded cars filled with workers whose body odors reflected the rarity of their taking a bath. Many of these men would have looked extremely dangerous to the uninitiated in that they wore razor sharp machetes at their sides. For these day laborers who earned their living by clearing fields, the machete was a simple tool of the trade that was usually as innocuous as the laptop computer carried by a commuter on a train. Only on occasion, usually a drunken Saturday night, was the machete likely to be used as a weapon.

The train also contained noisy small animals such as chickens that were being taken to market, and women called higglers who had huge baskets that contained fruits or vegetables that would be sold in the city. The fruits often included exotic varieties such as star apples, otaheite apples, naseberries, guineps, ortaniques, tamarind, sweet sops and sour sops, Bombay, St. Julian, or number 11 mangoes, and much more. The vegetables were quite mundane such as cho cho, yam, and gungo peas.

When he got thirsty, he would find someone with a water coconut whose cool sweet fluid could quench your thirst like nothing else. After drinking the fluid he would have the coconut opened so that he could eat the jelly next to the husk. If the coconut had matured a bit, the jelly became a solid and he settled for a filling, rubbery white meat instead.

The American train was nothing like that. The train was much larger and much, much cleaner, the trip was much longer, and although the scenery was more varied, it could not compare with the beauty that one saw through the windows of the Jamaican train as it noisily made its way through the lush green tropical foliage. In America there were towns much bigger than Port Antonio or Kingston. Instead of small plots of land that were occupied by makeshift shacks, he saw vast farms that seemed to stretch to the horizon where a large home was carefully constructed. Only when he went through the towns, close to the right of way, did he see homes that bespoke poverty, homes that were occupied by coloreds who often seemed to lack an interest in landscaping their yards in the fashion of their brethren in poverty in Jamaica.

He also saw huge swamps that dwarfed any that he had ever seen before, rivers that were as wide as the sea channel between Port Antonio and Navy Island instead of being easily fordable as were those back home, and bridges and tunnels that seemed to go on forever. The weather was not as predictable as he was accustomed to. Instead of a brief afternoon shower there was an afternoon long deluge in northern Florida and evidence of a drought in Alabama. The scale was epic, but mile for mile, he preferred Jamaica.

Fortunately the trip was uneventful in that there were no racial confrontations. As he traveled, he read up on the school that he would soon be attending. The colored educator, Booker T. Washington, had founded Tuskegee Institute in 1881. At first, the courses offered were very basic ones that were intended to teach the previously uneducated and recently liberated coloreds to be mechanics, tradesmen, teachers, and farmers. With the passage of time, more advanced studies such as a college of arts and sciences and a school of engineering were added to appeal to more highly educated students such as Bert.

In 1895 the country was experiencing a series of lynchings and the enactment of segregation laws in response to efforts by the colored population to achieve greater rights. In an attempt to reduce tension, Booker T. Washington gave a speech stating that coloreds should stop demanding voting rights and equality in public places. Instead, he advocated reliance on hard work and education. The white population agreed with this sentiment and came to view Washington as being the spokesperson for the colored population.

There were those who dissented with this approach to the problem of segregation however. The most prominent was W.E.B. Du Bois, the first colored to receive a PhD at Harvard University. He taught history and economics at Atlanta University in the early 1900's and in 1909 helped to form the civil rights organization known as the National Association for the Advancement of Colored People. This group was usually referred to by an acronym, the NAACP. Unlike Washington, Du Bois believed that coloreds, especially the college-educated ones, must speak out constantly against segregation and for equality. These conflicting views as to the best method of ending segregation each had substantial followings.

Tuskegee Institute was located in the center of the state, one mile outside the town of Tuskegee, and forty miles east of Montgomery on a site that overlooked all of the adjacent country. As the train pulled into the station, Bert surveyed the scene that slowly filled his field of vision as they decelerated to a stop. The first objects to catch his attention were the large signs that made it clear which waiting room was for coloreds and which was for whites. He knew from the stops along the way that while the colored waiting rooms were usually in need of paint and in a general state of disrepair, the white areas, glimpsed briefly from without, were maintained much better.

Outside of the colored waiting room was a young man wearing a dark blue coat and trousers, as well as a cap, an ensemble similar to that worn by the students in Jamaica. His dark complexion, medium stature, and Spartan musculature were typical of the habitus of a young West Indian male rather than of the taller, raw-boned, somewhat overweight Americans that he had seen since his arrival. However there was something, something that he could not quite put his finger on, something that was atypical for a West Indian.

As the train came to a complete stop he kept his eyes focused on the young man in an effort to determine what it was that was bothering him. Suddenly he realized that it was his demeanor that caused him to question his origins. Instead of displaying the buoyancy and animation that characterized the people that he saw on the street in Jamaica, this young man projected a cautious, subdued, almost fearful attitude. Most of the time he looked at the ground and not at those around him. Only on occasion did he glance in the direction of the train and then he did so for only a brief moment.

When Bert disembarked from the train their eyes met briefly and they approached each other in tentative recognition. "Are you the new Tuskegee student, Albert Forsythe?" asked the young man in a somewhat self-deprecating manner.

"Yes," said Bert as he looked straight ahead and simultaneously observed the young man, the crowd that was mostly white, and the physical layout of the station.

"I'm Hugh Paddyfoot from Gordon Town in Jamaica," responded the young man, his every word reflecting the lyrical accent that was characteristic of the West Indies. "I'm here to drive you to the Institute. Let's leave immediately. It's best not to linger in the town any longer than you have to."

Paddyfoot stowed Bert's small valise in the back of the buggy, took a seat on the left side of the buggy—which still seemed strange since those raised under the British customarily sat on the right and drove on the left side of the street—and shook the reins as he verbally urged the horse into motion. As they drove down the narrow road that led from the train station to the school, he explained to Bert why he had been anxious to leave town quickly without making any effort to show him around. The newcomer needed to be indoctrinated on the 'facts of life' for a person of color in the southern United States.

"It took me awhile to get used to life here" Paddyfoot confided in a voice that was stronger than he had used in town and with a posture that seemed much more assertive. "It is very different than back home. Everyone from the school tries to keep out of town as much as possible. The whites are suspicious that the students want to change the local way of life and are quick to interpret the slightest gesture that is out of the ordinary as a challenge that has to be met so that the colored always be kept in their 'place'. They don't expect any problems from the local colored, but are worried about what they call 'outside influences' and have been known to react with an anger that can be frightening."

With hardly a pause to catch a breath, he continued in the manner of one who was anxious to complete a distasteful task. "When you are in town, avoid looking in the direction of a white person for an extended period of time. The shorter you look, the less likely it is that someone will interpret the look as being offensive. If a white person challenges you over something that you said or did or something they say you said or did, never argue—apologize respectfully and back away without provoking a confrontation."

Bert thrust his tongue against his teeth and sucked in air in order to make the highly audible and distinctive sound that Jamaicans frequently used to instantly convey their displeasure. Then he cried out "*Chu mon!*" the Jamaican idiom used to express surprise, anger, or to simply emphasize a point. "I was told at home and in Miami about the craziness of the people here but this is totally ridiculous! How can the people here put up with such nonsense?"

"*Wha fe do*," came the reply as Paddyfoot responded in kind. "The signs they put up are insulting and humiliating, but pretty soon *yu* won't even see them. Get your education *mon* and let the Americans take care of their problems. This is not our country. The people who were born here don't like it any more than we do but them seem unwilling or unable to force changes. *Yu'd* best accept that things are the way that they are; I am serious when I say it is dangerous to do anything that might anger someone. That person might not do anything right at that moment but they could mention what *yu* did to someone who might decide to teach *yu* a painful or even fatal lesson; they could report *yu* to the police who have been known to beat coloreds without provocation. After the Civil War some whites formed a group called the Ku Klux Klan that often killed anyone who tried to stand up for their rights. They even went after whites who were sympathetic to coloreds. They got so bad that the government forced them to disband but they still have a lot of sympathizers and could rise up again soon. It's best that *yu* just listen to what I tell *yu* and do what I say. Soon you'll come to understand the situation here."

Bert grudgingly resolved to follow that suggestion, the same one that he had received in Miami and from his father in Port Antonio. Still he thought it sad that his countryman seemed to display a submissive attitude towards these people and vowed that he would never sink to that level. He listened without interrupting as Paddyfoot filled him in on what to expect when they arrived at the school. With his mind concentrating on what lay ahead, the trip to the Institute was quickly completed and the ignominy of prejudice was temporarily shelved in one of the mind's many folders.

After his arrival at the school, Bert, like all of the students, was given a brochure that pointed out that students were required to wear a uniform, to have a bible, to abstain from tobacco, alcohol, and gambling, and to refrain from taking part in any mass political meeting or convention. All non-resident male students were expected to board at one of the five dormitories set aside for them on the school grounds. To help defray the $10 per month cost of boarding, students had the option of working at the school, an option that Bert later took advantage of.

On September 13, 1911, as per his father's wishes, he was enrolled in a four-year course in Architectural Drawing. His first two years, he received almost perfect grades in mathematics, a subject at which he had a natural aptitude. In his first year he suffered to some extent from the homesickness that would be expected in a fourteen-year-old boy who was transplanted from a life of ease in familiar surroundings to one of discipline in a foreign and sometimes hostile land.

Bert was happy to learn that there were over a dozen West Indian students at the school. He found that he was quickly able to make friends with them, but that friendship with the Americans was a bit more difficult--both because his accent sometimes made it difficult for them to understand him and because they could not understand each other when it came to discussions about the relationships between the races in the United States. Nevertheless he soon fit in and made many friends.

During the next two years at Tuskegee, Bert came to know the symbols of segregation in the South as well as the effect that they had on the psyche. Signs in the town warned coloreds against using diners or drinking fountains or certain seats on public transportation. A colored was expected to look at a white deferentially and to speak respectfully. Sporadic stories of beatings, jailings, and lynchings attested to the necessity of obeying the mores of the community. His classmates recounted many tales of atrocities by whites against coloreds that were quite terrifying. No one that he knew of was ever affected by these extreme manifestations of cruelty, but all were affected by the reminders of inequality that they were exposed to on every trip into town. He began to take the signs for granted and to obey them without a conscious effort but subconsciously he was being wounded like a child who is constantly denigrated by a parent. Although he had the advantage of knowing that he was a *Forsythe*, a person of intrinsic value, it still hurt.

Race relations in the South were very tenuous at all times. Because simple words often expressed complicated relations, both whites and non-whites had to know what they could say, to whom they could say it, and when it should or should not be said. For example, the white population had assigned the word Negro, derived from the Spanish and

Portuguese word for black, to describe all non-Asians and non-Europeans who had *any* degree of sub-Saharan African ancestry. This word was generally used in a dispassionate way that suggested that the word entailed a scientific description despite the fact that many Europeans of Mediterranean origin had a significant sub-Saharan heritage but were not classified as being Negro.

When a white speaker wanted to be disparaging, they would use the word 'nigger', a corruption of Negro that was commonly used by uneducated whites in the South. Dark skinned Negroes were usually referred to generically as blacks. Lighter skinned Negroes might be referred to as colored, with the understanding that the presence of some European content was a plus. However a dark skinned person who was in favor might be called colored while an out of favor light skinned person could be a nigger. Unlike the situation in Jamaica where class was determined by more than color, it was understood that a high African heritage, as manifested by color, automatically placed the individual lower on the social ladder. This situation led to subtleties that were beyond the comprehension of a 14-year-old boy from the West Indies. If someone was called a nigger in town, they were offended. However if a friend from the Institute called them the same thing, no umbrage was taken.

As best Bert could understand, it was prudent to always use the word colored. Moreover, he noted that the primary civil rights organization in the United States had decided to name itself the National Association for the Advancement of *Colored* People. Since they preferred the word colored to the words Negro or black, he concluded that this would be his terminology.

In his first year Bert had a class that was taught by the principal of the school, Booker T. Washington. The scuttlebutt in the class was that although Booker T. Washington urged restraint in demanding civil rights in public, in private he fought the segregation laws. Since resistance is almost synonymous with youth, this reputation helped to endear Washington to his students.

There were many actions that confirmed Washington's commitment to the aggressive promotion of the advancement of coloreds. He organized a business league for coloreds in 1900 in order to help them start their own businesses; he often lectured on how to improve race relations; and he raised money for rural colored schools. It was said that he personally contributed to the cost of fighting segregation but did so discretely in order to avoid conflicts for the Institute.

As his exposure to the problems of segregation grew and his intellectual confidence matured, Bert gingerly challenged his teacher about the morality of the passive approach that Washington espoused.

"Shouldn't we be doing more to openly resist segregation?" Bert asked provocatively during one of his classes. "It's been more than forty years since the Civil War and things don't seem to be getting much better for the colored man in America."

Washington was accustomed to the impatience of youth and responded promptly with the fluid thoughts that had made him famous. "Slavery existed in Africa long before the white man came. It existed for three hundred years in the United States before being abolished, but it was abolished. The question is not whether segregation and discrimination should be ended. The question is, what is the best way to end it. It will take some time to eliminate the vestiges of slavery but they will be eliminated. Just as slavery was fated to come to an end, so are segregation and discrimination only temporary."

Bert persevered as he attempted to squeeze an admission from Washington that the previous generation, like the generation that preceded every new generation, was not acting with the wisdom that the current generation would undoubtedly display when it assumed control. "But what about right now! Three hundred years from now I won't be alive. Are you saying that we must put up with this while we live and hope that future generations will not have to?"

"I can't tell you how long it will take," Washington countered with the patience acquired from decades of successfully parrying thrusts from young men and women just awakening to their intellectual potential. "I can tell you that at this point in time the white man has all of the power. Those who push too hard are courting disaster. Even if aggressiveness resulted in segregation being ended a few years earlier than the gentle approach, what good would that be to you if you were not alive?"

His logic had its intended effect. Bert ceased his inquiries for that day even though Washington's answers had not satisfied him. However he periodically raised the same issues in future classes and tried to relate his Jamaican experiences to his American experiences. It seemed to him that there had to be some middle ground between passive acceptance of the status quo and the type of resistance that provoked hostility from the white population. He knew from his Jamaican history books that freed Jamaicans had successfully applied pressure on the English a century before while slavery still existed. Why couldn't ex-slaves in American apply more pressure than they seemed to be doing? He did not have the answers but he certainly had the questions.

These issues were often debated among the cadre of Jamaican students who came to Tuskegee. On Sundays the students would usually have dinner at the house of a Jamaican woman who welcomed the opportunity to enjoy the companionship of people who had experienced a similar upbringing and took a similar approach to life in general and race relations in particular. As students are wont to do, they debated the pros and cons of the different approaches of Du Bois and Booker T. Washington without ever reaching a single conclusion. More than anything at these sessions, they looked forward to a Jamaican meal.

When they entered their benefactor's house, they were invariably greeted with the odors of 'rice and peas' and curried meat—goat, pork, or chicken. Starting several hours before their arrival, their hostess would grate the white 'meat' of the coconut that was formed when the husk of the green coconut aged to a mellow brown and the sweetish watery fluid within condensed to a solid. Then she would soak the gratings in water, squeeze out this essence, and use it as the fluid in which rice was boiled along with some spices. When this was almost finished, some precooked gungo peas, would be stirred into the rice.

Plantains, pear—referred to as avocado by the Americans, and yams were the preferred side dishes. At other times she prepared green bananas, a fried bread called bammy, an amazingly fiery soup made from the conch shell, or a concoction of boiled coconut milk, cod or mackerel, onions, and scallions known as rundown.

Drinks varied, but at Christmas time they always managed to have a tart red drink called sorrel that was made by stewing the petals from the Sudanese shrub then adding some sweetening. After dinner there was usually a taste of homemade rum for the older boys to help get the debates going. Alcohol was not permitted at the school so their hostess was always careful as to whom she served and how much they drank.

After their meal the students invariably entered into lively discussions that covered a myriad of topics. Foremost among their subjects were items that involved England or the Caribbean, the centers of their social and political universe. Topics included the machinations of the great powers in Europe as the growth of the German navy threatened British supremacy over the oceans, the latest cricket scores, the activities of the royal family, or minor occurrences on one of their islands.

Also high on their oratorical repertoire were the activities of the country that they were now living in. The most important of these activities was race relations. While the students came from different islands in the British West Indies, represented different levels of prestige in their countries, and varied somewhat in the brown to dark brown color of their skin, they were monolithic in their evaluation of the status of race relations in America.

It seemed to them that white America had a very homogeneous view of colored Americans that failed to give due weight to differences in education and social standing. Perhaps this was due to the fact that the slaves in America had experienced less social stratification than in Jamaica, had not been allowed much social mobility, were only four and one-half decades removed from slavery, and lived in a society that had renounced the British system class system.

Moreover, at this point in time, most coloreds *were* similar in that they were either uneducated or severely under-educated and of low income. The disruptive effect that slavery had had on the integrity of slave families limited the possibility that the pedigree of a colored might provide them with some advantage. Some respect was *given* by white America to those colored who were educated or owned land, but there was not a significant cadre of colored Americans who *expected* respect by virtue of their genealogy, cultural heritage, education, and class.

In the absence of significant class, income, or educational differences, heterogeneity, in a society obsessed by race, was often supplied by skin color. Like a collection of early tintype photographs taken by an amateur experimenting in black and white, the spectrum of colored America showed a slight majority who were very dark in color, a few who were nearly white, and various shades of sepia that occupied the vast area in between. With very little economic or educational differences, the ex-slaves and their descendants were influenced by the prevailing idiocy and tended to pigeonhole each other on the basis of color. The fairer ones skin, the higher ones status. This only served to reinforce racial discrimination.

The West Indians knew that color mattered in the Caribbean, but believed that it mattered less. Their societies had adopted the British system of placing a great deal of importance on an individual's paternity and class. The fact that whites, lights, and blacks were all governed by class mitigated the potential for discontent in the West Indies. After slavery had ended, an English cockney in the Caribbean who tried to assume superiority on the basis of his color would have been put in his place by both whites and blacks. Not so in the United States. Color was king.

America seemed schizophrenic because of the conflict between an influential minority personified by W.E.B. Du Bois in his call for confrontation, and the majority as represented by the more passive approach of Booker T. Washington. There was some friction between the 'haves' and the 'have-nots' in the West Indies in 1912 that had some similarity to the racial conflict in America, but the level was minimal. The West Indians, descended from cultures that had experienced major revolts by slaves, at an age when testosterone floods the circulation and unleashes primal drives, wanted the American coloreds to be more aggressive.

These views were shared by the West Indians regardless of their class in their native countries or whether their heritage was pure African or a mixture of European, African, and East Indian. Those who had a European heritage that was several generations removed, and those who had none, considered themselves to be West Indians and thought like West Indians. The depth of an individuals color might be highly significant to white southerners but for the islanders, the bond of their common cultural heritage far surpassed the differences in their ancestry, their color, or their class.

The students recognized that both at home and in the United States they were living in a white-dominated world and were accepting of the fact that this denied them access to certain privileges. However on their arrival in the United States, they harbored some misconceptions that were common to the inhabitants of the Caribbean. Their limited exposure to American history in school was compromised even further by the fact that the official history that was put forth by white American historians had minimized the extent to which the slaves in America had resisted their subjugation. Moreover, the West Indians did not appreciate the fact that non-whites in the West Indies had been subject to a lower level of prejudice than in America because of several historical factors and not just because of an intrinsic fighting spirit that they possessed. These factors included their 30-year head start on freedom and the fact that they enjoyed a 20:1 numerical superiority in the racial ratio instead of the 1:2 disadvantage that prevailed in the South.

Had the students thought about these factors, they would have been less critical of the colored Americans reluctance to actively object to the demeaning reminders that coloreds were considered inferior, the physical threats, and the severe economic restrictions that prevailed in the South, and less convinced that they themselves would have been more proactive if they had been born in America.

Even though they might not have been justified in many of their assumptions, their attitude did create a certain bravado among the students, an attitude that made them more likely than the Americans to think in terms of concrete actions that could be taken to end discrimination. This was especially true of the young Bert whose family heritage and station in life made him very resentful of the indignities to which he was being exposed.

However the only action taken by the students was verbal and was rarely expressed outside of their group. They were proscribed by the schools bylaws against participating in mass political meetings, restrained by the knowledge that the American born students were not very supportive of aggressive efforts, unwilling to become involved because of their ages and their lack of resources, and secure in the knowledge that they could easily leave the problem behind.

At these suppers, the West Indians contented themselves by saying "We would never tolerate that back home". Then they went home on Sunday evening to study and prepare for the day that they could leave the South behind them.

In addition to discussing racism on Sunday afternoons and in Booker T. Washington's class, Bert was afforded a third opportunity to consider this problem. Because of his stature, Booker T. Washington was often called on to travel to New York or Washington D.C. to consult on civil rights problems. On these occasions Washington had the students drive him to the railroad station in a horse and buggy as part of the work that they did to defray the cost of their board. The time that it took to drive the five miles to Chehaw Station, a depot on the line of the Western Railroad of Alabama, gave the students an excellent opportunity to talk to the principal and learn more about his views on racial problems.

It seemed to Bert that he was given this opportunity more often than others were. In any event, at these times Washington would discuss the problem of discrimination in the South and give his opinion on the advantages of his go-slow approach to overcoming this legacy of slavery.

Once the horse was turned in the direction of the town he was on automatic pilot. Instinctively he would assume a slow pace at first as he moved away from the food and shelter of his barn and then later a more rapid pace after the journey to town was completed and the turn was made for home. The two occupants of the buggy had little to do except exchange ideas as their conveyance bounced down the dusty, rut-covered country roads.

In anticipation of Bert's launching his usual polemic, Washington initiated the conversation. "Look at the progress that we have made in the last forty years Bert. Besides being freed from slavery, coloreds can now own property, move to the North if they wish, get an education. I still remember when none of those things were possible. Don't be so hung up on what you don't have that you overlook what you do have."

Bert responded quickly to Washington's opening salvo on their favorite topic. "Those are certainly important things but they are all physical things. There are spiritual things that are equally important. How about the right to be free from fear and the right to dignity and respect. I think it must have been easier when people were slaves and had no rights. Its like a slow torture to allow some rights and deny others."

As always, Washington was ready with a response. "Remember that the whites in the South were forced to give up slavery. They resent having lost the war and take out that resentment on the coloreds. Since they can't have slavery they settle for segregation and discrimination. There are still a lot of people alive who fought in the civil war and cannot accept the change. As they die off you will see segregation get less and less."

"But why should we today have to wait for that?" Bert queried, the slight change in the timbre of his voice betraying the passion that he felt. "Slavery was never justified and the type of slavery enforced in the United States was even less so. We had slavery in the West Indies without the severe humiliation that you see in America and without the brutality."

"It seems that way to you now, but there was a great deal of brutality for the slaves in the sixteenth, seventeenth, and eighteenth centuries in the West Indies. Circumstances there led to an earlier abolition of slavery so the coloreds there have had longer period of time without slavery and are reaping the benefits of that passage of time. That's why I advocate that we temper our demands for equality and concentrate on educating our youth and starting up businesses so that the incomes of the coloreds will rise. As this happens you will see segregation lessen and violence against coloreds eliminated. The two greatest enemies of the colored man are the lack of education that puts us at a disadvantage in the first place, and the violence that is intended to frighten us into accepting that disadvantage. Equal rights in voting and equal rights in public places should not be our primary concern at this time."

Bert persisted, as youth always persists when its certainty is challenged by experience. "I read in the papers that whites think that coloreds are not capable of performing mentally difficult tasks. They then use that unproven conclusion as a justification for not spending enough to provide coloreds with a decent elementary school education. Next they complete the circle by using the fact that blacks have had an inferior elementary education to make it difficult for them to get into a public college where they could learn to do difficult tasks. That makes no sense and proves that whites are not as intelligent as they think they are. That some of these white farmers who never made it through high school should think that they are smarter than I am is ridiculous. That I should not be able to sit at any lunch counter or drink from any water fountain is humiliating!"

Bert persevered as the journey neared its destination and the debate was drained of new content. "In the South they're upfront in their discrimination but from what I have heard, the result is not much different in the North where they claim to be less prejudiced. Because coloreds in the North have to live in segregated areas, they wind up going to elementary schools that are poorly equipped and poorly staffed and have similar difficulties getting into the public colleges that they could afford."

The conversation followed similar channels on each trip. When they approached the train station, Washington would signal the conclusion of their discussion with essentially the same comments. "Obviously I sympathize with what you are saying. We both want the same ends. What we are arguing about is the means. No one can say with any certainty that one approach is better than the other. Its up to each of us to search our consciences and decide what road we want to follow. Just remember not to do anything that will jeopardize your life. Also remember that it would be wrong not to do anything at all."

Bert was favorably influenced by his mentor's quest to improve the quality of life for the coloreds and to subtly resist the racism that assumed that coloreds were intellectually inferior and incapable of performing a skilled occupation adequately. On the other hand, he was sympathetic to dissenting opinions such as those of Du Bois. Should educated coloreds simply set an example or should they take the lead in a prominent way in order to hasten the end of segregation? After dropping Washington off at the train station, in the solitude of his journey back to the Institute, he would go over their conversation and silently debate the question. His familial and cultural inheritance had predisposed him to resist injustice, now his education was helping him to develop the tools that he would use in that resistance.

From his conversations with the colored American students Bert gained other insights that often seemed to confuse rather than clarify. In the South, America's most segregated area, whites and blacks often lived in the same neighborhoods. There was a certain civility as long as boundaries were respected, but there was no social interaction. There was a tolerance to proximity, a proximity that had existed for hundreds of years and was accepted. In the North, the area that had shed the blood of its children in order to end slavery, there was an intolerance to proximity.

While signs in the southern cities carefully specified where each race was to eat, drink water, wait for transportation, or use the bathroom, white people in the rural areas were generally courteous and even friendly to their black neighbors although they would never consider going to school or church with them. The South that he saw on a train or in a town was much harsher than the South that functioned on a day-to-day basis. So many contradictions.

The problem of segregation was in some ways worse for someone such as Bert who had been raised in an entirely different environment, than it was for many colored Americans, especially those who had a minimal education and no exposure to a different way of life. While they obviously resented the restrictions imposed by segregation and debated as to the best method of overcoming them, it seemed to Bert that their historical circumstances made them more tolerant of intolerance.

Not surprisingly, the colored Americans did not see themselves as tolerating intolerance. They fervently wanted change, but felt that as members of a group that was outnumbered physically, economically, and militarily, they had to try to achieve change through group action rather than individual resistance to individual acts. In fact, given their situation, such pragmatism was probably the only sensible choice.

In 1912 Bert learned that his old headmaster, Major W. H. Plant, would be coming to Tuskegee as a representative of the Jamaican government at the International Congress of Negroes. When he arrived, Plant asked many questions about Bert's progress and was surprised when Bert told him that he was often called on to explain calculus problems to his class in mathematics—a class in which the slight 15 year-old Bert was dwarfed in size by the presence of men who were up to 25 years of age. Plant was happy to see that his former pupil was fulfilling the potential that he had seen, but was concerned that he might not be sufficiently challenged at a school where many incoming students had been denied an adequate basic education. He admonished Bert that he should keep in touch so that Plant could be assured that Bert was in the proper environment. This concern encouraged Bert to reconsider his options.

He had made every effort to avoid situations that might expose him to the indignities of prejudice. However, rather than continuing to adapt to the status quo as southern coloreds seemed to have learned to, he considered moving his studies to the northern United States or Canada where he believed that the problem would be significantly reduced. For Jamaicans of all social classes, their experience of being a majority rather than a minority, their history of having had a rebellion, and their longer experience with freedom than their American counterparts, made the acceptance of discrimination a difficult alternative.

Another factor was a letter from his father that discussed his return to Jamaica after he had finished his studies in architecture and civil engineering at the age of eighteen. Horatio had chosen a girl from a very wealthy and respectable family for Bert to marry. However, as Bert recalled her, she was quite ugly and very heavy and not someone he wanted to marry. Also, while his father had married at nineteen, an early marriage was not appealing to him.

In any event, Bert now felt that he wanted to remain in the United States where there were many more opportunities than in Jamaica. Moreover, he had concluded that architecture would not be a promising occupation in the United States because prejudice against coloreds would severely limit the quality and the quantity of the jobs that would be available.

Finally, Bert was also motivated to move because of his interest in studying medicine. Since Tuskegee did not offer the pre-med courses that he would need in order to apply to medical school, he wanted to transfer to a school in the North. When he wrote his father that he wanted to move to Illinois or Ohio and switch to a pre-med curriculum, his father was not enthusiastic. Eventually however he was able to convince his father that he should go to the University of Illinois to pursue a pre-med curriculum.

Undoubtedly his experiences at Tuskegee had a seminal effect on his evolving social consciousness. He had learned first hand about the teachings of Booker T. Washington, had read extensively about W. E. B. Du Bois, and had debated these issues with the passion that only a maturing college mind can display. The matrix had been formed for the foundation that would become the man. Now the experiences of his life would provide the finishing touches to this character.

4

The Midwest

Bert set out for the Midwest using money that he had saved from his allowance and the work that he was able to do at Tuskegee. The journey provided another opportunity for him to be impressed by the vast size of this new country and to glimpse a few more of the many variations in the landscape. The more that he saw, the more he became interested in seeing all of the wonders he had heard about. As the train entered the Midwest, he found that the countryside was much flatter than either Jamaica or Arkansas. This feature lent itself to large farms that were visually monotonous yet terribly impressive due to their size.

These behemoths displayed a homogeneous expanse of one crop such as wheat or corn instead of the mosaics that characterized the tiny parcels in the mountains of Jamaica or those of the larger farms that followed the irregular contours of rural Alabama. Once again, the scope of his trip was infinitely more impressive than a trip in Jamaica but the scenery was less esthetically pleasing.

One thing that did not change on the train as he left the South was the requirement that he take care as to where he sat, ate, drank, and went to the bathroom. The North would not be nirvana.

After Tuskegee Horatio no longer provided the majority of Bert's financial support. Generally he went to school part time and worked part time but on several occasions he had to interrupt his studies when he had ran out of money and go to work on full time basis. As a result it took him almost ten years to complete his undergraduate education. He began his studies at the University of Illinois and concluded at the University of Toledo. His circumstances in Toledo, Ohio in the early 1920's were typical of what he experienced during these years.

The relationships between the races were much less hostile in Ohio than in Alabama. A subtle system of segregation and discrimination was still a daily fact of life, but the 'whites only' signs were less frequent. Also, physical abuse was infrequent and usually took the form of being mildly hassled by the police, if you were unfortunate enough to come into contact with them, rather than being at risk for extreme violence from both the police and vigilantes as was the case for those who resided in the South.

Job discrimination and segregated housing were his biggest obstacles. With very little financial backing from home, Bert was forced to rely on a series of menial factory jobs in order to cover the basic costs of food and housing as well as the funds necessary to complete his pre-med schooling. This was quite a change for a boy who had never shined his own shoes or done any chores other than the few he had been assigned at Tuskegee.

Nevertheless he did what he had to do, driven by a goal and an almost obstinate determination to do what interested him and not what someone else dictated. He learned how to shop frugally and do without the culinary treats that he had taken for granted as a child. The clothing that had always been fashionable and kept freshly washed and ironed was now retained long after it had begun to fray and was worn without the benefit of regular laundry service. The living quarters that had been the envy of many when he was a child were now, to be charitable, less than desirable. In short, he learned to be the average colored American.

He realized that his circumstances were not very different than those of the average Jamaican but justified the plight of the average Jamaican by recalling that Jamaica was a poor country. America on the other hand was a rich country that deliberately tried to keep some citizens poor.

At one time he worked at a flourmill then, after work, rode the streetcar home with face and clothes whitened by flour. He thought how shocked his father would be to see his son like this. In fact, he felt ashamed that others would see someone of his social class in this condition. He did not have much time to contemplate these feelings however because he was usually so bone tired that he would fall asleep as soon as he got on the streetcar, and amazingly awaken precisely when it was time to get off at his destination.

This routine was most difficult for him in the winter. He was unprepared for the effect of the cold weather on his daily life. Scarce resources had to be devoted to purchasing heavy clothes that were supposed to keep him warm but never succeeded in recapturing the comfort that he had enjoyed in the tropics. The cold weather also forced him to divert money from his college fund in order to keep his apartment warm. In addition, the slowdown in traffic that occurred when it snowed caused him to spend more hours commuting and left him with fewer hours to rest and study. With less money and less time, he could only take one course at a time in the winter months. He realized that it would take him many years to complete his studies but he persevered.

An additional problem in the winter was a haze that covered a sky now subject to a much earlier sunset than he had been accustomed to in Jamaica. He did not realize it, but the lack of sunshine contributed to a depressed mood that affected him from time to time. He developed self-doubts about his wisdom in contradicting his father's wishes and occasionally considered returning home. If he had not had some definite goals in mind and a resolute character, it is likely that he would have returned to the warmth and security of his Jamaican home.

One goal of course was to complete his pre-med courses. The logic that he used to choose a college to attend was quite simple. After looking through a book that listed the colleges in the Midwest that offered pre-med courses, he chose the cheapest—the University of Toledo. He worked hard, attended school, and was able to save a little money for another goal that he had in mind.

Bert was concerned about the circumstances of his younger brother Roger who had also left home at fifteen to make his way in the world. Unlike Bert, he had not been offered an opportunity to go abroad to further his education. The arrival of three additional children into the family had caused Horatio to decide that he could not afford to send his second son to college although he was an excellent student.

Like Bert, Roger had sat on the beach and wondered what lay beyond. When he finished his basic schooling in 1915, he decided to satisfy that curiosity. With two others he embarked in a small boat for Haiti where it was said that the recently initiated occupation of the island by the United States Army had provided an opportunity for good paying jobs for English speaking people. Moreover, his father had a friend in Haiti who could house him while he looked for a position.

Haiti lay approximately 120 miles from Port Antonio. While most adults today would consider a journey of that distance in a relatively small boat on an open sea to be very hazardous, the trip was taken for granted by these three who were bolstered by the confidence of youth. On several occasions, oblivious to the dangers of the sea, they jumped from the boat and swam in waters that could have contained sharks. Fortunately their journey was incident free. After reaching the island, Roger made his way to the home of his father's friend and set about the task of finding a job.

With two years of French in high school to his credit, Roger was able to obtain a civilian assignment as a member of a branch of the United States Marines, the Gendarmerie d'Haiti, where he served as an interpreter for General Smedley D. Butler. After he settled in, he sporadically wrote to his brother and described what he had found in Haiti and how the country compared to Jamaica. Through his letters Bert was able to acquire an understanding of the situation there.

The country was quite similar to the land of their birth—warm, rainy, mountainous, and forested—yet dissimilar. There were fewer paved roads, fewer nice homes, and an entirely different social structure. As an employee of the United States, Roger led a comfortable life in Haiti with wages that were paid in American dollars. He made enough to quickly allow him to purchase a horse in order to ride to and from work and to visit friends. The horse, while attractive in appearance, had the unfortunate habit of stumbling. As a result, Roger, on more than one occasion, would arrive at his destination in a muddy state of disarray.

The small subset of the population that was educated and economically self-sufficient quickly welcomed a new member to their midst. He visited homes that had been constructed in the typical French colonial style with large porches, ornate grills, and interiors furnished with furniture made from hardwoods of rapidly diminishing availability. These homes were staffed by deferential servants who spoke a Creole version of French that he initially found difficult to understand. He had a good ear for languages however and soon mastered the dialect. Although he was experiencing very privileged circumstances for a teen aged young man, Roger was dissatisfied.

Abject poverty was infrequent in Jamaica. No search was required to find abject Haitian poverty. Moreover there was hopelessness in Haiti that he never felt in Jamaica. The Jamaican middle class made efforts to alleviate the poverty that existed by providing odd jobs for the unemployed. If someone knocked on your gate asking for work, you tried to authorize as much as you could afford. If one of Horatio's workers had to be laid off, he sent them to one of his suppliers with a note asking if they could give them a temporary job. Haitians were not accustomed to making such efforts on the behalf of the less fortunate.

There were several reasons for the differences between the two countries in the degree of poverty and the attitude of the middle classes to poverty. In Haiti, as in Jamaica, some of the mixed offspring of Europeans and Africans were granted freedom for a pragmatic reason--to enlarge the population that was available to take charge of the slaves. This freedom was granted in 1684 at which time 36,000 whites and 28,000 mulattoes oversaw a population of half a million slaves.

Haitians should have had an earlier start than Jamaica in reaping the benefits of freedom inasmuch as the French Revolution abolished slavery entirely in 1791, over forty years before it was abolished in Jamaica. Unfortunately the French planters in Haiti, in an action similar to those under-taken in the South after the American Civil War, passed laws designed to thwart the slave's freedom. This intransigence led to a slave revolt in 1793 that resulted in the death of all of the white planters who ignored the danger and did not flee from the island. In 1804, long before Jamaica's abolition of slavery and subsequent independence, Haiti became independent. However independence did not prove to be a blessing for the majority of Haitians.

Jamaica had an advantage in that it was able to gradually, over a period of 300 years, develop a stable, consistent, and politically modern form of government under the guidance of a single European power. In contrast, Haiti had a more schizophrenic and apocalyptic political development inasmuch as its rule was split almost equally between Spain and France, and independence came suddenly and violently before the proper political institutions could be developed. When Haiti found itself free of France, its leaders did not know how to lead.

The new leaders of Haiti proved to be very chaotic and more interested in lining their own pockets than in building a nation. One leader, Jean Pierre Boyer, crippled the country for decades after 1820 by incurring an indemnity to France in return for recognition of Haiti's independence. Coup d'etats and uprisings led to 29 different presidents in the 66 years following 1849. The end result of this instability was the intervention of the U.S. Marines and the imposition of American control.

An additional disadvantage for Haiti was the small size of its middle class. In Jamaica the large middle class was able to slowly gain political skills and perspective. They provided a buffer that allowed gradual reform in place of violent revolution. The slowness of the changes allowed the black and white populations of the island to be economically integrated in a way that shared resources, albeit unequally, and minimized the residual ill will of slavery. Moreover Jamaica did not have the severe demographical handicap that plagued Haiti where so much of the country was uninhabitable that the effective density of the population that occupied arable land was twice that in Jamaica.

The high population density, the expulsion of the whites and their expertise, and the fact that only a small percentage of the remaining population was middle class, destroyed the critical mass that was necessary in order to significantly alleviate the poverty of the lower class. The Haitian middle class was not large enough to hire enough servants, dispense enough day jobs, create enough businesses, or provide enough charity to significantly increase the standard of living for those at the lowest rung of the economic ladder.

Add to these problems a political system that thrived on exploiting the poor, the lack of mobility between classes, and a rudimentary educational system than did not come close to fulfilling the needs of the people, and it was not hard to understand why poverty in Haiti was a virtually hopeless condition.

In Jamaica, plots of land were large enough that a poor man could cultivate enough produce to support him and his family. Children could expect to receive a few years of education and to get ahead if they worked hard. There was the possibility of learning a trade then either saving some money or starting a small business. Families could usually scrape up enough cash to send one member to the United States where there was an opportunity to make enough money to repay the loan and bring over other family members. True, there was a large disparity between the poor and the rich in their standard of living, but at least the poor in Jamaican in 1916 were not always on the verge of starvation.

The only hope that a poor Haitian harbored was that he could squeeze enough sustenance out of his small plot of land to avoid starvation for yet another day and simul- taneously avoid the more severe aspects of the different dictatorships that took turns exploiting them. Every facet of their situation seemed to conspire against the possibility that the poor might escape from their poverty.

Roger had been in Haiti for almost three years when he sent Bert a letter that raised Bert's level of concern. After one of their expeditions into the jungle, the Marines captured the famous Haitian bandit Caco General Cudjoe and placed him in the jail where Roger worked. An ally smuggled a revolver and ammunition to Cudjoe who used the gun to shoot his way out of jail, dash to a picket line of horses, and then flee into the jungle. While Roger was only a bystander, the bullets flew perilously close as the escapade unfolded.

That story was the last straw for Bert. He did not want his brother subject to that level of danger. Moreover he felt that the atmosphere in Haiti was not one in which one should spend their most impressionable years. Consequently he wrote instructing Roger to come to the United States where he could get an education and fulfill their shared ambition and become a physician. Bert offered to provide Roger with a place to stay at no cost until he could find a job. Once he was working, the pair would share living expenses and thereby reduce their overall costs.

The exposure to gunfire combined with his general dissatisfaction with Haiti caused Roger to accept with alacrity. He gave notice to the Marines, bought his ticket, said his goodbyes to the friends that he had made, and traveled by ship to Miami. Then, as his brother had directed him, he traveled by train to Toledo, Ohio.

Bert had been in the United States long enough to know that although it was cheaper to travel by bus, it was safer to travel by train. Bus travel was local with multiple stops and multiple opportunities to encounter local police and local peculiarities. The longer you were exposed to segregation and bigotry, the more likely you were to run afoul of it. This was especially true for a newly arrived West Indian naïve to the mores of prejudice. This approach had worked well for Bert years ago when he arrived in America and was placed on a train by his father's friends.

The trip to Toledo was fortunately very uneventful. Like Bert, Roger marveled at the size of the country, the many changes in scenery, and the many changes in the weather. While he had been in Haiti, he had been in a climate very similar to that of his childhood and in a social position very similar to that to which he was accustomed. Along with the change in climate and scenery in America, he was to experience some significant social changes. In his letters Bert had repeatedly warned him of the problems that he should expect, but one has to experience prejudice to appreciate its full impact.

Bert met Roger at the train station on his arrival and took him by streetcar to the small room that he rented in a private home. It was a common practice for homeowners and apartment dwellers, especially in the colored community where segregation often placed a severe limit on the availability of housing, to rent out a spare bedroom in order to supplement their income. They were fortunate in that the housing was provided by an acquaintance of their father. After his brother had settled in, Bert wrote Horatio to let him know that Roger had arrived safely.

The summer was just ending when Roger arrived in Toledo. Soon he experienced for the first time the glorious colors of the leaves as the maples, oaks, and other deciduous trees cleansed themselves of their unwanted leaves in preparation for their winter hibernation. Later he felt for the first time the bitter cold of winter gradually develop after the autumnal equinox when the suns rays were diminished in intensity as they sank below the equator and traveled ever-longer distances before weakly warming the northern atmosphere.

Roger found, as his brother had previously, that the job market was limited by his color. In Jamaica, a middle class young man who had completed his basic education could expect to get a white-collar job as a clerk in a business or a bank. In Toledo, a part of the northern United States that had deemed the inhumanity of slavery to be so intolerable that it had fought a bloody civil war to achieve its elimination, the inhumanity of discrimination was accepted. White-collar jobs were reserved for whites while coloreds were expected to accept the fact that only menial jobs were made available to them. A man of color who had been eagerly hired by the United States Marines in Haiti would never be considered for a similar position in the northern United States.

Gone for the brothers was the maid who washed and ironed their clothes and laid them out for them to wear. Gone was the cook who knew your favorite dishes and made every effort to provide the type of meal that a young man should have in order to keep his strength up. No longer was there someone to clean and wax the floor, take out the garbage, wash the dishes. If you wanted to make something of yourself in America, you had to be willing to change your entire perspective--both towards your home life and towards your job options.

Every day before dawn Roger boarded a streetcar for a trip to a factory that would occasionally have a job for a colored man. Every day he came back without a job. Weeks went by and autumn gave way to early winter. Now he was shivering from the unaccustomed cold as he waited in vain to be singled out for a job in a city with multiple factories and multiple jobs—if you were the 'right' type of person. Then an acquaintance told him that if the man at the glass factory where he was applying asked if anyone had experience in stoking an oven, he should say yes.

At the next opportunity Roger raised his hand when the question was asked. The hiring boss told him to come with him to a furnace with a roaring fire. Then, without any further instruction, he told him to tend the furnace. The heat from the furnace was intense; breathing was almost an impossibility; his eyebrows felt as if they were about to catch on fire. His clumsy effort to perform this seemingly simple task was an abysmal failure. Fortunately the foreman took pity on him and gave him a menial job to perform. He stayed on in that position until he heard that the railroad was hiring.

A job on the railroad was sought after because it was fairly steady work that was not terribly demanding physically. If you were white, you could aspire to work on the railroad as an engineer or a conductor at good wages. If you were colored, you worked as a porter or in the dining car for low wages and inconsistent tips. Roger's job in the dining car turned out to be better than Bert's job in a factory in that waiters had a fair amount of free time that could be used to study. However the job called for long hours, many of which were spent on your feet. As a result, fatigue limited the effectiveness of studying.

There were other problems. Little or no attention was paid to the effect of the schedules on the lives of the employees. An employee who suddenly learned that they were needed to take over a run in another city might have to abruptly leave their family and find a new place to stay. To refuse was to have your job given to some one else. Moreover, colored employees risked dismissal if they complained about an insult from either the passengers or their white co-workers. Unions provided some protection for white workers, but at this point in time, colored railroad workers had no leverage.

Despite the problems that they faced on a daily basis and their intense dislike of the social system that controlled their lives, their inherent strength of character allowed them to tolerate setbacks in order to eventually achieve their goals and to gain sustenance from some of the seemingly insignificant pleasures that exist in all of our lives.

When the warmth of the sun's rays was at its weakest and icy winds swept south from the Artic, Roger had his first exposure to snow. Bert used the occasion to wash Roger's face in snow and baptize him with a handful of the cold crisp crystals that he shoved down the back of his coat. That energized his younger brother and instantly cleansed his mind of the misfortunes that they had experienced. After a few minutes of reciprocal ablutions, they agreed to a truce and proceeded to engage in some of the other winter rituals that were ingrained in all northern children but were a source of wonder to a newcomer from the tropics.

Bert next created an arsenal of snowballs that he used to introduce Roger to the mock combat that was to replace the 'last lick' ritual of playful punches that they had used as children in order to show their affection. Roger quickly caught on to the art of ducking and twisting to avoid Bert's missiles while simultaneously scooping up his own supply of snowballs and firing them back at his harasser. Since he was totally unaccustomed to the properties of snow and ice, he often found himself thrown jarringly to the ground when his feet slid on the snow covered ice and he was rudely launched into the air before crashing heavily onto the ground.

Later that day Bert spontaneously created a wintry hybrid of cricket and baseball as an additional method of participating in the rites of winter. In cricket a ball is pitched (bowled is the accurate word) so that it bounces on the ground and knocks off one or both of the two horizontal sticks (which are known as bails) that rest on top of three upright sticks (which are known as wickets). A batter tries to hit the pitched ball in order to simply prevent the dislodgement of the bails (which would cause him to lose his turn) or, if possible, to hit it between the fielders so that he can dash from one stump to another and score one or more runs.

In Bert's version, a narrow flat piece of board served as a bat, a stick was imbedded in a small snow bank and used as a wicket, and an icy hard snowball took the place of a regular ball. With a ground that was covered by snow and a ball that disintegrated on contact, Bert had to forego the bounce and simply pitch the ball through the air the way that the Americans did when they played baseball. In Jamaica the brothers had delighted in playing the English game of cricket, a sport that had been the inspiration for the creation of baseball many years ago. They thoroughly enjoyed this improvised version of an old favorite. At these times, homesickness did not exist, bills were unimportant, and discrimination was immaterial.

When they tired of cricket, Bert showed Roger how to continue rolling a snowball until its circumference grew to one or two feet, pile up three of these giant balls in descending order of size, add branches for arms, clumps of coal for eyes, nose, and mouth, and then top the resultant snowman with Roger's cap. Then, fatigued from all of this activity, they eventually slumped to their haunches and watched the children who ran down the street at full speed then threw themselves down onto their sleds where they coasted along the slippery surface for several yards. The seasons, like the culture of this new land, presented some problems but also offered some rewards.

The snows of winter gave way to the slush of March, the rains of April, the humidity of summer, and the glory of fall for a span of several years. Courses were taken and passed, pay was received and paid out in rent and groceries, problems were met and solved, dreams were retained and nurtured, and boys became men. Ability, ambition, and resolve combined with a solid moral upbringing to see them through the obstacles that they met due to a lack of funding and due to the impediments that the American society had constructed from the vestiges of slavery.

Along with the difficulties there were friends, parties, and days of leisure. Somehow, under the most adverse of circumstances, people of character seem to thrive. On a Sunday, a picnic by the Maumee River or a trip to the Toledo Zoo, one of the nation's finest, could provide needed respite from the trials of the past week without the expenditure of vital cash.

When one of the members of their social group was experiencing a cash flow problem, a favorite method of replenishing their resources was to invite a few friends to what was termed a rent party at which the host supplied food and drink and the guests paid a little for each drink or sandwich. In this way, enough money would be scrounged up to meet the rent for that month. By recycling their cash among themselves, they made it go farther.

In 1920, after the 18th Amendment to the Constitution ushered in the Prohibition Era, the alcohol that they consumed was usually a homemade brew known as "bathtub gin" or "white lightning". These drinks were nothing like the smooth blends of rum that Bert remembered from his days in Jamaica, but they were often all that could be afforded.

When times were a little better and the cash flow more robust, they would go to a club called a speakeasy where alcohol was sold illegally and jazz was often played and sung. Jazz was an outgrowth of the rhythms of West Africa and the spirituals of slavery days. Some jazz was known as ragtime, an energetic form of piano playing that often was comprised of three different sections, each with its own melody. Other versions concentrated on the blues, mournful notes that were accompanied by sad reflective lyrics.

The magnetic rhythm of the music and the beautiful baritones of the colored singers attracted many whites to jazz. It became very fashionable for white audiences to go to black clubs where artists such as Bessie Smith and Louie Armstrong played and sang and began to develop a national reputation that allowed them to begin to perform for predominantly white audiences. These renowned artists and musicians still experienced a great deal of prejudice in their travels but their talent was a valuable commodity that gave them leverage and contributed to a steady but infuriatingly gradual diminution in segregation and discrimination.

The quality of the alcohol in these speakeasies was a little higher than that of the homemade variety but the main attractions of drinking out was not the quality of the alcohol but the cachet engendered by the illegality of the establishment, and the opportunity to mingle. The speakeasies provided an opportunity for women, another group that was rebelling against its minority status, to escape the cocoon that society had spun for them.

When Bert and Roger had their picture taken in one of their college classes in Toledo, there was one colored student besides Bert and Roger, six women, and eighteen white males. Had a similar picture been taken two decades

UNIVERSITY OF TOLEDO 1922
BERT TOP RIGHT, ROGER 3rd ON RIGHT

earlier, almost everyone in the class would probably have been a white male . Changes were occurring, albeit slowly. Throughout this time Bert was showing signs that he was going to be a man of talent and a man of involvement. In 1920, at 23 years of age, barely supporting himself, he paid to have a six-page analysis done that purported to explain how he could improve himself. The analyzer wrote that if Bert had any faults, it was that he was "too bookish" and concluded that he should learn how to speak publicly and become involved. Bert seems to have taken the advice because on January 12, 1923, he received a letter of commendation from the Frederick Douglas Community Center in Toledo because of the efforts he had made there. He was poor, he was both working and going to school, but he made the time to help his community.

While one experience can not explain why a person chooses a given path in life, a picture of Bert riding on a trolley with a face whitened by flour and an inner shame that he, a Forsythe, should be forced to take such a menial job, be restricted to the rear of the trolley, and be reduced to appearing in public in such a disreputable state, would have gone a long way to explaining his later decision to risk his life in an effort to open up jobs in every field to blacks.

Eventually Bert's perseverance was rewarded and he received a Bachelor of Science degree from the University of Toledo on June 14, 1923. As is usual with pre-med students, Bert hedged his bets and applied to several medical schools for admission although his first choice was McGill University in Montreal, Canada where, as a citizen of one of the countries in the British Empire, his national origin was an advantage and his race was not a disqualifying factor. He had applied himself so his grades should have guaranteed admission to most universities in the United States but admission to U.S. medical schools, with the exception of the two black schools of Howard and Meharry, was unlikely.

Because slavery had never taken hold in Canada as it had in the West Indies and in the southern United States, it was easier for a colored to be admitted to a predominantly white graduate school in Canada than for a colored, foreign or American, to be admitted to a predominantly white graduate school in the United States.

After months of waiting, the long hoped for letter arrived. The following year Bert would be enrolled at McGill, a school with an excellent academic reputation in a country that was known to be fairly race neutral. The schools in Ohio, the state where he had completed successfully completed his pre-medical education, did not proffer an acceptance. Prejudice still prevailed.

Roger was overjoyed at his brother's good fortune. The two brothers went out and treated themselves to a meal at a West Indian restaurant. A trace of sadness intruded on their celebration however since they knew that this would cause them to have to separate. Roger would have to remain at the University of Toledo in order to complete his undergraduate education while Bert journeyed to Canada.

As the time for their separation approached, they reminisced and recalled the paths that their lives had taken. Bert, initially the recipient of financial support from a father who wanted him to be an architect, had eschewed that support, worked and paid his own way through college, and would not return to Port Antonio or marry the woman his father had selected. Roger had left home without any financial support, made his way first to a land where French was spoken and he was a member of the elite, then to a land that denigrated him because of his color and relegated him to jobs that were beneath his intellectual capabilities. Yet both were satisfied inasmuch as they expected to realize their dream of entering medical school.

5

MONTREAL

Inasmuch as the trip to Montreal involved the northernmost part of the United States and Canada, an area where segregation was mild, Bert decided to travel by bus. He reasoned that this would afford him an opportunity to closely experience the magnitude of two of the Great Lakes, Lake Erie and then Lake Ontario. He found that the lake that had seemed large from its shores in Toledo was in fact gigantic when one tried to go around it. In Jamaica he had thought of lakes as being small bodies of water that allowed you to see from one side to the other. These lakes were like the ocean or a sea, so wide that it was impossible to see the other side.

As he had expected, no significant racial problems were encountered on his trip by bus. He received a few curious looks when he got off at a depot to purchase food or enter a bathroom, but there were no confrontations. A variety of people struck up conversations with him—coloreds who were happy to have someone of their ethnic origin to provide the security that comes in numbers and whites who were curious or just plain friendly. Most passengers were seasoned bus travelers who simply sat and minded their own business until their stop arrived, then departed without exchanging a word. No doubt there had been some who had made it a point to sit elsewhere but their prejudices were of no concern since they had not taken any action that affected him.

On arrival in Montreal he went straight to the University. After settling in, he looked up some Jamaicans whose names he had been given. They agreed to take him around town and provide a short history and geography lesson while he was waiting for his classes to begin. Typically immigrants simplified the problems that they might face in a new city by obtaining from family and friends the names of some countrymen in the area. Usually these compatriots were delighted to return the favor that they had received on their arrival, and to meet people who shared their language or accent and their cultural values.

His new acquaintances pointed out that Montreal began as a French colony called made Ville-Marie that was formed in 1642 at a spot on the Saint Laurence River named Pointe-a-Calliere. The large square in that area was named Place Jacques Cartier in honor of the Frenchman who in 1535 first sailed over 1,000 miles from the Atlantic Ocean, up the Saint Lawrence River to the site that would be the city's location, a triangular island near where the Saint Lawrence River joins the Ottawa River. The city fell under British rule after its capture in 1760. All of Canada was then ceded to England in 1763.

Bert saw that McGill University was much larger than Tuskegee in size and very different from both Tuskegee and Toledo in ambience. The school was located several miles from the river at the base of Mount Royal, a mountain thought to be one of the oldest in the world. The city derived its name from this dominant feature of the topography. His friends first took him along Sherbrooke Street at the base of the Mount Royal and then, as students are wont to do, to a street that was a favorite hangout for the students, the Boulevard St-Denis.

There was very little overt racial prejudice in Montreal since slavery had never established itself in Canada as it had in America. However prejudice of some sort seems to be a universal facet among the multitude of potential relationships that comprise the veneer that is presented to the world by the different societies. In the case of Montreal, the primary prejudice that aggravated a portion of the population involved language rather than race. Although the majority of the population of Montreal continued to be French-speaking after the capture of the city by England, English became the language of business and was the language at McGill, established in 1821 as a private, English-speaking university.

As a result of the primacy of English, French-speaking Canadians often found themselves being discriminated against in the quality of the jobs that they were likely to get and the salaries that they were likely to command. Hence even though he personally was usually not the target of prejudice while he was in Montreal, in this instance, as in Jamaica, Bert found himself the beneficiary of an arbitrary difference that the society had created between its various groups. In one country the barrier was language, in another it might be class, in others it might be religion. The linguistic prejudice that prevailed made it easier for him, a foreigner, to find a reasonable part time job that would allow him to pay for both his living costs and his education than it would be for the French speaking indigenous inhabitants of Montreal to get a job that would adequately provide for their basic necessities.

This was similar to the situation that had prevailed in Toledo where immigrants from Europe found it easier to get a job than did American born coloreds. There was one major difference however. The colored Americans spoke the native language of English while the immigrants often did not. In America, the handicap of race trumped the handicap of language. Prejudice, a demeaning human peculiarity, was inconsistent but ubiquitous.

There was an irony in his circumstances that he did not appreciate. In Toledo the colored students had pointed out that liberal whites decried the unequal salaries paid to coloreds but condoned the status quo by paying 'the prevailing wage' to the coloreds who worked for them. For example, a colored maid would be paid the prevailing low wages paid to a colored to care for a household. If a white were hired to perform the same function, they would expect and would receive a larger salary. When the same work is compensated by different salaries because of factors such as color, class, language, or religion, that is prejudice and the beneficiary of the differential, in this case Bert, perpetuates the prejudice. However he did not develop that insight until later.

The improved prospects for income in Montreal led him to conclude that the physical and mental strain that he had labored under for the previous ten years would be removed. He knew that he had to be frugal however, and generally limited his recreation to inexpensive activities. On campus he visited museums such as the Redpath, a museum of natural history that also housed a large collection of Egyptian antiquities. At other times he hiked along Le Serpent, a switchback bridle path, up to Parc Mont-Royal at Chalet Lookout where there was an exquisite view of the city, or to Lac des Castors where he admired the skill of the ice skaters in the frigid Canadian winter.

When spring came to Montreal he found that it was quite different from the springs that he had experienced in Toledo. In a city with French origins, food played a much more prominent role than he had become accustomed to in America. When the dreary overcast of winter began to be replaced by the lengthening days of spring, the sidewalk cafes on Boulevard St-Denis slowly came to life with students who sat for hours over coffee and pastries while they studied for their classes. Later, when the air began to warm and the birds began to sing, retirees returned to their favorite haunts to discuss politics with life long friends over a lingering glass of wine.

At this time of year the sap that ran from the maple trees was collected from the woods, condensed, and then converted into delicious syrup that the café patrons could generously pour over delicate crepes that were made from batters that could contain anyone of a large assortment of berries or nuts—blueberries, blackberries, strawberries, walnuts, pecans, and many other choices were always available. Alternatively, the café might present the delicately sweet flavor of the maple in the form of an irresistible sugar pie that seemed to melt in your mouth as you sat and observed the young girls who walked by wearing inexpensive imitations of the latest fashions from Paris.

Montreal, like other Canadian cities, held an attraction to Americans that was unrelated to the scenery or the culture. Canada flirted briefly with prohibition from 1917 to 1919 but then repealed it. Shortly after Canada's repeal, it was instituted in the United States. This of course made Canada a magnet for Americans desirous of having a few drinks or those willing to risk carrying a case or two across the border. In any event, Bert appreciated the fact that he did not have to settle for bathtub gin but could get a decent drink of Jamaican rum on those rare occasions when he wanted to splurge.

Most of his time was of course spent on his studies. Medical school was as challenging and as satisfying as he had expected. His first class had been gross anatomy, an opportunity to dissect a human body and learn firsthand how it functioned. When the students arrived at the lab on the first day of school, they quickly changed into the clean white uniforms that they had purchased, eager to begin the dissection of the body that had been assigned to their team of four. Their professor however had a few words to say before allowing them to proceed.

"I know you are all anxious to get started in anatomy. This is the reason why you often went without sleep during your four or more years of pre-med. You should however pause and consider how fortunate you are to have a human body to study. In order to have a body to dissect years ago, the medical schools had to employ people to steal bodies from graves. This led to some terrible practices. Now society is more advanced. Some of the bodies that we use are unclaimed, usually paupers whose remains we use with government permission. We also get some that are willed to us by people who are grateful for what physicians have done and want the students to learn what the human body can teach them. Whether your body is that of a derelict or the result of a donation, respect it. That was once a living person with all of the hopes and fears and feelings that you now have. Throughout your career, remember that you are not dealing with an object or a disease or a source of income but with a person. We have the names of the people who you will be working on and will give them to you if you so desire."

Those words had a profound effect on Bert and the other students. As they had looked at the cloth-draped protuberances that lay before them on the laboratory tables, they had unconsciously been dehumanizing them in an effort to steel themselves for the upcoming sight of the cadaver. Now they were reminded that they were to be healers and that this exposure to death was but a prelude to sustaining life.

Every student took advantage of the professor's offer and asked to be told the name of the person that he worked on. The students would forget most of the minute details that were presented to them over the next four years but they would never forget the name of the individual who benefited them and their future patients by sharing the intimate details of their bodies with a first year medical student.

Anatomy had been his favorite class during his first year. With relish he learned the muscles of the body, the variations that could exist between one individual and another in the location and pattern of their arteries and nerves, and the organs of the chest and abdomen that could be mutilated by disease. Every time a student had a finding that differed from the textbook, the rest of the class would be called over to remind them that they should always expect the unexpected.

In that first year the curriculum also included other classes that were described as being in the laboratory or basic sciences—neuro-anatomy, histology, pathology, and biochemistry—in contrast to the clinical classes that the students would enter in their third and fourth years when they would be introduced to patients. At times things seemed quite logical and he felt that he was being given a series of building blocks and asked to stack one upon the other. On other occasions the material seemed unconnected as if the professor had thrown a puzzle with missing pieces on the floor and then expected them to rapidly assemble it.

The second year of medical school was far preferable to the first in that the curriculum progressed to subjects that seemed as if they would have more practical applications. His favorite topics were microbiology where they learned about bacteria and infections, and pharmacology where they learned about the drugs that were used to treat infections. He enjoyed the subjects but like all of his classmates he did not enjoy the exams.

Written exams were given frequently to ensure that the potential physician was capable of retaining the volume of knowledge that a practicing physician must be able to recall and utilize. The information that had to be memorized was being presented in a short period of time with the expectation that it would be assimilated quickly so that the student could quickly progress to the next field. Courses that doctoral students spent a year on would be covered in one semester.

The rapid pace and the vast volume of information proved to be unmanageable for some of the students; in the first year, several of the students flunked out. One day they were your partners in perversity, the next day they were gone. Whether these unfortunates took the time to say their goodbyes or disappeared without being able to face their classmates, their departure left both a void and a profound sense of discomfort as even the brightest of students felt a gnawing fear that somehow the axe would one day fall on them.

Bert had the ability to perform well in his studies but it soon became apparent that there was a world of difference between working ones way through college and working ones way through medical school. He realized that he had been premature when he had concluded that he could work on an almost full time basis while attending medical school. The strain began to take its toll on him. He spent less time sleeping than he should have and his recreational time dwindled to zero.

Since he also knew that Roger was having similar difficulties, he decided that the practical thing to do was to quit medical school and go back to Ohio where he would get a job and allow Roger to quit his job and devote his attention to entering medical school. It did not seem reasonable to him that they should both have to worry about whether or not they would have enough money to meet the rent and pay for the groceries and tuition.

Bert knew that if he mentioned his plans to his brother, Roger would certainly try to talk him out of it. He therefore left school at the end of the term without telling his brother and took the train to Toledo. With his limited income he had not accumulated many worldly possessions so it was fairly simple to pull up stakes and head back to America.

On arrival, Bert found that Roger had also dropped out of school! His brother had developed a severe case of influenza, missed a lot of school, decided that he could not catch up with the curriculum that year, and intended to work and send Bert through medical school. Not wanting to worry his brother, he had not written Bert about his illness or his intentions about working to support him. The strong bond that they shared caused each to want to sacrifice for the other. Now they were both out of school with no chance of realizing their ambition to become physicians.

Fortunately a letter arrived from their father in response to messages that they both had written detailing their progress and inquiring as to whether or not he could offer any financial assistance. Horatio replied that he wanted to help, but could only afford to help one of them. Since Bert was the oldest and had not yet missed any significant amount of classes, the two decided that he should get the aid from their father, and go back to McGill to complete medical school. Roger would remain in Toledo where he would study pharmacy, a less demanding subject that would allow him to both work and go to school.

There was not much time for goodbyes as the next term in medical school was about to start and Bert did not want to fall behind. He returned to Montreal, applied himself to his studies, and found that by reducing his outside job to a few hours on the weekend, he was able to complete his studies and do well on his exams without feeling stressed. In his studies, as in all other aspects of his life, he was somewhat of a perfectionist. Things had to be done right, not almost right, but right.

Things went well for several months but before long another problem arose. During the third year of medical school he noticed that he had to take his belt in by almost one inch. At first he attributed this to his poor eating habits and resolved to pay more attention to his diet. However, although he increased his caloric intake and began to weigh regularly, there was no improvement in either his weight or his strength. Then gradually he developed a weakness in his legs that was accompanied by strange sensations. At times it felt as if dozens of fine needles were being stuck into his flesh; at other times he noticed an uncomfortable numbness that shifted from one site to another.

The most seasoned hypochondriac does not experience the degree of agony that is experienced by a medical student when an unexpected symptom appears. The hypochondriac takes the normal variation in the signals that are sent to their nervous system and magnifies them until they are interpreted to be a warning of impending disaster. With time, the victim becomes superficially knowledgeable about the potential causes for their symptoms. Their salvation is that they realize that they do not truly know how to compile a proper list of the potential diagnoses or how to perform a proper battery of tests in order to confirm or rule out an illness. Because they must rely on a physician to do these things, they are forced to bring someone else into the equation, share their fears, and alleviate their anxieties to some extent.

On the other hand, while the medical student shares with the hypochondriac the knowledge and the fear that a lethal cancer may be causing their unexplained symptoms, the student is unique in being able to conjure up a long list of other ostensibly plausible entities that could be the cause. While the hypochondriac quickly runs to a professional for reassurance or diagnosis, the student suffers alone for a longer period while they contemplate the possibilities so that they can approach their physician with diagnosis in hand. Every medical student goes through the disease known as sophomoritis, a circumstance in which dire consequences are attributed to benign findings or sensations.

However there was nothing benign about Bert's situation. At first he attributed his weakness to the stresses that had become familiar over the preceding fifteen years—too little sleep, too many money worries, too much studying. In the beginning the symptoms were non-specific and did not elicit much concern. Then, as he developed entirely new sensations and findings he began to consider cancer, the greatest threat that any human faces. As the weight loss continued he became more and more convinced that fate was about to cheat him of his life long ambition to be a physician. He made out a will that left his few possessions to his brother Roger and prepared for the worst. However, when the problem progressed to the point that he began to urinate frequently, he realized what was wrong, diabetes!!

A diagnosis of diabetes was almost as lethal as a diagnosis of cancer. In the mid 1920's, so called juvenile diabetes, the form that began before the age of 35, often resulted in death within a few years. That situation was expected to change since in 1922 the Toronto physician Banting and the medical student Best had isolated the hormone called insulin that controlled the metabolism of carbohydrates. This discovery made the treatment of diabetes possible. For this seminal accomplishment they were awarded the Nobel Prize for medicine a year later. The rapidity with which this prestigious award was conferred was recognition of the importance of their discovery.

However isolation was not the same as availability and despite the fact that insulin had been discovered nearby, there was none available to treat him. In the absence of insulin his body was unable to utilize the calories that he took in, the level of glucose rose in his blood and urine, dehydration began as water accompanied the glucose through the kidneys and into the bladder, and toxins became concentrated in his blood as fluid was lost. Bert's outlook was grim. Once again he dropped out of school.

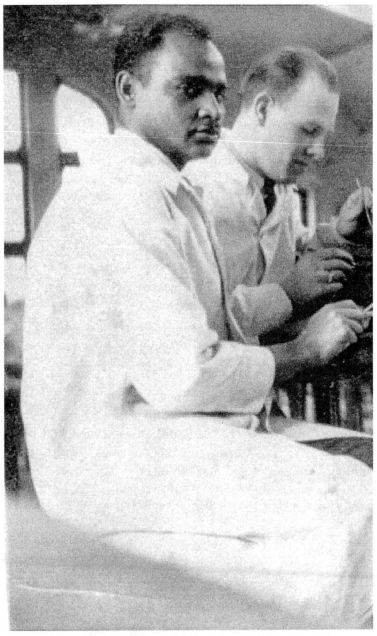

MC GILL MEDICAL SCHOOL, 1927

6

JAMAICA

The plane slowed, began to descend, and traced an oval path in the sky as it prepared to land. The larger dots below became houses and the smaller dots became people as the pilot adjusted his flaps, checked his instruments, and completed the routine of what was now second nature for him. His sense of security was somewhat unjustified inasmuch as he was not landing on a runway designed to accept a plane and known to be free of foreign objects, but on a surface that might contain unexpected hazards that could rip through the underbelly of the plane. The pilot peered at the landing surface as best he could to see if there would be a last minute need to abort. When nothing was discerned that seemed hazardous, he made his final descent.

Bert had to be helped off the seaplane after it landed in Port Antonio's West Harbour. The diabetes had weakened him so much that he had been unable to care for himself on his own in Montreal. On hearing of his dilemma, his father had written enclosing funds for a ticket and insisting that Bert come home immediately so that the family could care for him. Bert gladly accepted the invitation; he was anxious to get back to familiar surroundings, to leave the cold of the northern hemisphere for the warmth of the Caribbean, to taste the cuisine of his childhood instead of the high calorie diet necessitated by the marrow-chilling cold of the north, and to begin his recuperation.

As a medical student Bert understood that a strict diet was the primary treatment for diabetes. Consequently he decided to undertake a diet that consisted mainly of milk and refused the well meant but potentially deadly importations of the maid who tried to get him to eat some rich foods in order to regain his strength. This rigid program was remarkably successful; with rest and the strictest of diets he was able to bring his diabetes under control within a relatively short period of time.

The first sign that he was getting better was the cessation of his urinary frequency. His weight, which had been plunging, stabilized then gradually recovered from its nadir. However the strange sensations in his legs, referred to by physicians as paresthesia, were slow to resolve. For months he was tormented by alternating sensations of numbness, tingling, and burning in his extremities. Tiny electric shocks in his arms and legs that were more annoying than disabling, alternated with invisible tongues of flame that licked at his arms or legs and caused him to writhe in agony. At night, when his mind was deprived of most of the visual and auditory stimuli that might have distracted him and suppressed his awareness of these sensations, the discomfort was particularly acute. Moreover, from time to time the temporary loss of sensation caused him to develop a sore over an area of his buttocks, hips, or heels that had been temporarily rendered insensitive to the pressure caused by the weight of his body.

The determination that he had shown in defying his father in his choice of a professions and his decision to forego an arranged marriage, in working his way through school, and in helping to support his younger brother, was in evidence in his efforts to overcome the weakness that now restricted him. Every day either his father or one or two of his friends from his kite-flying days such as Osmond Petrie,

Danny Nairn and Leslie French, would take him down to the beach where he exercised in the warm salt water. The warmth relaxed his muscles; the buoyancy reduced the work that the weakened muscles had to do; his refusal to give in to the viscidities of life provided the drive that sustained him as he fought this terrible disease. Weeks elapsed, then months as the paresthesias slowly faded and the strength returned to his legs.

On occasion his family took him to Bath, the hot springs that they had visited in his youth. The spring had been discovered by a runaway slave in the 1690's and had rapidly became a very fashionable retreat named The Bath of St. Thomas the Apostle or Bath for short. The waters of Bath, warm and high in its content of sulfur and lime, were reputed to be curative for skin diseases and rheumatic ailments. Horatio felt so confident that they would bring strength to the weakened muscles of his son that on several Saturdays he gladly made the hours long drive there in his horse and buggy, spent the night, and returned the next day.

Another attraction of the Bath area was the Botanical Garden, the second oldest in the Western Hemisphere. It was here that some of the breadfruit trees brought to the West Indies by Captain Bligh had been planted. A slow walk through its grounds, with many pauses to rest, allowed him to exercise his muscles, enjoy the beauty, and indulge in flights of fancy about the life style of the gentry who had visited two hundred years before. Both the garden and the spa were not as well kept as they had been during the era of slavery but they were still impressive. He always felt much better when he returned from a visit to the spring that ran both hot and cold water and left your skin feeling tight and invigorated.

During this hiatus from medical school he occasionally practiced what he referred to in later years as bootleg medicine. Physicians, especially Jamaican ones, were in short supply in a country town such as Port Antonio.

The government sent a physician to serve at the local clinic for only one day each week. The rest of the time a nurse staffed it. When the physician came, anyone who wanted to be seen could expect an all day wait culminating in a brief "What's wrong with you", followed by an equally brief opportunity to answer, and then some homeopathic advice from a physician who was often much too busy to keep up with the advances in medicine.

After he had given some free medical advice to several of his fathers workers, Bert found that others were offering to pay him a shilling or two for advice in order to avoid the long waits and the impersonal atmosphere of the government clinic. They preferred to accept advice from one of their own, the son of 'Chief' Forsyth, even though it was well known that he was still only a third year medical student.

On several occasions he was able to perform a true service by diagnosing a serious problem that was then referred to the physician at the public hospital. For the most part he spent his time giving basic advice on procedures such as the application of a poultice to one of the frequent sores that developed from poorly cleaned wounds or perhaps in recommending some simple gastrointestinal remedies from the local pharmacy. This practice allowed him to accumulate some of the money that he expected would be needed on his return to Canada.

In Jamaica a moderately sized town such as Port Antonio had a quality usually found only in very small towns elsewhere. When you were born and raised there, you could go away and return years later and be treated as if you had never left. As an example, when he got his strength back he went into the local post office to buy some stamps for a letter that he planned to send to Roger in Toledo. On seeing him coming, the postmistress automatically reached for the family mail and gave it to him with a personal comment that revealed the attention that she paid to the mail that passed through her hands, her knowledge of the affairs of the community, and her recognition that he was still a part of the community.

"Here you are, Mr. Bert," she said offhandedly. "Not much mail today. Your brother don't write very often. I happy to see that yu are up and about."

This familiarity and sense of concern imparted a feeling of belonging that he suddenly realized had been missing while he had been in the United States. In a large North American city one usually was made to feel insignificant, tolerated, or most objectionably, inferior in the case of people of color. Coloreds suffered from both the universal indifference experienced by the inhabitants of a large city and the added discomfort of overt prejudices. In large cities there was often as much recognition accorded to those in a line of people at a local post office as that accorded to the members of a herd of water buffalo waiting their turn at the water hole in Africa. Here in Port Antonio he was at home, he was a person, he was a Forsythe.

His intense dislike of the treatment that he had received in America made him aware that the class system in Jamaica had resulted in seating arrangements on public transportation and in movie houses that had the same effect as segregation in the United States. However there was a difference in that there were no signs that reserved one section for the privileged. Discrimination in this society modeled after the long practiced British system of class snobbery, generally relied on the disincentive of money to separate the classes. Downtown Port Antonio boasted one movie theater. If you were upper class, middle class, or lower class you could sit wherever you desired, as long as you were willing to pay the cost of that seat. Needless to say, the poor chose the cheaper seats thereby leaving the well to do free to sit as an undisturbed social grouping in the more expensive seats. There was separation, but color was not the limiting factor.

Bert now recognized that this was a subtle system of segregation that had seemed quite acceptable to him in his youth. Even now, he accepted this differential inasmuch as it did not have the dehumanizing quality of overt discrimination intertwined with the frightening threat of physical abuse.

His long recuperation gave him ample time to ponder the differences between the class system that he was the beneficiary of in Jamaica and the racial discrimination that he was the victim of in the United States. Could one complain about the latter while participating in the former? Were the two very similar or were they fundamentally different? He rapidly concluded that the similarities were far overshadowed by the differences.

As in the United States, he did not socialize with whites to any extent. They had their cricket clubs that were for members only but he never felt debased by this because the signs said members only, not whites only. He was excluded not by force but by what seemed to be a perfectly understandable desire to associate with ones peer group. Customs, not the police, enforced the separation.

On the other hand his family did not have any social contact with the working class. The gulf was different from that between whites and middle class Jamaicans, but it did exist. It was a class differentiation not a racial one and in Bert's mind, this made a world of difference. He recapped mentally. There were no signs that proscribed where you could sit, no desire by one group to have access that was being denied, and no fear of police intervention. No, the situations were not at all similar.

On other occasions he thought back to the conversations that he had with Booker T. Washington during the times that he had driven him to the train station more than a decade before. Should those in America fight racial discrimination by relying on self-improvement, acquiring property, and avoiding overt confrontation, or should they follow the admonitions of W.E.B Du Bois and openly push for equality? Was there some middle ground to follow—get an education, acquire some wealth, but don't just rely on the beneficence of the whites to grant equality? Should one instead take some concrete steps to hasten equality? He had no idea what those steps would be but it seemed to him that some concrete action was necessary. Without realizing it, he was undergoing an evolution in his sociological thinking.

He began to think about the different manifestations of discrimination that he had seen in Alabama, Ohio, and Canada and what Roger had told him about in Haiti. The vivid nature of segregation in Alabama stood out as being indefensible. Prejudice and discrimination in Ohio was less threatening but equally demeaning. He was not quite sure what to think about Haiti in that it seemed to occupy a position somewhere between Alabama and Jamaica and was not a situation of which he had first hand knowledge.

The other situations that he had experienced were not clear-cut. French Canadians in Montreal were not in danger of physical abuse, not subject to restrictions on where they could sit or what fountains they could drink from, but what of their relegation to lower paying jobs because they did not speak the language of their conquerors?

As an English speaking person he benefited from this type of discrimination in Canada in that he was able to get jobs that the native born French speakers could not. He benefited in Jamaica by being financially able to sit in the more desirable section of the theater. Can one complain about not being allowed to sit in one section of a theater in Ohio when some one else does not sit in a given section in Port Antonio because of a financial barrier whose unspoken purpose was to separate one group from another?

When he had tried to discuss these quandaries with his relatives and friends who had never left home, he had met a dead end. One had to experience southern segregation to appreciate its horror. One had to sit in classes with a nationally famous speaker and enjoy hours of private conversation with him in order to open ones mind to the questions and the possibilities. The information gained by hours of conversation with your brother about a backwards country such as Haiti, combined with your own experiences in a country such as Canada that had an almost slave-free history, contributed to a richness of experience that most of his peers in Jamaica would never have and could never understand.

While he saw the societal structure in Port Antonio in a different light than he had in his childhood, he did not feel any compunction to attempt to change anything. Whatever prejudice the English exhibited towards Jamaicans or light skinned Jamaicans had towards dark skinned Jamaicans was inconsequential in comparison to the prejudice that he had encountered in the Southern United States and was relatively minor when compared to that present in the Northern United States. Whatever envy or hostility the poor Jamaicans might have had towards middle class Jamaicans was much less than the class antagonism that existed in Haiti. That the 'haves' would resent the 'have nots' seemed both understandable and universal. That those who worked hard and made an effort to get an education would have more than those who did not seemed quite justifiable.

The existence of these newly recognized frictions did not propel him to conclude that a philosophy such as social-ism should be embraced in an effort to achieve total equality. He had worked his way through college while enduring great physical discomfort and knew that other Jamaicans of all classes had done the same. Consequently he did not believe that everyone should be paid equally. Instead he decided that the functions of a society should be to respect the dignity of all individuals, provide its people with equal educational and economic opportunities, and not assign them in perpe-tuity to one class but allow them to progress from one class to another through education and hard work.

His dream in life was not to be a politician who would assume the Sisyphean task of trying to address all of the problems of a society over a period of decades, but to be a physician who could expect to achieve day-to-day tangible accomplishments. He knew instinctively that while social change was important to him, it would never be the focus of his life.

Horatio, originally upset by his son's decision to drop architecture, was delighted to see that he would be entering the prestigious profession of medicine. Periodically he would bring their conversations around to Bert's future and encourage his son to return to Port Antonio and enter the government service as a physician. The usual pattern for a young physician in Jamaica was to enter government service, slowly develop an after hours private practice to serve the middle class who might pay as much as ten shillings for your service and the working poor who could pay up to five shillings to avoid the long waits at the public hospital, and then, when ones reputation had been established and the practice had grown enough to stand on its own, leave the government and open a full time private office.

Bert however saw that he had outgrown his boyhood home. The idea of spending years in the government service, subject to their decisions as to where he would be located, and limited to prescribing what they agreed to provide, was not acceptable to him. Moreover his experience in treating a small number of Port Antonians made him realize that the type of medicine that he was being taught at the prestigious Mc Gill University would not be possible in this rural setting. Most of his patients would be poor people who were unable to afford the modern medications and treatments that he was being taught to employ. When he tried to balance the good that a well-trained physician could do in Jamaica against the problems he would face if he remained, he concluded that his future lay elsewhere.

As he lay in the buoyant warm waters of the Caribbean, absorbed the heat of the sun, and exercised the muscles made weak by the ravages of diabetes on his nervous system, he considered his options. The sub-zero Canadian winters were not very appealing at those moments. He knew that he could easily obtain Canadian citizenship and build a successful practice in an urban English speaking area such as Toronto. Besides the many West Indians there who would be anxious for his services, there would be whites that were not burdened by the stereotypes of the United States and would be willing to enter his practice.

Alternatively he could go to a rural area in Canada and have little or no competition. He would be treating patients who were reasonably educated and sufficiently affluent to allow him to engage in the type of practice for which he was being trained. These sites were blessed with many virgin lakes that would provide him with one of his favorite recreational activities, fishing, that rivaled the fishing available in Jamaica. But there were shortcomings. At the height of the summer season, the lake water could never compare to ocean water. It lacked the warmth, the buoyancy, the salty taste in your mouth and the salty tingle on your skin that vitalized your body when you swam.

Despite America's shortcomings racially, it seemed to be the most attractive option. However he never considered a location in the South to be a viable choice since he was unwilling to tolerate the degree of discrimination that he had found there during the two years that he spent at Tuskegee. He was favorably disposed to the Institute, the place that he had spent his formative educational years, but completely opposed to the culture that surrounded the school.

On the other hand, the northern part of the country provided many choices. Salt-water fishing was available on both coasts and the Gulf of Mexico. Warm temperatures were available in Florida, Texas, and California, and tolerable temperatures were available along the East Coast. People had enough money to afford the type of medicine that he wanted to deliver. The degree of prejudice and discrimination in the North was much less than in the South and was improving. All things considered, northern America seemed to be his best choice.

From time to time the admonitions of Booker T. Washington entered into his decision-making. Since Bert accepted that coloreds should become educated, demonstrate their abilities, and thereby encourage the white majority to end segregation and grant full civil rights, he would have to make some contribution if he decided to move to the northern United States. He still had no specific plan, but he knew that inaction was not an option and that radical confrontation was not his style.

Time seemed to pass very slowly as Bert went through the restorative process. His milk diet was successful in bringing his diabetes under excellent control. He thought about insulin but it seemed as if he would have no need of it—as control of his diabetes increased, his strength increased, as strength increased, physical activity increased, as physical activity increased, control increased.

After approximately six months had passed, the sustained fall in the level of his blood sugar allowed the small blood vessels in his legs to heal. This healing led to an increase in the flow of the blood that nurtured the nerves that supplied his skin and his muscles. Gradually the pins and needles sensation in his skin abated, became intermittent, and then disappeared. The weakness in his muscles receded first from his thighs, then from his legs, and then from his feet like a gentle morning tide.

After noticing the improvement in his health, his friends Osmond, Leslie, and Danny concluded that he was up to a series of short weekend trips. They trudged up the thirty stairs to the Forsyth house and paused on the veranda where Horatio was observing the activities in the harbor below.

After exchanging the expected pleasantries, they and put the question to Bert's father.

"Chief, on Saturday we plan to go to Kingston for a few days and would like to take Bert with us," said Leslie as he rocked gently in the comfortable cane-backed chair that Horatio had made from native mahogany. He looked out at the beauty of the harbor below without truly appreciating it and continued speaking as he flicked the ashes from a cigarette. "He needs to see a different part of the country-side, meet some new people, and enjoy some of the activities that are only available in Kingston. Do we have your per-mission to take him?"

Horatio had recognized that Bert had improved to the point where he was becoming restless. He had included him in many activities but understood that his son was at an age that does not relish extended contact with parents. He had been wondering what he could do to alleviate Bert's increasing boredom and saw this as the perfect solution.

"Certainly Leslie," replied Horatio as he leaned back and conversed easily with the men who would forever in his mind be the boys who had flown the kites on the beach, brought home fish that they caught on a Saturday, and gotten into one scrape after another. "However you have to promise that you will not let him overextend himself. He has to stay away from the rich foods also. And he can't stay up too late. We'd hate to see all of our efforts over the past months be undone."

Bert was of course very enthusiastic about the idea. As his strength had increased, he had begun to feel as if he were being confined even though he left the house almost daily. After all of these years on his own in big cities like Toledo and Montreal, the life in his fathers house in Port Antonio that had seemed so idyllic as a child now seemed very monotonous. Day after day he repeated the same exercises. The only significant addition was that he now walked to the nearby beach every day and rarely used his father's horse and buggy. At the beach, he still spent an hour sitting in the shallow water and exercising his legs then another half hour swimming at a leisurely pace before getting dressed and returning home.

Before going home he would walk around the city and visit with various merchants that he knew. As a child, he would have delighted in enjoying some of the culinary treats that were available but with his strict diet, this was not possible. Instead, he derived his greatest pleasure from going to the wharf and seeing what activity was transpiring. He would spend hours watching freighters unload industrial supplies and take on agricultural cargo. Sometimes they would also leave elegantly dressed tourists for the Titchfield Hotel. This would remind him of the alternate life that was available-if one had the money.

When he tired of these rounds, he would stop in at his father's office briefly to discuss his fathers pending projects or the latest political uproar. If he had not already done so, he would read an ever-present copy of the *Daily Gleaner* especially the comic strips where the latest adventures of *The Yellow Kid* were recounted. Then he was off to the post office to pick up the mail. It was however a routine that had lost it's interest.

His evenings were even less active. After everyone had taken their pre-supper bath, the family would sit down to a dinner that was prepared and served by the maid. Again his enjoyment of the food was severely limited by the restrictions that he had placed on himself. He ate very slowly and listened as the various children recited the momentous events of their day. Afterwards he would join his father and Juanita on the front veranda for some more serious conversation—the problems of his father's business, the latest gossip, or, at times, Bert's future.

There was some variation on the weekend. Usually someone, somewhere had an open house on Saturday evening. However the majority of the attendees were older people--friends of his father whose conversations centered on business or family. In this small community there was not an abundance of younger middle class singles or even couples who might share his interests and concerns. In addition, his ability to participate fully in the primary local ritual was limited by his decision not to drink any rum until his health had fully recovered.

Sunday morning invariably began with a trip to church. As one of the city's most prominent citizens, the family had an area reserved for it in the front of the church. In fact, many years later, the church would inscribe his sister's name on one of the seats in recognition of May's many services. May donated land at Anchovy to the church and later her son George added to the donation. For some, church was primarily an opportunity to wear your best clothes and to catch up on what was happening. For his father, it was meant to express your devotion.

After church they would travel somewhere in a horse and buggy caravan. At first the trips were designed to facilitate Bert's recovery. Later, they began to include areas of interest to the smaller children and visits to various friends and relatives, especially his sister May.

In his absence May had gotten married and now had three children, two boys and a girl. She was the only one of the ten siblings who had married at this point in time. Whenever he reminded her of this, she blushed and stammered, a reaction that was sure to provoke further teasing from her brother. The two thoroughly enjoyed their opportunities to relive old experiences and share confidences. Despite the satisfaction that these routines provided, Bert missed the excitement and the attractions of a larger city. As a result of this restlessness, he gladly agreed when Leslie and Danny suggested the trip to Kingston.

When he had been in Jamaica before, the usual method of transportation was a horse and buggy. Occasionally one rode the bus or a train. Now, in the late twenties, middle class families often had access to a motorcar. This added flexibility allowed his friends to debate as to what route to take on this first trip. Should they take the coast route to the east, should they go west along the coast, either cut inland as soon as possible and drive over the Junction route, or should they continue along the coast to Ocho Rios and go then inland?

The east route was quickly ruled out. Bert had already traveled over a fair portion of that route on his trips to the different beaches and to Bath and the Botanical Gardens. The Junction was quite scenic and somewhat exciting. It was the most mountainous of the routes to Kingston and afforded some spectacular scenery similar to what one saw on the railroad. It consisted of one hairpin curve after another, narrow roads with sheer precipices, and complete uncertainty. When you came around a curve, would you find a donkey cart on your side of the road? Would there be a rockslide? Would the potholes break an axle? Then, as now, young men in their twenties had a spirit of adventure that had to be satisfied.

One never knew quite what to expect on the Junction in the way of hazards, but you could always be assured that you would see something that you had never noticed before. Shallow rivers coursed over a rock-strewn bed along the base of the mountains that were enshrouded in strands of bamboo. Here and there the countrywomen could be seen washing their clothes. Then there were the waterfalls, waterfalls that were especially beautiful after the rain. Since it frequently rained in the mountains, their full beauty was seen on almost every trip. The confluence of the mist from a waterfall, the bright tropical sun, and the clear blue skies often produced a delicate rainbow that never failed to catch your eye.

At a mostly subconscious level, Bert recognized that colors were much more in evidence in Jamaica than they had been in Toledo and Montreal. In Jamaica there was a profusion of color against the dark green foliage and the bright blue skies that far surpassed the beauties of American and Canadian landscapes. The scenery resurrected the childhood memories that he had recorded from his journeys on the train. He truly appreciated the effort that the poor country people made to beautify their humble homes with hedges of crotons, bougainvilleas, or hibiscus and beds of coleus. He contrasted that with the bleakness he had seen in the rural South where oppression seemed to have drained the poor population, both colored and white, of an appreciation of beauty while also robbing them of their potential.

After mentally reviewing the options, Bert suggested that they take the route through Ocho Rios. They drove along the North Coast to that city then stopped at one of the many small beachside restaurants before heading inland. Bert limited himself to a lunch consisting of a small helping of rice and peas, a bit of snapper, and sliced Bombay mangos for desert. His companions added breadfruit, salt fish and ackee, and a generous rum and coconut water. They debated as to whether they should go to the falls at Dunn's River or to the caves further along before resuming their trip but both options were ruled out as being too time consuming.

Instead they headed inland through the area known as Fern Gully. Here the road curved snake-like through the rock for almost a mile. On either side of the road, ferns had been planted that had grown up to a point where they almost blocked out the sky. The rest of the trip was not as visually sensuous as the Junction route, but Fern Gully alone was a sight to behold with its giant fronds of green.

If one approached Kingston from the north, there were other landmarks that were as well named as Fern Gully. When you came to Stony Hill, the origin of the name was evident. Outcroppings of pock marked volcanic rock punctuated the hillside in such profusion that it seemed unlikely that man could find any site to build a home. Yet many did. However the scalping of the hillside created a hazard for the travelers below. At times, especially after a downpour, the uprooted rocks that had been pushed aside to create home sites could hurtle down the hill and do serious damage to your car.

Kingston was also close to the famous Blue Mountains whose color reflected an altitude that combined with its soil and perfect rainfall to produce what was reputed to be the most delicious coffee in the world. To the right of the city were the Red Hills where a heavy concentration of bauxite ore created a deeply red soil. As the mountains came into view Bert thought, 'In Jamaica, even the earth exudes color'.

Eventually the road into northern Kingston led you to Matilda's corner. No one remembered Matilda, the woman who had sold her produce there many years ago, but for some reason the appellation stuck over the years. Similarly a tree that had been located half way between the mountains and the ocean and had been used to provide a name, Half Way Tree, for the intersection of roads at that location. Somehow these names seemed so much more romantic to Bert than the names of places in the United States and Canada where names were often mutations of those bestowed by Indians or self-commemorations created by developers.

After they reached the city they easily made their way to the house of one of Leslie's relatives. Although Kingston was a much larger city than Port Antonio, was not visited very often by the country people, and did not have very good road signs, the drivers never seemed to have any problem in reaching their destination. Once someone had gone to a home, their internal radar was infallible in its ability to guide them back again. If the home had never been visited before, the traveler could usually reach their destination by simply asking the first person that they came upon as they neared the vicinity of the home. If that person were a local, they would undoubtedly know where the people of importance lived.

However if the individual asked did not know the area, their directions could be very non-specific and unintentionally misleading. Inasmuch as working class Jamaicans did not have cars, they had no need for the spatial skills of a driver. Distances were denoted by phrases such as 'down the road awhile'; directions were given in terms of landmarks that would have no meaning for a stranger. It could be frustrating to try to follow such advice, especially in a rural area where the inhabitants typically never strayed as much as ten miles from home and could not be counted on to be very helpful even though they wanted to be.

One skill that seemed commonplace for those usually described as 'the common man' was the ability to immediately place everyone they met in their appropriate slot in the social hierarchy without any knowledge of their lineage. The new individuals color, clothes, and conveyance would provide an initial impression but this would be quickly adjusted based on a few observations, often intangible to an outsider. For example, someone like Bert, a man whose medium brown complexion could darken quickly at the beach, would still be recognized as being a person of quality as he stood in a bathing suit, bereft of any accoutrements of class such as expensive clothes or a car. His direct gaze and assertive posture would be enough to mark him by sight. His distinctive diction and ingrained confidence in making a request with authority but without disrespect would confirm his status. In Jamaica, unlike in America, deference was not given just on the basis of color. When deference was given, it was given voluntarily and not by coercion for the simple reason that those who were most deserving of it did not have to demand it.

The habit of being deferential to someone of a higher social group would gradually fade in the decades that followed as the British followed the example of the French and the Americans and discarded their class system. At this point in time however, this was the system that was in place and was the system that shaped the attitudes that Bert developed. He was accustomed to being respected and was resentful that in America respect was withheld simply because of his color. Moreover, having worked as a common laborer for over ten years, he had come to appreciate the fact that respect had to be secured not just for himself as a member of the middle class, but also for all people of color.

When they arrived at their destination, they would be welcomed with the inevitable invitation to have a drink of rum. The hosts also understood that after the long hot trip, a bath and a change of clothes was a necessity before the guests could feel comfortable. By the time that they had all completed their ablutions, it was time for a dinner that, as custom dictated, consisted of much more than they ever could have eaten.

The dining room, like the rest of the house and the veranda, was tiled throughout with a locally made cement based tile that was kept at a high state of luster by layers of wax that had been assiduously applied by the maids once each week over a period of years. Burglar bars enclosed the verandas in testimony to the fact that paradise was not without its problems. Petty thievery was always a possibility if one was careless enough to provide the opportunity but violent robberies were fortunately rare.

After dinner they retired to the veranda in anticipation of the arrival of guests who were uninvited yet expected. The middle class in Kingston seemed to differ from their rural counterparts in several important ways. First, there seemed to be a noticeable division into two groups—hosts and guests. Drop in at any host Jamaican house on a Saturday evening and the same scene would be repeated. Throughout the evening guests would arrive: single males, young couples who could not yet afford to be hosts, or a couple with an eligible female friend or relative. This format provided an acceptable form of introduction for unmarried men and women and an opportunity for couples to renew acquaintances and make new friends.

In general, the gathering was split into a male and a female contingent that were not so widely separated that each could not keep abreast of the conversation of the other. When the gathering threatened to become too large to permit an intimate level of conversation, the early arrivals, in response to an unwritten code of standards, would depart and make their way to another location.

With each new arrival, in recognition of the fact that two entirely different families bore the prestigious name of Forsyth, Bert would invariably be asked, "Which branch of the Forsyths are you related to? The surveyor or the builder?"

Once the answer was given, the questioner would usually follow up with a statement such as "Oh, I met your brother Lorenzo once" or "Your father did some work for my uncle" or "My cousin who is at Wolmer's knows your sisters Dottie and Kathleen". There was always a connection to be made.

After these words, often spoken as a self informing soliloquy rather than as part of an interactive conversation, the speaker would then enter Bert into a mental catalogue replete with files and sub files as complex as those found in a modern computer and subject to an instant recall button. It seemed that every middle class Jamaican, regardless of his or her level of education, had this remarkable mental facility.

If your family connections were sufficiently impressive, you would be entered into the positive side of the ledger. If no connection could be made, you might be placed in taxonomic limbo to be resurrected at some later date if the situation warranted. If the connection was a negative one, you were so labeled and were apt to receive scant attention for the duration of the individual's stay. In Bert's case, he was doubly blessed in that he was the son of H.A. Forsyth, known even in Kingston as one of the leading citizens of

Port Antonio, and was in addition, soon to be a physician. He was immediately accepted and spoken to frankly. After a round of drinks, the conversation would become more animated. Most males were capable of heated debate, but usually there was one who eclipsed the others. As the rum lubricated the portion of his brain that supplied his tongue, he might say to the maid "Get me another drink *nuh.*" This was intended to provide him with an adequate prop with which to gesticulate since he was unlikely to pause and partake of his drink and allow someone else to speak before he had finished. Then he would subtly signal his intention to monopolize the conversation by coming forward in his chair and raising his voice to command attention before proceeding to hold center stage.

The conversations that ensued were always much livelier than those in Port Antonio. Middle class Jamaicans, especially Kingstonians, were never at a loss for an opinion. No, theirs were not mere opinions but were pronouncements made with the certainty of an Evangelist at a Sunday Revival meeting. "This country is going to hell man. People don't want to work anymore. When they do work, they want way too much money. The next thing they will want to form unions. It's all the American's fault. Our people go up to Miami and pick up those foreign ideas that don't do anyone any good."

Speakers were equally certain whether making comments about Jamaica or about places or situations with which they had no personal experience. "Segregation in the U.S. is a disgrace! Those white southerners ought to be horse-whipped. I hear they hang colored men just for looking in the direction of a white woman. If I go there, there will be the devil to pay. No one is going to tell me where to sit or what direction to look in. You were crazy to stay in Alabama for two years. That is why you moved to Canada."

Any questions that might be asked tended to be rhetorical since the speaker clearly knew all of the answers and did not feel the need to learn anything from the receptacle of their verbal barrage. Bert would be told, not asked, why he had left Tuskegee or taken some other action. The fact that the listener might have some first hand knowledge while the speaker had none was irrelevant.

After a particularly vituperative outburst, Bert made an observation based on his fifteen years of experience in the United States. He chose his words carefully and spoke in a matter-of-fact tone. "I can see how the common man in Jamaica might be attracted to a union. Most don't have a steady job and a steady paycheck the way middle class Jamaicans do. Their wages are low yet they have families to feed. Alone they have no power but in a union they can achieve change. Right now my brother Roger is in charge of some workers on a train in the States and he tells me that they are all supporting a fellow named A. Phillip Randolph who formed a union of colored porters called the Brotherhood of Sleeping Car Porters a couple of years ago. Until they got the union, the porters were at the mercy of the railroad. Now they are beginning to see some changes. If Jamaica doesn't give more consideration to its workers, it will force them into a union within the next ten years. Jamaica has to be careful not to treat the common man they way the whites treat all coloreds in the U.S."

"You can't be serious man!" came the excited rejoinder as his protagonist's voice rose by several decibels and his body assumed a more engaged posture as if he were a prize fighter balancing his body in preparation for throwing a knockout punch. "The two situations are not the least bit comparable. The common man here is not starving like they are in America. All he needs here is a little plot of land to grow some food and a piece of string to catch some fish. What's more, no one in Jamaica is trying to kill him or tell him where he can sit. We have public schools for those who want to go. Let him learn a trade if he wants to do better."

As he listened to these words, Bert was reminded of the ambivalence he had when he tried to compare the two countries. It was not a simple matter. He thought about trying to counteract the dogmatic statements of the speaker but thought better of it. The speaker had never been to the United States much less lived there subject to the indignities that he had experienced. He had never gone months without a steady job, powerless to affect his economic future. More than likely he had gotten his well paying job in the usual manner of the upper middle class--from the friend of a friend--without any competition. If he had had a few adverse experiences, he would have appreciated the fact that although the situation in the America was indeed worse, the principle was the same. Any denial of equal opportunity, whether moderate and class driven as in Jamaica, or severe and race driven as in the America, created an undue hardship that could not be justified and should be rectified.

Instead of trying to rebut his challenger, Bert turned the conversation to topics that were just a fiery, but generated less heat. The day before there had been a football match between Kingston College and Jamaica College. In a city with limited forms of entertainment, such clashes were the equivalent of a World Series baseball game in America. Offices generally let out early in order to let their white-collar employees root for their alma maters. An exodus of men in long sleeved white shirts with dark ties was joined by separate groups of women in white blouses and ankle length dark skirts who walked briskly to the playing fields. Spectators lived and died with each kick or save and relived the game for days afterwards. The strong school loyalties often provoked spirited discussions after a game.

An alternative subject for contention was the Saturday afternoon horse races. The sport of kings was enjoyed by all classes in Jamaica. The best horses were owned by the English and ridden by short wiry Jamaican jockeys who inspired deep devotion or endless criticism depending on their success at that particular moment. Whenever a favorite lost, there was an immediate cry of collusion. Emotions always ran deep but never actually erupted. Still, the inevitable upsets made for some impassioned commentary that could rapidly divert a conversation away from an inflammatory topic.

Within less than two hours, the guest would have had their obligatory drink or two and left for the next house where they would renew and cement relationships and learn the latest gossip. The arrival of overlapping participants in this social merry-go-round ensured that there was never a lull. Later, when the titer of rum in their systems had reached a level that resulted in a recognizable slurring of speech or a change in the ferocity of the debate, the gathering would break up as the wives of the deteriorating males would emphasize their own fatigue and request that they now call it a night.

Various alternative activities were available for Sunday. Church in the morning was a matter of routine. For the afternoon one might choose lunch at the Myrtle Bank where one could see and be seen, a few hours at one of the nearby beaches, or an excursion to places like Port Royal, the earthquake destroyed headquarters of the olden pirates. Other alternatives included a trip to Hope Gardens to stroll through the manicured acres of trees and flowers, a trip to the downtown square known as Parade where the military band, resplendent in brilliant red and black uniforms was performing, or else a short sojourn to the nearby hills to Papine or further out to enjoy the enchanting beauty of Castleton Gardens

With the recent onset of talking motion pictures, new movie theaters were springing up to join the Ward Theater where previously only silent movies had been performed. The cheap section of the movie theater was often somewhat annoying but somehow endearing in their vociferous response to the movie. Action on the screen would provoke loud comments from an audience that never seemed to feel embarrassed about describing what was obvious to everyone. With loud shouts they would warn the heroine, comment on the ineptitude of a hero, or otherwise demonstrate their total involvement in the proceedings.

For the middle class in Jamaica, going to the movies was the equivalent of going to the opera in New York. One dressed in high fashion and sat in the box seats where friends and relatives were likely to be seen. When you did meet someone, you took advantage of the opportunity to update your knowledge of what was going on in his or her life and to make arrangements to visit at some later date.

If you were ever so naïve as to ask anyone what time to expect their visit, you would likely to be answered with the phrase "Soon come mon." Any question that required someone to commit themselves to a specific time frame would elicit this most non-committal of responses. For example, if you wanted to know when a contractor would return to complete his job, 'soon come' let you know that it would be whenever he got around to it. This ubiquitous response was the equivalent of the Spanish word mañana.

After completion of the afternoon's activities, it was usually family time. Either one had dinner at a relative's house, or vice versa. People in the 'right' social circle rarely ate alone on Sunday. After the meal, the group would again to the veranda for drinks and conversation. Since these were family gatherings, the conversation usually dwelt on family matters. Cousin so and so has been going out with that girl who lives in Hagley Park; Alex left his job at Grace Kennedy; and so forth. There was usually nothing of real interest in these conversations to a non-family member such as Bert.

As he sat and listened to the conversations, Bert was constantly analyzing the participants and making comparisons with his experiences abroad. On one occasion he made note of the fact that the complexions of the participants in these gatherings encompassed the entire range of the black and white spectrum. Most families of this era were large in size and could expect to find marked variations in the color of their siblings, children, grandchildren, cousins, nieces and nephews. Moreover, with increasing frequency, family gatherings included in-laws who were white.

As in many societies, men tended to choose a wife based on looks while women placed more emphasis on the prospects of a prospective mate. Hence white men in Jamaica, with the demise of slavery, were able to marry attractive women of color without breaking the law or being ostracized. White women in Jamaica were in short supply, highly sought after by white men, and rarely married colored Jamaican men. However when a Jamaican man went to England to study, his primary exposure was to white women. Consequently they not infrequently returned with an English wife. In general, class more than race regulated these marriages. With many of its members having in-laws who were not white, the Jamaican white society would have found it impractical had they attempted to practice American style discrimination.

These opportunities to intermingle socially with people of all colors contrasted sharply with the situation that existed in the United States where many states had laws against interracial marriages. This re-exposure to a more tolerant approach to race relations reminded Bert that there was an alternative to the combination of color based discrimination and complete segregation. It nurtured the seeds of discontent that had been implanted in him during his years in the United States.

After all visitors had left on Sunday the guests exchanged a half-hour of pleasantries with their hosts before retiring. Monday morning would start with an impressive breakfast that offered a large variety of fruits. While their host would be scheduled to work, he would never give the appearance of being in a hurry to leave. Just as a New

Yorker considered the *New York Times* a vital part of their daily existence, the Jamaican could not do without their copy of *The Daily Gleaner,* the venerable newspaper that had been a staple in every middle class Jamaican household since 1834. Without fail, everyone read the obituaries in order to update their mental catalogues on the islands population. A complete reading of the newspaper in the morning was combined with the evening broadcast from the *British Broadcasting Company,* usually referred to as the BBC, to provide the Jamaican with a thorough knowledge of what was going on in the island, the highlights of the empire, and a smattering of the world. If your name appeared anywhere in the *Gleaner,* for any minor reason, everyone of your friends would be sure to have seen it.

Eventually the host would leave for work. At this point in time expatriates from England filled the top positions in most companies and made the strategic decisions. Upper middle class Jamaicans held the secondary positions that were responsible for implementing the decisions. Lower middle class Jamaicans held the clerical jobs. Jamaicans categorized as of the lower or working class performed messenger or porter duty if they were male. A primary duty of the working class female, other than clean up work, was to provide everyone with their afternoon tea. There was not segregation or discrimination in the American sense, but there was a definite British style class system that in some ways functioned like segregation.

After work, many middle class Jamaican males were often delayed in their return to their home. For some, the delay was due to a stop at a club for an hour of socializing with other males over a drink of rum and coconut water. For others, especially the financially secure middle-aged men with wives who had lost interest in sex, there were primal urges that would be satisfied by the system established in the days of slavery. For these men the delay was occasioned by a stop at the home of their mistress, a mistress who often had children. As men migrated abroad in search of opportunity, the imbalance between the number of men and women was exacerbated so that for many women, their best hope for companionship was with a married man. In these instances, the lengthy absences of the husband and father were usually a silently accepted fact for the family.

In due course, the houseguests would prepare to take leave of their hostess and begin the return trip to the country. After their departure, the hostess would begin her household duties--supervising the house staff in cleaning up behind the visitors, and replenishing the supplies that had been used up over the weekend. Many of these supplies were obtained without leaving the house inasmuch as the street provided a steady parade of women selling fruits, vegetables, and poultry, and fishermen peddling the day's catch. Any fish or poultry that was purchased would probably be used that day due to the limitations of refrigeration by ice.

After having been away for so many years, Bert found· that he was repeatedly taken by surprise to hear middle class women slip into the local dialect when they spoke to the 'higglers' who peddled their wares from door to door. It wasn't just that they added words to their vocabulary that Bert had long forgotten—their posture and their intonation changed completely. There was often an angry aspect to the woman's voice and demeanor as she bargained for the best price. Yet, at the end of the transaction, both seller and buyer seemed highly satisfied. He wondered why the need to go through this ritual when both sides knew going in that the final price would be as it had been the week before and the week before that. Episodes such as these reminded him that the Jamaican and American cultures were different in many ways and that he was now more attuned to the American way.

Some purchases had to be made at a store rather than from a peddler. On these occasions one could count on seeing some friends and making plans with them for the coming weekend. In making these plans one would be sure to reach as high on the social ladder as possible. The class system did not consist of a simple division of upper, middle, and lower but was a complex of divisions and subdivisions whose constituents were constantly changing. Although the boundaries of these divisions could not be defined, everyone was cognizant of their existence, capable of pigeonholing everyone else accurately, and anxious to enter into the next strata by virtue of a change in their position in the business world, a marriage that could change the circles into which they were accepted, or the cultivation of judicious friendships with influential people.

As the hostess became involved in her daily rituals, Bert and his friends would leave. After each trip to Kingston, they always tried to take a different route back to Port Antonio in order to add to the enjoyment of their trip. At times they detoured to have lunch with friends who lived on one of the estates in the central and western parts of the country. Bert's surprise about the ability of his friends to navigate poorly marked streets in the city was miniscule in comparison to the admiration he felt for their skill in utilizing an invisible road map that led them down totally unmarked narrow back roads that the navigator had not traversed for a year or more. After his years in large cities with clearly marked streets and transient populations, he had not developed either of the local skills—an innate local positioning satellite for travel, and a facility in cataloguing and recalling the social status and connections of all of the middle class individuals whom they had met.

When the weather was hot their preferred destination was Mandeville, a city located at an elevation that made it several degrees cooler than in Kingston. The return trip from Mandeville took them by the famous Bamboo Drive, the perfectly straight one-mile stretch of road that was enclosed by bamboo that had grown up on either side of the road until it met twenty meters above in a high arc. The majesty of this location was so impressive that Bert made sure that they stopped and took a picture that he could show to his friends back in Canada when he returned.

When visiting one of the large estates, one was reminded of the heritage of the country. Ownership of these estates was often vested in a large corporation with headquarters outside of the country, or in a family whose primary residence was elsewhere. Jamaicans of mixed heritage who could trace their ancestry back for a century or more usually conducted the day-to-day management. The fieldwork was done by the Jamaicans whose ancestry was generally almost pure African. Again, differentiation was by class, but class and race were closely intertwined.

The main house on these estates was set on the highest point of land in order to provide an observation point for the management. The result of positioning the house for business reasons was usually a wonderfully unobstructed view of the natural beauty of the area. For those houses located near the sea, one had a mixture of an ocean view and the colors of the plantation—densely packed acres of dark green in the case of bananas, broad fields of a lighter color for sugar cane, and distinct strands of tan trunks topped by tufts of green and yellow in the case of coconuts. A visitor always received a genuinely warm welcome at these outposts where the contact with ones peers was relatively infrequent. The group would sit on the veranda, sip rum and coconut water or a rum punch served by the maid, and cover all of the gossip known to the hosts and the guests.

"So Leslie, you spent the weekend with the Forbes? How is the old man doing? Is he still with Cable and Wireless? I hear he got a new Vauxhall a few months ago. And how is his brother? They just had a second child I hear. And you, young Forsythe. How is your father? I understand that he is constructing a house for Dr. Walsh in Kingston. Your father is a fine builder, a man to be trusted."

The breadth of knowledge that the rural Jamaicans had about the relationships and activities of the people in Kingston and around the island was astounding considering that they only occasionally went into Kingston and less frequently to other parts of the island. On reflection, Bert realized that although the island had a population of around one and one-half million, the class that he moved in consisted of only a few thousand people –people who always remained in a relatively small area whose boundaries were circumscribed by a sea. It was much easier to keep current in this environment than in the North America where many of the cities that Bert had lived in had populations that exceeded that of the entire island. Moreover, there was very little constancy in America. Populations were constantly changing because of migrations between cities. Conversely, if you left Jamaica and returned ten years later, the vast majority of people would be right where you left them.

When they prepared to leave, their hosts would insist that they take a large supply of any of the plantations available produce. In addition to acquiring these staples, Bert and his friends would stop along the way to pick up some of the variety of fruits and vegetables that were available from the roadside stands that they passed. In due course they would arrive back in Port Antonio and resume their regular routine.

After a trip to the larger city of Kingston with its new faces, spirited arguments, and wider variety of choices, Bert often felt a bit letdown. He had become accustomed to the more cosmopolitan attitudes of the inhabitants of a large metropolis. Although he thoroughly enjoyed the childhood reminiscences that had been stimulated by his stay in Port Antonio, he missed not being in a larger city such as Toledo or Montreal with their ready access to good roads, automobiles, acceptable public transportation, and an extensive choice of leisure activities.

He was thankful that in his year at home he had an opportunity to rekindle his relationship with his sister May and the stepsiblings that he had left in 1911, and to begin to know the stepsiblings who were born in his absence. May had been an especially great comfort to him. As a deeply devout person, she had read to him from the Bible every Sunday while he was confined to bed and unable to go to the local church, and prayed every day for his recovery.

His relationship with his half siblings was at a different level. Their memory of him was limited for the two oldest, and non-existent for the others. There were three new faces that were added to the group that had previously seen him off--Kathleen, Harvey, and John. For years the new siblings had heard stories about this brother who had the nerve to choose a profession other than the one dictated by his father and had instead worked like a common laborer to support and educate himself. They recognized and respected the determination that he displayed in overcoming the illness that had forced him to come home, and were impressed that he would soon be a physician. As they gradually overcame their shyness and he gradually regained his strength, they began to first sit on his bed and then to physically interact. By the time he began to think of leaving, they were playing with him as if he had never been away.

On one particularly pleasant Saturday, Osmond suggested that they should get a small boat and invite a couple of young ladies to go with them to Navy Island for a picnic. The few eligible young ladies of the area had shown some interest in the physician-to-be, especially when it became clear that his health was improving. He knew that he was feeling well when the suggestion of female companionship stimulated his interest.

Bert and Osmond supplied the muscle in rowing to and from the island in a boat laden with four people, a small feast that the women provided, and all of the equipment they girls thought necessary to insure a successful picnic. The men ate with relish after the effort of rowing; the young ladies, ever intent on attaining a suitable match, engaged in subtle flirtations.

"Bert, you know you really ought to return to Port Antonio after you finish your studies," said the comely nineteen-year old who had occupied most of his attention. "Port Antonio really needs well trained physicians such as you will be. What's more, think of how much nicer life is here compared to the United States. From what you have told us, the weather is terrible and the white people there are even more terrible. I could spend a couple of years there *if someone asked me to*, but Jamaica will always be my home."

Bert had already decided that his future laid in the United States and did not respond to her broad hint. Instead he complimented her on the excellent meal that they had just enjoyed and silently reminded himself of the importance of resuming his studies and not getting caught up in any romantic attachments.

When a small child waits for a birthday or Christmas to come, a young lady waits for a special dance or event, or a young man waits to be eligible for a driver's license, the future seems terribly distant. When that next phase of your life does arrive, you wonder how the time passed by so quickly and regret missing out on the things you meant to do but never did. So it was that the year in Port Antonio passed and it was once again time for Bert to take leave of his family although there were still places to visit and people to see.

His goodbyes were easier than they had been on his first departure. He was not an untested stripling somewhat hesitant to leave his family and friends but a man who knew what he wanted to achieve and was on the verge of doing so. He shook his father's hand vigorously, gave May a long hug, and said goodbye to each of the other siblings. This time there was no Roger to administer a 'last lick.'

No one quite trusted the plane to safely come close to the dock without creating waves that would smash the small boats against the dock or generating a noise that would deafen the townspeople. Consequently the seaplane, like the ship he had taken years ago, was reached by a transit boat from the wharf. On his trip to the island a year ago he had been too sick to enjoy the flight in. He was therefore determined to miss nothing on the flight out. After reaching the seaplane, he quickly scrambled aboard so that he could commandeer the seat with the best view. He sat down and contracted his thin frame into a seat by the window where he could savor the takeoff and the sight of the island from the air.

The plane was quite small and cramped for a large adult. Had his father been there, he would have found both the headroom and the legroom to be very confining. Bert however was quite slender and had no trouble fitting his legs into the space between the seats. He peered through the porthole-sized windows that were obscured by the constant splash of salt water towards the tiny figures on the dock several hundred yards away, picked out everyone in turn, and waved even though he knew it was unlikely that at such a distance those waiting on the dock would be able to see through the small aperture in the body of the plane and into its dimly lit interior.

It never ceased to amaze him that attaching a motor to a metal hull could result in men flying through the sky. The whole process was fascinating to him. He looked around and found that the pilot and his controls were clearly visible from his seat. He was able to watch each step of the departure process with fascination.

With everyone on board, the pilot started the engines. At first there was a mild cough and a low rumble as if a phlegmatic fat man was in the early stages of sleep. The rumble grew into a deafening roar as the pilot revved his engines prior to take off and the small plane shook until everyone on board began to look at each other in order to be reassured that this was normal and not a precursor to disaster. Gauges were checked, switches were thrown, the throttle extended, and the steering wheel tilted towards the pilot as the plane gathered speed and rose into a sky that was clear blue except for the inevitable afternoon clouds that were visible in the distance. With a shudder the plane began to hover over the waves and head towards Navy Island. As the coconut trees that dotted the island grew larger and larger and collision seemed more and more imminent, the plane began to rise and gain altitude. It cleared the trees with plenty to spare, dipped a wing in homage to those watching from shore, and headed north to Miami.

Bert had been excited at the thought of flying in a plane over Port Antonio. Planes were still a rarity in this small city on this small island in the Caribbean. As a small boy he had read about planes, and had dreamed of actually being on one and seeing the island from above. He was not disappointed. The people on the wharf became tiny specks like the flies that one sees on a rock that lies far below while you are ensconced in a tall tree full of ripe mangos. Most of the buildings in the town itself were made invisible by the coconut trees, fruit trees, and bananas that either grew wild or had been planted by the inhabitants in order to provide a tie to their agrarian roots after moving into the city. The island itself was a tangled mass of green against a backdrop of high mountains that contained speckles of cultivated land around makeshift huts that he knew were constructed from discarded sheets of metal and odds and ends. On the better plots of land in the distance were the large estates that grew sugar cane and bananas.

The ocean presented a panorama that was similar in configuration to the patches of quilt work that he had seen on the land. Off to the right was the deep blue of Blue Hole. Around Navy Island were shallow transparent turquoise waters that covered bright white sand that was scalloped with dark projections of coral. Further out was a sparkling royal blue that contained sporadic breaks--white-capped waves that looked like ripples in desert sand. On the horizon a smoke that was white with wisps of black rose lazily from a ship towards the pastel blue sky. The plane rose to meet the fluffy white clouds that he had previously admired from far below. The people, the city, the country all faded from view. The experience was everything he had anticipated yet much more. He was defying gravity and soaring upwards like a bird. Distances that took days to cover in a horse and buggy and hours in a car were being covered in minutes. If he had the controls, he would have swooped down to the ocean top like a sea gull, tilted right and left to catch the currents, and then climbed to explore the mysteries of the clouds that loomed in the distance. He was on his way back to his dream.

7

ATLANTIC CITY

Money was an important factor in every decision that Bert made so it seemed quite logical when he chose a lengthy train ride in coach rather than saving time by taking a plane flight from Miami to Montreal. After his experiences as a passenger and an employee, train rides were now second nature for Bert. After arriving in Miami he made his way to the train station where he boarded the train for Montreal, sat back in his seat, observed the scenery for a brief period, and then settled down to alternating brief views out of the window with extended catnaps or periods of reflection.

He felt confident that his diabetes would not be a problem in the future. His regimen of diet and exercise had been a complete success. As a result of the disappearance of the paresthesias from his legs, he felt as strong as ever. Moreover, inasmuch as he had tried to keep up with what was going on in medicine while he was out of school, he knew that the synthesis of insulin was becoming available commercially and reasoned that this would be available in Montreal if he needed it to help avoid any repetition of the incident that had forced him to abandon his studies for a whole year.

He therefore looked forward with confidence to completing his schooling at McGill and going out into practice. The money that he had made from his 'bootleg medicine' in Jamaica had been spent but his father had agreed to continue to contribute to his support. He concluded that this income plus that from some part time jobs should relieve him from any financial worries, was confident in his ability to master the studies, but was still not sure where he would set up practice after graduation. That bridge would be crossed later.

The next two years passed uneventfully. Now his classes concentrated on individual systems of the body rather than overall themes such as anatomy or pharmacology. He learned about the heart, the lungs, blood, the urinary system, the reproductive system, the nervous system, the eyes, the bones, the skin and the ears. Time was spent on the Pediatric Ward so that the differences between adults and children could be appreciated and on the surgical ward. There was training in radiology and laboratory testing.

He enjoyed all of these subjects thoroughly and was pleased to find that the emphasis on rote memorization and rigorous written examinations had been replaced with an emphasis on problem solving and oral presentations. The oral presentation of a case could be humiliating since certain professors delighted in making life difficult for the medical students. Most of his time was spent on hospital wards where he had an opportunity to apply what he had learned in his basic science courses to the clinical problems that patients faced. His routine was still vigorous, but he now saw the light at the end of the tunnel.

Bert continued the time management patterns that he had developed in his first two years. The majority of his time during weekdays was spent in studies while weekends were spent on part time jobs and social engagements with the friends that he had made. As he neared the completion of his studies, he began to correspond with a Jamaican physician who was acquainted with his father. Dr. Lucas, a physician practicing in Atlantic City, New Jersey, was in need of an associate. This was of great interest to Bert since the economy had entered a depression that had exacerbated the already difficult possibility of opening ones own practice. As the value of stocks plummeted, banks cut back on their lending, factories ceased to hire, and workers found that jobs were hard to come by. Since coloreds tended to be 'the last hired and the first fired', they were especially hard hit by the economic decline.

While in Jamaica it was commonplace for newly graduated doctors to enter government service, the accepted course of action in America was to enter into association with an established physician whose practice had grown so big that they needed some help in making house calls and handling the office load. In 1930, the art of medicine, the ability to project an air of competence and compassion, was more important than the science of medicine, a science that was still quite rudimentary. Patients did not want to be treated by a physician who had limited experience unless there was a competent back up. With money at a premium, working class people did not go to a physician unless there was a serious problem that needed expert attention.

Despite the potential difficulties caused by the depression, Bert was happy to enter a private practice in the United States rather than enter government service in Jamaica. He had heard that Atlantic City was an attractive town with a moderate climate. This seemed a very good alternative to him after a total of over fifteen years in Ohio and Canada. After some correspondence with Dr. Lucas, an agreement was reached. He graduated medical school in May of 1930 with honors in medicine, bade his farewells to the friends that he had made during his years in Montreal, and set out for his new destination.

Before beginning practice, Bert had to pass the New Jersey boards and obtain a license. He studied for several weeks, took the boards, and in due course was told that he had passed. Years later he was told that he had received the highest score of anyone on that examination. One would never have heard this from Bert however because he was a very modest man.

Anyone who met Bert was immediately struck by his appearance and his intellect. His build was not as commanding as his fathers. Now in his thirties, he was less than five foot ten inches in height, usually weighed around 150 pounds, was slightly balding temporally, had straight black hair, and had a chocolate complexion. The most striking feature of his countenance was his eyes, deep set and best described as piercing. They seemed to twinkle and thereby reveal the marvelous subtle sense of humor that he frequently displayed. His gaze would dart quickly around a room in a way that made you immediately understand that this was a highly intelligent man and nothing would escape his attention.

Bert had heard that Atlantic City, located 140 miles south of New York City on the ten-mile long Abseon Beach Island, was world famous for the boardwalk that had been built to take full advantage of the wide beach that nature had created. The attraction of the beach was so great and the influx of visitors so marked, that many amusement areas, shops, restaurants, and hotels were constructed along the boardwalk's seven-mile length. These types of businesses required a large number of maids, busboys, bellhops, and similar personnel in low paying jobs. In the 1930's, in this city located on the fringes of the south, coloreds traditionally filled such jobs.

For many coloreds their lack of qualification for more highly skilled jobs was a self-fulfilling legacy of their southern heritage. Because older coloreds were totally denied an education under slavery, their illiteracy doomed them to menial jobs for the rest of their lives. Most of the younger coloreds who had moved to the northern and east coast states from the South, had received a very rudimentary education in dilapidated schools with poorly trained teachers and were therefore very limited in their capabilities.

These circumstances showed little sign of changing although over sixty years had passed since the civil war and thirty had passed since Booker T. Washington advocated forbearance and education as the path to progress. The lack of significant progress was due to the mindset that prevailed in the white population overtly and subliminally. To many white northerners, the menial jobs that coloreds occupied made it self evident that their mental capabilities did not justify their occupation of more highly skilled jobs. Their perceived low mental abilities made it unnecessary to give them the equal education that would prepare them for higher paying skilled jobs. The unequal nature of their education justified maintaining a separation from them. The separation perpetuated the stereotypes. The Gemini of demagogues, discrimination and segregation, were very efficient in maintaining the status quo.

As in Ohio, the situation was not as bad as it had been in Alabama. However while a colored person did not feel like they were under a constant threat, there were daily reminders that segregation existed, especially if you had a job that placed you in daily contact with the white society. The slightest mistake for a maid or a porter could result in their being fired or at least receiving a severe tongue lashing that would heap every imaginable insult upon them. Children were not spared but were raised amid constant reminders of their supposed inferiority. Even if they were geographically close to a white school, they were expected to attend a colored school. If they went to the beach, they had to stay in the area set aside for 'coloreds', an area that seldom received any maintenance.

As the businesses of Atlantic City prospered and the volume of colored workers swelled, a cadre of colored professionals such as Dr. Lucas then followed. As Booker T. Washington and W.E.B. Dubois had advocated, it was this group of educated coloreds that were in the forefront of resisting the discrimination and segregation that was imposed on all coloreds, regardless of their level of education. Support was primarily manifested through financial donations to organizations that fought discrimination. At this point in time, there was very little open resistance by either the middle or working classes.

As an example of the ubiquity of discrimination, any colored person who wanted to stay overnight in a town where they did not have a friend or a relative would have to ask around to acquire the name of another colored who would be willing to put them up. This was necessary because mainstream hotels did not accept coloreds as guests. Informal networks had to be set up to provide lodging or other services that were either denied totally or provided under undesirable circumstances.

Meals were similarly difficult to obtain. When making a trip that lasted for more than two or three hours, coloreds would routinely prepare a lunch to eat along the roadside. What was a picnic for a white family was a matter of necessity for a family that might not be allowed to eat in a diner, or might be asked to occupy a less than desirable seat, or made to wait while a later arrival who was white was shown preferential treatment.

Because coloreds usually made these accommodations as a matter of second nature, there often was not a conscious realization that discrimination had played a role in a decision that had been made. However these circumstances all contributed to a building resentment and hostility that would eventually have to find an outlet.

When it came to moving into an apartment or buying a home, the discrimination was not subtle. In northern cities residential areas were often segregated not simply by custom but also by restrictive covenants that legally prevented the rental of a dwelling to a non-white. As a result of the limited access to housing, colored areas usually experienced a high population density and a resultant high crime rate.

Periodically the growth of coloreds escaping the rural South would overwhelm the availability of housing and the least desirable white area that adjoined the colored ghetto would open to one colored family. This would result in a sudden cascade of white flight by the balance of the neighborhood and an easing of the population crush in the colored neighborhood until further growth caused the cycle to be repeated again.

It was ironic that the first white families to sell were usually rewarded with a premium price by coloreds anxious for housing, while later sellers ran the risk of having to sell at below market value as the volume of housing suddenly put on the market temporarily overwhelmed the availability of qualified buyers and the prejudices of lending institutions against lending to coloreds.

At times this cycle was deliberately initiated through a phenomenon known as 'block busting' in which unscrupulous realtors would move a colored family into a white neighborhood, scare the remaining white owners into selling at below market rates, then rent to colored families who were forced to live in overcrowded conditions in homes that degenerated into slums when the realtors reduced maintenance in order to maximize profits.

It was usually easy to recognize the colored area of town, especially the part occupied by lower socio-economic groups. The densely populated dwellings encouraged the inhabitants to spend more time outside of their homes than inside. The result was an increase in the volume of trash since these neighborhoods did not receive very much in the way of services from their local government. A society that was anxious to avail itself of their low salaries and willingness to take menial jobs had concluded that the low tax base that resulted from these low salaries precluded any claim on quality services.

Conversely the white areas never lacked for good schools, good sanitation, polite policing, and all of the accoutrements that made a neighborhood a desirable place to live. The contrast in appearance between these neighborhoods provided further justification to the majority that the minority did not have the proper ethos and had to be kept separate in order to maintain property values.

In Atlantic City, the colored area of town was located on the north side of the city; the better homes were relatively few in number; the number of hotels and apartments was insufficient to meet the demand. A young professional man such as Bert had very few options as to where he could stay. Generally a room was rented from someone in your social sphere. In this case, Bert had a bed and breakfast arrangement in the house of Dr. Lucas. Evening meals were usually taken at a nearby boarding house.

This pervasive prejudice extended to Bert's profession, health care. In most communities, colored physicians could not admit patients directly to a hospital, they had to refer the patient to a white physician who would then hospitalize the patient. The colored physician could visit the patient but was not supposed to be involved in their care. Once admitted, the colored patient was often relegated to a ward style room that was not as attractive or as well maintained as the rooms that were reserved for whites. All too often the physician or nursing staff treated these second-class citizens with indifference or rudeness.

Periodically an article would appear in the paper detailing the fate of a colored who was denied emergency care at a white hospital somewhere and then placed at an undue risk by being told to travel a distance to a county or a colored hospital. Even if this denial resulted in a fatal outcome, the hospital was never held liable because entities such as hospitals were deemed to have a right to choose whom they would serve. In this peculiar game known as Prejudice, property rights trumped human rights.

Here and there an outdated hospital would be closed and turned over to colored physicians. While the facilities that the colored community received under these circumstances were antiquated, the increased access that resulted allowed professional skills in the minority community to develop rather than atrophy, dignity for the minority patients, and a gradual erosion of the status quo. Unfortunately, Atlantic City did not have a colored hospital.

Bert learned to tolerate the indignities that he experienced under this system. As in Tuskegee, he noted that tolerance seemed easier for those who had been born into these circumstances than for those who had migrated to the United States from the various islands of the Caribbean. While there were activists working for change, many American coloreds seemed somewhat resigned to the situation as it was and willing to leave it to their leaders to make the effort to improve things. This perceived passivity among his acquaintances stimulated him to consider being more proactive in increasing racial equality.

However, on reflection he realized that Jamaicans had really not been any more proactive than colored Americans. Perhaps Jamaicans were more strident in expressing outrage over inequities and certainly they did have a cultural history of action, but the students that he had debated at Tuskegee and those Jamaicans who had pontificated at cocktail parties in Jamaica during his year of recuperation had relied on words rather than action. Bert, like others, had nothing specific in mind.

The primary outlet for the indignation of the colored middle class in Atlantic City usually came during social gatherings when vociferous objections to the status quo were commonly presented, but efforts to achieve some remedies were seldom proposed. After one individual had lamented the latest indignity that they or a friend had experienced, others would provide additional examples. With an air of resignation rather than of defiance, the assembled group would then move on to another topic.

"Can you believe it?" was the opening comment as one participant began the ritual of complaints. "Mary and I went to the movies the other day and the ushers there really gave us a hard time. The theater was very crowded so the only seats available together were one row out of the colored section. When we sat down together in those seats, the white man two seats over from us got up, went and got an usher who made us get up and move back into the colored section where we had to sit apart. I was so mad I could have spit nickels! I paid the same money that the white man did. What difference does it make if I sit two seats over from him or one seat back?"

"That's really crazy" came the follow up from an individual who was eager to make his contribution to the conversation. "But the problem is everywhere. The Johnsons had a nasty problem last weekend when they took their children to the beach. During the week a lot of broken bottles were tossed onto the part of the beach that was roped off for the coloreds. No one ever made an effort to clean it up so that it was safe. Naturally the Johnsons told their kids to use the white part of the beach just outside the ropes where it was safer but when they did, the lifeguard came over and made them leave the beach. The kids only got a chance to swim for about five minutes. Do they think that small kids should cut up their feet in the water? Would they let one of their kids walk around on the beaches where they ask our kids to walk? Something has to be done before something really bad happens. "

By now Bert had been fully indoctrinated in the tempo of this social routine, a routine similar to the one he had participated in on Jamaican verandas. He had no difficulty in coming up with an example that confirmed what everyone knew all too well. "I run into this sort of stuff in my medical practice all too often. Mrs. Tate needed to go to the hospital a week or two ago because her diabetes was out of control. They put her in a room with three other patients then gave them all the same sort of meals for two days. When she questioned what she was getting the nurse rudely told Mrs. Tate not to bother her and eat what she was given. She said whatever she was getting was what the doctor ordered. Of course with the wrong diet her diabetes got worse rather than better. Fortunately I dropped in to see how she was doing and was able to tell her what to do. However it could have been a disaster. I told Mrs. Tate not to let her doctor know that I had given her any advice. If they knew that I had, they might have put her out of the hospital just to put her in her place. They certainly would never have let me back in there again if they knew what I had done. It is hard to believe that those doctors took the same Hippocratic oath that I did."

Twenty years of residence in the United States was causing Bert to replace his tendency to at least consider active resistance to segregation with a resignation that was all too common. As a student under Booker T. Washington, Bert had concluded that individuals had a responsibility to actively promote racial equality, but in a manner that did not engender confrontation. Now he merely cited examples of injustice without suggesting any action. Was he becoming like Paddyfoot--the Jamaican who had picked him up at the train station when he first arrived at Tuskegee—unconsciously giving in to the mores of the status quo to a greater degree than he realized? Were the circumstances of the society and the era in which he lived overcoming his genetic and early cultural predisposition to be assertive and resist an unjust authority?

As a person who had an extensive exposure to several different cultures, he had a unique perspective that in the past had allowed him to recognize and reject the social fallacies that different cultures tolerated but to also adopt the strengths of these cultures. For example, during his year of recuperation and reflection in Jamaica, he had rejected the financial inequalities perpetuated by their class system but embraced the absence of demeaning restrictions on any group. He decried the empty eloquence that was commonly expressed at social gatherings by participants who were unlikely to suffer from discrimination, but was proud of the fact that the island's history suggested that action would occur if the appropriate occasion arose.

On the other hand he embraced the American ideal of a classless society in which all men were created equal but was outraged by the extent to which those in positions of authority ignored this ideal. He applauded the efforts of the unions and the civil rights organizations that fought for change but was saddened that many middle class colored Americans seemed to prefer to leave the battle to these organizations while accepting the discrimination that they were experiencing, instead of making a personal effort to eliminate it.

The indignation of youth was evaporating and being replaced with the complacency of the middle years just as the light slowly evaporates when the sun sets in the West. Bert, despite the limitations that were placed on his ability to fully practice medicine, enjoyed the practice that he was developing in Atlantic City. His patients were by no means rich but, unlike most poor Jamaicans, they had enough disposable income to afford ordinary medical care and enough education to want a modern approach to that care. Between his growing office practice and a willingness to take on extra house calls, Bert developed a comfortable life style, began to save some money, financially supported organizational efforts to promote civil rights, and found time to engage in recreational activities.

In the area of civil rights, the discrimination that so concerned everyone was under attack, but not primarily at an individual level. The risk of retaliation against an individual was so high, especially in the South, that the colored population relied on the efforts that organizations such as the NAACP and the Urban League made to either modify or eliminate these vestiges of slavery. Their activities were a source of great encouragement.

People were most familiar with the legal efforts of the slightly older NAACP whose actions were more sweeping and publicized than those of the Urban League. The NAACP worked to pass and enforce anti-lynching laws, fight discrimination in housing, and prevent unjust legal penalties or job discrimination. The organization grew rapidly and received significant support from the colored population and from various philanthropic groups.

The Urban League fought discrimination at a more grass roots level. Founded in 1910, the Urban League, in an approach similar to that advocated by Booker T. Washington, urged coloreds to become involved in efforts to demonstrate their capabilities and promote both their social and economic status. Rather than stressing the immediacy of achieving legal equality, they helped to set up tutoring and apprentice programs, helped set up small colored-owned businesses, assisted in providing housing, and promoted voter education programs.

Perhaps because this approach mirrored that of his mentor, Booker T. Washington, Bert was attracted to the activities of the Urban League. Although he participated in a pattern of cocktail party verbal opposition combined with financial support for organizational efforts for change, it still seemed to Bert that every individual had a responsibility to be involved in a personal way in the struggle to eliminate discrimination. At this point in time he had no specific goal in mind but he kept abreast of the activities of the different organizations and looked for something that he could do. There was no sudden moment of inspiration, no compelling inner drive that had dwelt within him since childhood, just the strength of character and the background that gave him the potential to be one of those infrequent individuals who has the ability to recognize an opportunity to effectuate change and the diligence to act upon it.

As always, life was more than work and politics. The east coast presented many recreational choices for its inhabitants. Ocean fishing was available year around. Bert, accustomed to the relaxing 80-degree warmth of the Caribbean, limited his swimming to the month of August when the temperature of the shallow waters of the Atlantic beaches crept towards seventy. He dated, but did not meet anyone that he wanted to marry at this stage of his life. Then in 1932 he found an activity that captured his attention.

In 1927 the nation was captivated by the flight of Charles Lindberg from Roosevelt Field in Garden City, New York to Le Bourget Field near Paris. The impetus for this non-stop flight was a prize of $25,000 offered in 1919 by the New York City hotel owner, Raymond Orteig. Ten days before this flight Lindberg had set a record by completing a one-stop coast-to-coast flight from San Diego, California to Long Island, New York in 21 hours and 20 minutes. He followed his transatlantic flight with a new transcontinental record in 1930 and a flight to the Orient in 1931. His fame led to a request by Pan American Airways that he set up their air routes to South America and across the Pacific.

Lindberg's exploits made the country and the world acutely aware of the potential of the airplane. Young men who had previously aspired to own a car now aspired to own an airplane. To help pay for these small planes known as 'jennies' the pilot would offer rides for five or ten dollars. Bert, who had been fascinated by his trips on the seaplane, took several short flights on these jennies and developed a desire to become involved in flying.

In this land known as the home of the free and the brave, a land of opportunity, but also a land of discrimination and segregation, nothing was simple. Bert was a man who had the intellect to be admitted to and graduate with honors from one of the top medical schools on the continent and a man who had the financial means to take flying lessons. But he was a man who had the handicap of being the 'wrong' color.

The flying schools that existed were under the aviation branch of the Department of Commerce. Neither this branch of the United States government nor the aviation agencies for the state governments wanted to accept coloreds as commercial pilots or private pilots. Architecture had been a vocation in which he would have found it difficult to earn a livelihood because of prejudice. Now flying was being added to the list of forbidden fruits. Flight instruction was precluded because instructors were sure that coloreds were not intelligent enough to master the complexities of flying. Training for less skilled jobs in aviation such as that of a mechanic was similarly off limits. The door to this activity was nailed shut just as so many other doors had been.

Even though he had been unable to receive flying lessons, Bert persevered. He went to Maryland where he inquired about purchasing a 95 horsepower, Ranger-powered, three place Fairchild 24. Perhaps, perhaps if the instructors knew that he would be the owner of a plane they would exhibit some forbearance. It was not to be. Every instructor that he asked refused.

There had been colored pilots before, pilots who had distinguished themselves despite the prejudices they faced. Eugene Bullard flew with distinction as a member of the French Lafayette Flying Corps during World War I until his unit came under American control and his flight status was canceled; Bessie Coleman, rejected when she tried to enroll in flying schools in the United States, had worked, saved, learned French, solicited sponsorship by the colored newspaper *The Chicago Defender*, and gone to France where she received an international flying license in June of 1921; Hubert Julian had had to go to Canada in 1923 in order to learn how to fly; J.C. Robinson had made a flight at Tuskegee in a homemade biplane in 1924; a colored Aero circus named after Bessie Coleman had toured the West and

Southwest after 1929 and shown great skill; William Brown had entered the 1932 National Air Races and did well until the old plane that he flew gave out. Despite pervasive discrimination, there were colored Americans who refused to submit to prejudice or to be denied participation in an endeavor that attracted them.

Once again contacts were invaluable. The husband of his partner's daughter had heard of a colored man named Al Anderson who had managed to obtain a pilot's license and was making a small amount of money by flying newspapers from Philadelphia to Atlantic City. When Bert heard of this, he became very energized. If this fellow had been able to find a way to get a license, there was no reason why he should be denied one. Bert, a man who had worked his way through school and disciplined himself to overcome juvenile diabetes, was not to be permanently discouraged by an obstacle such as discrimination. As soon as he heard that Al Anderson was in town he sought the pilot out.

After getting directions from a mutual friend, he drove to the outskirts of the city. Presently he came upon a light-complexioned, slender man in his middle twenties who was digging a ditch along the side of an infrequently used road. "Are you Al Anderson?" Bert queried hopefully.

"Yes I am" came the reply as Anderson, sweat pouring from his forehead, took the opportunity to pause from his labors.

"Man with your qualifications, what are you doing down there in that ditch?"

"Making a living."

....

Charles Alfred Anderson had seen his first plane in 1913 when he was an eight-year-old farm boy. It captivated him so completely that being an aviator became his life's ambition. It was an appropriate choice in that he came to be recognized as a natural—someone who took to flying the way that a baby duck immediately takes to swimming on its first exposure. He seemed to intuitively know just how much speed was needed to achieve takeoff, how the plane would react to a headwind, how steeply to bank when making a turn, and how to execute a perfect landing every time.

He was born in Pennsylvania and raised by his aunt Probes in Virginia where he had been unsuccessful in his efforts to get someone to teach him to fly. Both the local flying schools and the Army told him to forget about flying because there was no future there for him. Nevertheless he managed to save $500, borrowed $2,500, bought his own plane at age 18, then tried to teach himself how to fly by first reading about it, then attempting flight. These efforts resulted in two crashes, one of which left a severe scar on his scalp. This frightened his aunt so much that she unsuccessfully tried to destroy his plane. She then sent him back to his parents in Bryn Mawr Pennsylvania.

He finally was able to get some instruction from an unlikely ally. Ernie Buehl was a retired World War I German fighter pilot who owned a small airfield known as the Flying Dutchman in Sommerton outside of Philadelphia, Pennsylvania and was willing to teach a colored man to fly. Under his tutelage Al quickly assimilated the fundamentals on the ground and then the skills in the air.

Additional flight time was obtained from Russel Thaw, the son of a millionaire, who asked to rent Al's airplane so that Thaw could fly to Atlantic City on weekends to visit his mother who ran a nightclub there. Thaw refused to teach Anderson to fly, but Anderson carefully watched what Thaw was doing so that he could learn.

On August 8, 1929, Anderson was finally able to get a private pilot's license, number 7638. In 1932 Buell cajoled flight officials into giving Anderson a written and flight test for a transport license at Buell's airfield. On the examiners arrival, he took Buell aside and berated him for being involved in trying to get a colored man a license.

"You can refuse to test him if you want to," said Buell slyly. "I'm just a foreigner so it won't impact me, but if it gets out that you refused to test him, it might create problems for you."

The examiner felt trapped. He put Al through an examination that was twice as long as usual in an effort to avoid giving him the license. In the end, he could find no justification for refusing the license and Al became the first colored aviator to obtain the United States transport license that made him eligible to fly commercially.

Jobs for a colored pilot were few and far between so Anderson was elated when he got the opportunity to fly newspapers from Philadelphia to Atlantic City. This was not enough to provide him with a livelihood however so he supplemented his income with jobs such as the one he was engaged in when Bert first met him. If you were colored and had ambition, you had to be willing to accept whatever work was available; you had to have a spirit of perseverance.

....

"I understand that you have a pilots license," Bert continued in a voice that was edged with anticipation. "I want to learn how to fly but have been unable to find anyone to give me instruction. Worst of all, the United States Government, the government that is supposed to protect the rights of all of its citizens, actually puts barriers to achievement in the way of those citizens who are colored. They believe, despite many examples to the contrary, that coloreds are incapable of mastering such technical matters. Obviously you have proved them wrong. Could you help me to learn how to fly?"

"Glad to," Anderson replied, his broad smile reflecting the genuine pleasure that he felt in meeting a kindred spirit. "It's lonely being one of the few colored pilots. The more of us that there are, the more obvious it will be that it is ridiculous to try to deny coloreds the right to fly. I know this pilot who has an airport in Pennsylvania and will help us. Between the two of us, we will make a pilot out of you in nothing flat. If you can drive over to Sommerton next weekend we can get started."

At his first opportunity Bert went to Sommerton where he received flying lessons from Al and Ernie Buehl. He proved to be an apt pupil and quickly mastered the skill of flying. A private license was much easier to obtain than a commercial license so he had less trouble in becoming licensed to fly a private plane than Anderson had had in obtaining his transport license. Bert then bought a plane from Buehl.

About the time that Bert received his license, Al tried to enter the Pennsylvania National Guard so that he could have an opportunity to fly. Given the prevailing attitudes, it was not surprising that he was rejected. After Bert heard about this, an idea began to form. In time, he shared his thoughts with Al.

"For some time I have been thinking about what I could do to help bring an end to discrimination and segregation in the United States. You are a perfect example of the problems faced by colored people. You are an exceptional pilot, yet your own government refuses to give you an opportunity to fly. What I want to do is to publicize the fact that colored people are not the incompetents that many whites think that they are. The average white is guided by stereotypes that make him believe that coloreds deserve to be restricted from many activities because they lack the mental ability to perform anything other than menial tasks."

"We both know that any lack of ability on the part of coloreds is due to the inferior education that they are given coupled with their being denied an adequate number of opportunities to advance. Unfortunately the problem is so severe that many coloreds are resigned to their fate and unwilling to exert the mass pressure that is needed to effect change. It is not enough to just rely on the colored elite such as the lawyers at the NAACP. It *is* important to try to achieve legal equality but it is also important to try to instill a feeling of pride and confidence in the general colored population."

"My idea is this," Bert continued, totally caught up in the enthusiasm of the moment. "Look at all of the publicity that Lindberg gets on the flights that he makes. No one doubts his ability. If we can make some noteworthy flights, the whites will be unable to deny that coloreds have ability and will have to admit that we should be allowed to participate in all professions rather than always be limited to low paying service jobs."

The concept appealed to Al immediately. Anything that had to do with aviation was of interest but it was especially sweet to consider using aviation to combat the prejudices that had held him back from pursuing his primary passion. Once the possibility had been raised, the two proceeded to discuss the issue at length. Words flew around the room as if they had been compressed into a balloon then suddenly allowed to escape in a stream of consciousness. Emotions that had been suppressed for decades now had an outlet as the planners considered what might be.

"That sounds like a really good idea," interjected Al with an excitement that was evident in both his voice and his body language. "If we can generate some publicity I think that it will inspire a lot of young coloreds to go into aviation. I know that there are many others who have the same dream of flying that I did. Right now they tend to become discouraged and give up--I almost did several times. If we can let these young kids know that the two of us became pilots even though almost everyone tried to prevent us, it will encourage them to persevere. How should we go about this?"

Bert did not need much time to formulate a reply to a question that he had silently asked himself for several weeks. "Lindberg got a lot of publicity by setting a coast-to-coast speed record. There is no way that we can compete with that. Our planes are not powerful enough. I suggest that we make a round trip to the West Coast and back. We are not interested in speed but in maximum exposure and publicity. We should try to stop in as many different places as we can, perhaps 25 going and 25 different ones coming back. The more stops we make, the more publicity we will get. We can take turns at the controls so that we don't have to worry about fatigue as Lindberg did. I suggest that we take my plane since it is newer and has the power that we will need in order to climb over the Sierra range."

Al's response to Bert's elaboration on their course of action was instantaneous. "Terrific. That should be a fabulous flight. Can you imagine seeing the entire country from the air? That is what I dreamed about when I was an eight-year-old kid and ran across Aunt Probe's field trying to chase an airplane. What a thrill it will be to fly over the Mississippi River then on to the Pacific Ocean. Think of all the magnificent scenery we will see. Do you have any other ideas?"

"Yes," was Bert's studied reply as a thoughtful look replaced the animated one that had been present up to that point. "One flight alone won't do it. We need several in order to keep the issue in the public's eye. I have a couple of ideas as to how to accomplish that but I need to think about them a bit longer. To be successful, we need to plan carefully. For example, we will need to have arrangements in place for food, lodging, and fuel when we land. Also we need to arrange to get as much publicity as possible."

"How can we get the money and the publicity?"

This question caused Bert to pause for a moment before responding. He had thought about what was needed but had not decided as to which course of action would be best. "The biggest expense will be the plane. As I said, I will donate mine but we should also try to get some extra equipment to increase our safety. Right now all I have is a compass and an altimeter but we should try to get parachutes and a radio and perhaps a few other items. There will also be the expense of the fuel and food and housing. The publicity must involve both whites and coloreds. Whites in order to eliminate their prejudices, coloreds in order to encourage their involvement in aviation. And our publicity must make it very clear that Anderson and Forsythe are not the story. The story is all coloreds and the discrimination that holds them back."

"The first step will be to get the colored community involved. I have already talked to a few of the colored professionals and businessmen in the area and found a great deal of enthusiasm. I proposed to them that we set up a group called the 'National Negro Aeronautical Society' to coordinate our efforts. We needed a business address so I agreed to use my office address at 44 Kentucky in Atlantic City. I was sure that you would agree but I wanted to talk to you before going any further."

"I'm absolutely in agreement," was the brief response as Al, always more of a doer than a talker, awaited more information.

"I'm going to contact Eugene Kinckle Jones, the National Secretary of the Urban League. Hopefully they will be able to provide some funding. Even if they can't, they will be a good source of contacts and advice. We also need to get other civil right organizations, the colored churches, the colored schools, and the colored press involved. They need to see that it is possible for colored men to do things they were told they could not do."

"Of course, we won't accomplish anything if only the coloreds are involved. We need to give the white community a stake in this. I'm going to contact the Atlantic City Board of Trade and play up the publicity that Atlantic City will receive if it is involved in a first, and the value of that publicity to the reputation of the city and the volume of business on the Boardwalk. There is civic pride in any kind of first, even if it is a first by a colored, so when dealing with the city I will stress the benefit to the overall community along with the economic benefit and will downplay our major goal, the opening of aviation to coloreds."

"In order to help get publicity in the white media I plan to name my plane the 'Pride of Atlantic City', to leave from Bader Airport in Atlantic City, and to visit the bigger city of Newark on return. By using the phrase 'The Pride of,' in naming the plane, we evoke memories of Lindberg and his plane the "Spirit of Saint Louis'. By naming the plane after Atlantic City we will give that city publicity and encourage its participation. By going to Newark we will appeal to another cities pride and turn it into a state project not just a one-city project. The more people we involve, the more we will accomplish."

"We won't use our usual Pennsylvania airport for either departure or return" Bert elaborated, "but we will stop in at your hometown in Pennsylvania and give your friends a chance to see you off. If we plan this really well there is no reason why it should not be a success. I think that we can make a real contribution to the cause of civil rights with this."

The thoughts kept pouring out as Bert continued without giving Al an opportunity to comment. He was now a synthesis of his ancestry, his culture, his educators, and his experiences. He was exerting leadership and standing up for his rights as the Forsyths had always done, demanding the dignity that West Indians had enjoyed for decades, exerting pressure in the manner advocated by Booker T. Washington, and battling, not just for himself but for all colored Americans, against the prejudices that he had experienced in the United States. The problems of America were now his problems.

Eventually the pair exhausted all of the possibilities that came to mind and parted company. In the days that followed, they had to devote all of their spare time to the project in order to begin the tasks necessary to accomplish their goal. They contacted the Urban League but learned that there was not any money available for their project. However the League was enthusiastic about the idea and offered to involve the colored press in the cities that they planned to land in that had an Urban League branch. The press would turn out a crowd and see to it that there was adequate press coverage. In addition, the League promised to see to it that Bert and Al had free housing and lodging in cities where they would spend the night

The duo got out a copy of the Rand McNally Atlas and looked up all of the airfields they could find close to those cities that had an Urban League branch. As Bert had suggested, they agreed to stop at one set of airports going and another set coming so that they would have an opportunity to be seen by the largest number of people. A southerly route would be followed on departure and a more northerly route on return. With these parameters in mind, they slowly came up with an itinerary.

Bert enlisted the help of several civic organizations that he had joined in gathering donations. He spoke at local colored churches about the need for everyone to participate as a method of fighting discrimination. At times he received contributions of as little as twenty-five cents but these small contributions added up until it began to look like the trip would be economically feasible. As time passed the level of acceptance for the project increased and the two men felt that they had initiated a worthy endeavor. They gave little if any thought to the possibility that significant dangers awaited them despite the fact that their plane was very inferior to those used by white transcontinental fliers. Besides the lack of safety equipment, the Fairchild carried only 24 gallons of gasoline as opposed to the hundreds of gallons carried on other planes.

The risks of aviation were not unknown to them. Al himself had already been in two crashes. The most famous colored in aviation, Bessie Coleman, had broken several bones in a 1923 crash then perished in 1926 when she fell without a parachute from a plane that then crashed and killed her copilot. Bessie, publicized by Robert S. Abbott who was the publisher of the colored newspaper *The Chicago Defender* and one of her financial sponsors, had become an international celebrity after obtaining her international flying license in France and returning to America in August of 1921 where a black Broadway musical was created in her honor.

A very contemporary death occurred in April of 1933 when J. Herman Banning, who with Thomas Allen in October of 1932 was the first colored to fly from the west coast to the east coast, was killed in a jump from an airplane. The early aviators experienced a very high mortality.

Danger was not a deterrent because of their intense desire to promote racial equality. This made it possible for them to sublimate their concerns and apply themselves to their project with the certainty that comes from the combination of being at an age that juxtaposes the self-confidence that comes with experience with a remnant of the sense of invincibility that is found in youth. Moreover, they were convinced about the importance of their undertaking, and had complete trust in each other. Finally, Bert was confident because of his planning. While Banning and Allen had started their flight with only $25 in their pocket and had raised contributions along the way in order to buy fuel and effect repairs, Bert was starting with a newer plane, a fund raising effort that he expected to provide added safety features to his plane, and a clearly outlined schedule. At this point in time, fear, the aviator's nemesis, did not exist.

8

COAST-TO-COAST-TO COAST

The idea for this adventure first arose in 1932 but it was not until July 17, 1933 that the two adventurers were ready to go. In June they had obtained a letter of confidence from the local airfield and a letter from the mayor of Atlantic City, Harry Bacharach, stating that the flight was being sponsored by the Board of Trade. These official letters helped to finalize the acceptance of their project and insure publicity within the white community.

True to their word, the Urban League made arrangements for families in the overnight cities to provide housing and meals. This avoided the problem of discrimination in public accommodations and eliminated a potential expense. The League also made sure that the newspapers, especially the colored ones such as the *Courier* in Pittsburgh and the *Defender* in Chicago, had been advised of their arrival. Local colored churches encouraged their congregations to attend and support the project. It was a formidable undertaking.

Mayor Bacharach gave Bert a letter to deliver to Frank Shaw, the mayor of Los Angeles, on his arrival on the west coast. The mayor of Newark was also involved. He told the duo that if the flights were successful, a parade would be arranged in Newark after their return. The pre flight planning that Bert had done was very successful in raising the awareness of the general public.

Early in the morning on Monday July 17, 1933, a crowd of hundreds gathered to see them off at Bader Field in Atlantic City. With the excitement that Lindberg had generated in the last eight years, anything that had to do with aviation was big news. The coloreds in the crowd realized that aviation was a very risky undertaking but their racial pride overcame their reservations; they felt sure that the flight would be a success and would promote the cause of civil rights. Some of the whites had deeper reservations that were caused by their prejudices; they doubted the ability of coloreds to perform this feat.

In recalling that day and the reporters assembled, Bert later said, "...some of them were looking to see how far these guys were going to fly before they got killed and they were running out to get a good story—somebody breaking their necks, calling themselves aviators."

With Bert at the controls the Fairchild took off into a light blue sky that contained scattered clouds. The winds were minimal and the weather looked good. Their capabilities were quite limited however. Their fund raising had been sufficiently successful to cover their fuel, but they had not raised enough to purchase a radio, lights, or parachutes. A compass and an altimeter were their major instruments.

Like all early fliers, they knew that since compasses were not always accurate, it was wise to find a railroad line, a major road, or a river and then either follow it or at least use it to verify your position. Essentially their flight plan consisted of following Route 66 on the trip west and Route 80 on the return journey. They started out with their Rand Mc Nally atlas but that blew out the window.

Another problem was the availability of landing sites. Many cities did not have adequate airports. In fact, at times racetracks or roads were used as runways. Also, because small airports did not have landing lights, flights had to be timed to arrive before dusk. A third restraining factor was the limited flight range that was available due to the size of the gas tanks on their small plane. These shortcomings were ignored because of their overriding enthusiasm, but contributed to the very real danger that they faced.

Since publicity was their goal, they planned to make proportionately more stops on the densely populated east coast than in the sparsely populated western states. An unscheduled stop at Camden, New Jersey was added soon after takeoff when they ran into a dense fog. With no radio, they had no way of knowing the extent of the fog and were wisely unwilling to risk flying blind.

The fog quickly cleared and allowed them to resume their flight. In less than an hour they made their first scheduled stop, a very important one in Bryn Mawr, Pennsylvania, Al's hometown and a city that had raised contributions for the trip. Of course Al was at the controls for that landing and the subsequent takeoff. He also gave a short speech to the friends and family that had assembled.

After Harrisburg, they made their third Pennsylvania stop, at Bettis Field in Pittsburgh, a city of almost 700,000 that was located where the Allegheny and Monongahela rivers met to form the Ohio River. Pittsburgh was known as the Steel City because of its many factories, factories that had attracted a very large colored population from the South. The forced segregation of this large population created a severe housing shortage.

An active branch of the Urban League had grown up in Pittsburgh in an effort to deal with the prejudice that the people faced. Pittsburgh was also the home of the *Courier*, a very influential colored newspaper that gave them very good coverage. The importance of the League was recognized in the more detailed speech that Bert gave to the crowd that met them. The response of the crowd made it evident to the pair that their trip had already accomplished something—an increase in racial pride.

Once again they were in the air where the view from this low flying small plane was spectacular. They intermittently used the rivers that wound their way through this huge state to confirm their position. As they passed over the Allegheny and the Appalachian mountain ranges they marveled at the huge dark green forests. Conversely they felt depressed by the sight of large areas that had been denuded by mining that had left an ugly scar on what was once pristine beauty.

One state gave way to another and at 11:45 AM they arrived in Columbus, Ohio where they were met by a photographer and Lawrence La Marr, a representative of the Pittsburgh Courier. At every stop the aviators were pleased to see the turnout and to receive the well wishes of the coloreds who had so much pride in these aviators and so much hope that their efforts would succeed in improving their lives and demonstrating their value as human beings.

During the next leg of the trip they encountered the next of the many obstacles that they would experience due to the effect of Nature on their small aircraft. As they passed over the plains of the Midwest, their speed slowed significantly as they encountered some severe gales with winds that they estimated to be over 40 miles per hour.

"Bert, it's getting difficult to control the plane," said Al in his matter of fact fashion, seemingly unconcerned with the buffeting that their small plane was taking from the winds that gusted with irregular spurts of ferocity. "Be prepared for some rough weather. We don't have anywhere to sit down so I'm going to change course a little bit so that the winds don't toss us around so much."

"Do what you have to but try not to get too much off course," Bert replied in a voice that displayed no evidence of concern. He had complete confidence that the skills that Al had previously demonstrated would get them through this without any problem. "I hope this doesn't last too long. This next leg of the trip is rather long so we don't have much fuel to spare. Now is when I miss not having a radio. If we knew what the weather was like up ahead, we would know where to go to avoid things like this."

Al allowed himself the luxury of a small smile. His face seemed totally relaxed and without a care as his mouth parted slightly and his eyes darted from the instrument panel and over to Bert. "Not to worry. Just pretend you're back on a roller coaster ride in Atlantic City. This is no worse. As long as you have a strong stomach you can handle a little up and down."

A 95 horsepower plane fighting a 40-mile an hour wind was much more than the ups and downs of a roller coaster. It required constant attention to the controls and produced a great deal of physical strain. It was in situations like these that the natural skills of Al Anderson were truly tested. He had never been on a simulator to experience what it would be like under these conditions; he had never gone up in weather like this when he had been taking flying lesson; he had had some exposure to winds when he was flying newspapers into Atlantic City, but then he had the luxury of knowing that he could land at one of several airports if the need arose. Here he had no choice. He had to go on and risk the danger that he was encountering.

The more that he was tested, the more skillful he became. Soon he forgot about trying to remember what he had been told should be done under these circumstances. Instead he relied on 'the feel' of the plane to determine how fast to go, how much to anticipate, to what degree he should overcorrect. While the danger was quite substantial, there never was any doubt in either of their minds that they could handle anything that came their way. In due time the winds abated and the pair settled down to the routine of flying, landing, greeting, and taking off again.

After a stop in Indianapolis, Indiana, they arrived in St. Louis where they spent the night at the home of a colored family that had volunteered to take them without charge. The excitement of that first day filled their minds with so many memories that many were lost. Bert remembered how difficult it had been to fall asleep on that first night. Eventually he did, and awoke feeling fully energized.. They were offered a large Southern style breakfast that included coffee, ham, eggs, grits with gravy, and biscuits enhanced with large pats of butter. After the meal they thanked their hosts and departed for the airport and a routine that would not vary. Check to make sure that the gas tanks were topped off, go over the itinerary and check for possible alternate landing sites in case of an emergency, then say your goodbyes before turning the ignition and ending conversation. The engine would cough then reluctantly turn over, several minutes would pass by while the oil overcame its morning lethargy, and then the days adventure would begin.

In the Midwest Bert saw the same sort of scenery that he had seen from the train years ago but from a different perspective. Again, moderately sized farms, often with multiple crops, gave way to vast acres devoted solely to one crop such as wheat or corn. Small cities quickly came and went. Occasionally a small child would energetically wave at them, awed by the miracle of flight. If Al was at the controls when that happened, he would invariable dip a wing in recognition of the salute. At these times he thought of himself as an eight year old boy, looking up at a plane in the sky, and longing to be up there--a bird effortlessly riding the air currents, a cloud drifting lazily through a pastel colored sky.

After a stop in Kansas City, they proceeded south by southwest to Wichita, Kansas. Then they dipped south towards desert country, Amarillo, Texas. Now it was Bert's turn to be at the controls when Mother Nature decided to test their mettle once again.

Al had closed his eyes and availed himself of the opportunity to rest after completing one of his shifts at the controls. He had not been asleep, but neither had he been awake. His thoughts had been floating from one inconsequential memory to another when he heard Bert speak and sensed the concern in his voice. "It's beginning to get dark up ahead Al. I think a storm is coming. I don't see any rain yet and the winds aren't too bad so I don't anticipate any trouble. Still, look sharp and let me know if you notice anything that could be a problem."

Between their speed and that of the storm, it did not take very long before they found themselves in the midst of one of the most awesome displays that nature can provide. Far ahead, a bolt of lightning zigzagged its way through a foreboding sky. It began in the upper reaches of the visible atmosphere and crazily arced its way to the ground. Had they thought about it, they might have been more prepared for the bone-chilling clash of thunder that followed. Instead they jumped involuntarily when it arrived seconds after the lightning traced its erratic pattern across the sky.

An aviator can have confidence in their physical ability to wrestle with the wind and emerge victorious; their judgment can help them to decide what airspeed should be attained as they taxi prior to takeoff into a headwind; their skill will help them to hold a steady course or to descend for a landing under adverse wind conditions. But there is not much that they can do when their craft encounters an electrical storm that thrills you with its beauty while frightening you with its power.

Soon after the first bolt appeared in the distance and emphasized its might with a distant clap of thunder, a second bolt was seen significantly closer, and was accompanied by a significantly louder blast as the air expanded in response to this mighty electrical discharge. There was a strobe-like effect as electrical flashes intermittently illuminated the sky and returned the brightness of day to the gloom that otherwise prevailed. Photographic images of the landscape below were received by their retinas then recorded in their memories for the rest of their lives as the intense light briefly passed through their corneas, shuttered their pupils, and etched proof of its temporary existence on their mental photo albums.

A series of closer bolts and louder discharges continued for nerve-wracking minutes until the two pilots confidence began to be displaced by a gnawing in their guts. They felt a fear that was engendered by their helplessness during this onslaught by nature. They were totally silent. No comments were made, no questions were asked, no jokes were forthcoming. Silent prayers were offered as they realized the danger that they were in, the possibility that their odyssey might end before it had barely begun.

Again and again the sky exploded with forks of lightning that seemed perilously close and explosions of thunder that jarred them to their souls. Had they thought about it they would have realized that they were fortunate that their area of the storm did not contain torrential rain. They however did not consider themselves to be the least bit fortunate. They were totally at the mercy of the elements.

After what seemed like an eternity the proximity of the forked bolts of lightning to their fragile craft began to lessen and the volume of the gargantuan thunderclaps became less intimidating. The interval between occurrences that had shortened so rapidly as they flew towards the storm now seemed agonizing slow in lengthening. Gradually the display receded into the distance then disappeared as the roar of their engine muffled the sound of thunder and the clouds hid their tormentor. Ahead, rays of sunshine illuminated fleecy white clouds that announced the end of their ordeal.

"Man I've never been in anything like that before in my life and I never want to be in it again." Bert exclaimed as he shifted nervously in his seat and looked back at the darkened sky and the fading eruptions of illumination that were receding behind them.

"You can say that again," Al agreed in a voice that betrayed the concern that he had been able to mask in his face. "It's one thing to be on the ground in your house looking out the window at these things. It's completely different to be up among all this juice and right next to those explosions. There were several times I thought my heart was going to stop beating. And the worst part is that you are so helpless. You can't go over it and you can't go under it. If that ever happens again, I'm turning around and landing somewhere, anywhere. The next electrical storm I see, I want to be on the ground looking up and not in the sky looking out."

It was quite awhile before the pair recovered from their ordeal. After their initial exchange of words following the storm, they maintained a silence that allowed them an opportunity to contemplate their mortality. Aviators, especially one like Al who enjoyed pushing the limits of his plane and testing his skills, only rarely gave a serious thought to their danger. Accidents happened to the 'other guy', the less skilled, not to those who maintained their plane properly and possessed a natural ability. With an episode such as this, it was impossible to deny the truth. Flying was dangerous, there were things beyond ones control, and it was possible for a brave man to experience fear.

After the great plains of the Midwest they entered the panhandle of Texas. They had started at the Atlantic Ocean, skirted the Great Lakes, were passing within a few hundred miles of the Gulf of Mexico, and would eventually reach the Pacific Ocean. The scenery changed constantly. Now they saw wide plateaus that loomed on the horizon, vast prairies with widely dispersed herds of cattle grazing on miles of a range grass that seemed colorless in comparison to the deep green grasses of the Midwest dairy lands, fertile land planted in swaths of cotton and wheat, and oil extracting derricks that populated the landscape like giant tinker toys. They were constantly being amazed by the variety of sights that passed underneath them.

Almost in the middle of the panhandle was Amarillo, Texas, their next destination. After an uneventful landing at 4:30 P.M. and a short speech, they took off for the town that would be their destination for their second night, Albuquerque, New Mexico.

Here they had an opportunity to observe the beginnings of a western sunset from the air. This was a sunset that was unlike any they had ever seen in the east. Swirls of peach intermingled with patches of orange as if an artist was creating multiple pastels for his pallet. The horizon seemed to go on forever, its magnitude adding to the grandeur. After landing, as nature's display progressed to its conclusion, they witnessed a red-orange glow that was followed by tinges of purple as the giant screen faded to black. Then twinkles of light gradually appeared in this broad sky in a multitude that far exceeded that found on the light polluted east coast that they had left. At these times they did not speak but visually inhaled the sights before them and experienced a satisfaction they had never known before.

Their hosts for the night conversed with them in a lazy drawl that reawakened Bert's memories of his days in Alabama. At dinner they were given a choice of collard greens with bacon fat, barbecued chicken, ribs, corn pone, and a soup-like liquid called pot likker. After ascertaining that the etiology of chitterlings was pig intestine, Bert declined the helping that was offered.

The main courses were followed by a large helping of a deep-dish apple pie that seemed to taste better than any he had ever had before. The memory of that pie made all subsequent apple pies suffer in the comparison. Perhaps the future pies were actually better, but they could not compete with the feeling of well being that was simultaneously incorporated in his memory during this evening of satisfaction and serenity.

The hospitality that they had been shown at every stop was impressive. There was a genuine appreciation for the effort that they were making, and an unspoken expectation that it would lead to a more dignified life for the small children that watched from the sidelines not quite knowing why the arrival of these strangers was so important. In later years however, several colored professionals and ordinary people told them that as children they had been among the crowd that had welcomed them or seen them off and that the memory had stayed with.them. The children were being exposed to the fact that their color should not be a handicap. They were being prepared to participate in a generation that would have many more opportunities for advancement than the one that was currently continuing the process that had begun with the Civil War—the destruction of segregation and discrimination.

Once again they finished breakfast, proffered their thanks, received the well wishes of their hosts, went through their pre-flight rituals, warmed their engines, and taxied down yet another runway. To the west lay Arizona with its amazing rock formations that at twilight were bathed in ever changing shadows. The variations in color that were produced by the shadows were unique from one minute to the next so that one never tired of looking at them.

At the border of Arizona and California they flew over the Colorado River at a point south of its passage through the Grand Canyon. They were on the last leg of a journey of over 2,500 miles. The fatigue that had threatened to overcome them on the day before did not seem very significant with their goal almost at hand. The Colorado River disappeared into the distance as they headed for the Mojave Desert, towards the lower portion of the Sierra Nevada mountain range that was the last major impediment to reaching the Los Angeles basin.

The airplane had been climbing for several minutes before Bert decided that it was necessary to voice his concerns to Al. His attempt to disguise the gravity of the situation failed as his intonation betrayed his dilemma. "We have to land the plane or we're going to crash! The temperature of the outside air is so high that the engine is beginning to overheat. When I tried to increase our altitude in order to reach a cooler temperature, the strain on the engine was enough to cause it to get even hotter and start to sputter. This is only going to get worse if we don't do anything. We have to land and jettison everything that we can so that the engine will not have to work so hard. If we do that, I think we should be able to climb above the heat without making things worse"

As he spoke these words Bert realized that once again he was experiencing an uncomfortable sensation—fear. His fear was not occasioned so much by the danger, the electrical storm that they had passed through a day before had been of that sort. His current fear was instigated mainly by the realization that they might not succeed. If they could not climb, they could not make it over the upcoming mountain range and all of their efforts would have been in vain. True, the overheating and sputtering of the engine did provoke some anxiety, but he felt confident that this was not a physical danger but an obstacle that could be overcome.

Somehow the heat that he was now experiencing combined with the excitement of the moment triggered memories that had long lain dormant. He had a vivid mental image of that hot day when he first left Jamaica from Boundbrook Wharf in Port Antonio. He recalled the faces of his family, not as they were on his last visit several years ago but as they had looked in 1912. The view from the boat as it left Port Antonio, his thoughts, his feelings, all seemed as real as they had then. All of this transpired in seconds as he simultaneously struggled with the controls.

Bert and Al had been sweltering in the small cabin of their plane as the sun rose in the summer sky and the temperatures over the Mojave Desert steadily climbed toward a daily high that exceeded 110 degrees. The ripples of heat that radiated from the sands of the desert made the barren landscape seem even more desolate, distorted their perspective of the horizon, and caused their eyes to ache. An intense perspiration streamed through the pores of their skin and dehydrated their bodies as nature relied on evaporation to maintain an inner temperature that was compatible with life. Their own attempt to stimulate evaporation by opening the windows of their cockpit was unsuccessful.

In order to counteract the heat Bert had raised the altitude of the plane by over 500 hundred feet. This maneuver had taxed their small engine and caused it to overheat even more. Because of the overheating, at times the gas in the fuel lines vaporized and became over diluted with air. As a result the engine occasionally hesitated as it awaited the delivery of the vital energy source that kept it functioning.

There was one factor in their favor on this occasion. Unlike the situations they had faced during the gales that buffeted them or while the electrical storm had enveloped them, they now had the option of finding a suitable landing site. But to what avail? If they put down on a deserted road, they would encounter a heat that was even more suffocating than the heat they were currently experiencing. The two pilots considered their options. If they were having trouble climbing now, what would it be like when they came to the mountain range that lay ahead? Al provided a couple of alternative choices.

"We could land and take off early in the morning when the weather is much cooler. Or we could avoid the heat by heading north away from the desert. I'm not sure if lightening our load will do the trick and allow us to cool off by climbing because I'm not sure that we can jettison enough to make a difference. What if we discard as much as we can and it is still not enough? Then we would have discarded some perfectly good items that we might need later."

"If we do either of the first two options, we will fall behind schedule" Bert pointed out. "A lot of the people waiting for us have made plans that will be difficult to change. Even if they do change them, rescheduling will cut down on the size of the crowd that meets us and on the amount of publicity that we get. Besides, I don't want those who might want us to fail to have any excuse to belittle what we have done. If we are not on time, they could use that against us and say it was because we were not skillful enough. As to what we discard, we can always replace it later. The cost is not important. Under the current circumstances I'd rather waste money than waste time."

Al responded immediately as he moved about the small cabin and put their thoughts into action. "Agreed. Besides, trying the discards first is probably the best idea anyway since if it looks like that approach is not going to work, we can always go to plan B, find a place to overnight, then take off early in the morning. You keep on with the flying and I'll try to figure out what items can be discarded."

Bert scanned the countryside on the off chance that he might see a potential landing site. He found his thoughts uncontrollably drifting back to the path that had led him to this place. In rapid succession he relived his arrival in Miami and the train ride to Tuskegee. He saw himself on a buggy ride with Booker T. Washington. Then his visual playback jumped to a particularly cold wintry night when he came home from work, fatigued, half asleep, and covered in flour as he rode on a Toledo streetcar that was swaying from side to side in between its many stops and starts. He relived his first day in anatomy class at medical school in Montreal and then re-experienced the frustration that he felt as he journeyed, weakened by diabetes, back to Jamaica. He remembered the peace that he experienced during his recuperation at home and the picnic on Navy Island. Finally he recalled his first sight of Al in a ditch, the words that Al spoke, and the scene as they took off from Atlantic City to begin this trip. So much had transpired. Then Al broke his concentration and the moment was lost. His time machine had reversed course and brought him back to the present where he would live until some future stimulus sent him back to the past. "I found a map of this area," Al explained. "It is pretty unpopulated around here but there is a nearby area called Badly Mesa where we can land. It's so deserted around here that I think we could safely land on a road but you never know. An unexpected pothole could do us in if we tried that sort of landing. If anything went wrong, there might not be anyone around to help."

Al did not expect any reply to what both knew to be factual. Without a pause, he continued his update. "When we land we can have something to eat and drink but then we should leave the rest of the food and water behind. There isn't that much that we can get rid of otherwise. After we land I'll look in the back and see what else can go. There are some ropes and small tools and other junk that isn't essential. We can probably leave some of our clothes at the airport and ask someone to ship them to us or we could buy some new ones in Los Angeles. Since we are going by a northerly route on our return trip we will not have the same problems with heat and altitude so the weight of the plane will not be a factor."

They circled the landing site twice before landing in order to alert anyone there of their arrival and to give themselves a chance to examine the poorly maintained runway for any evidence of a significant rut or an obstruction that could disrupt their landing. After an unremarkable landing, Al followed through on his offer to reconnoiter the rear of the plane for disposables. In due time he had a pile of items that he believed could be safely removed.

The temperature on the ground was just as severe as it had been up in the plane. Their discomfort was made worse by the complete absence of a wind that might evaporate some of the perspiration that flowed copiously from the pores of their skin in nature's effort to cool their bodies. They quickly completed their task and were able to gain some respite by moving to the shady side of the small building that served as an office. Then they bathed their faces and chests in uncomfortably warm water, ate and drank what was available, and mentally steeled themselves for what lay ahead.

They did not spend very much time in the heat of the desert. In less than twenty minutes they were back in the air and checking their compass to be sure than they were headed in the right direction. The cooling of the engine that occurred with their brief stop combined with the reduced strain on the engine that they achieved by discarding pounds of clothing, food, and equipment produced the intended effect; the plane was somewhat easier to handle; the engine no longer seemed to hesitate; the temperature gauge began to creep out of the red portion of the scale.

Previously they had spent most of their time looking down—observing the animals, the people, the cars, and the fabulous scenery. Now they were constantly looking up towards the mountain range that loomed before them. The mountains were scenic in their own right, but this was not what currently held their attention. The first priority had to be clearing the mountains that reached as high as 14,000 feet in a plane designed to operate below 10,000 feet.

Fortunately as they approached the mountains, the shrubs and trees on the foothills below adsorbed some of the heat that had been radiating from the sand and rocks of the desert and gave them some relief. It became noticeably cooler in the cockpit of the plane and the temperature gauge on the instrument panel continued to remain out of the red zone. They took care to maintain an altitude that was sufficient to provide a substantial margin for error in case a sudden downdraft occurred and forced them down towards the mountain. In this desolate area with no radio, with the majority of their food and water back at the last airport, they would not have been able to survive even if they were able to walk away from a forced landing.

After the fog, the gale, the electrical storm, and the effect of the heat on the performance of the engine, they were pleasantly surprised when the journey over the Sierra Nevada range proved uneventful. They easily cleared the pass in the mountains and headed towards the ocean. As they passed over the range, they were surprised to see that what was labeled a forest on their map looked like nothing more than a few rather anemic looking pines. In Jamaica or in the Allegheny Mountains, a forest was a dense collection of trees and not a scattering of scrub. In California, the word forest seemed to have a different definition. They continued their flight over a series of such mountains, occasionally seeing a dirt road, but never seeing any cars.

"There is the railroad line Al," said Bert with both excitement and relief as he spotted the familiar pattern of longitudinal steel tracks and horizontal wooden ties on a bed of rocks—a pattern that had guided them so often in the past. "That should lead us into Glendale and the airport. The rest of this should be a cakewalk!"

Al nodded as he too looked with surprise on these semi barren mountains. They were impressive in their size and number, but not as impressive in their color as those he was accustomed to back east. His gaze shifted from the map to the compass and then to the railroad tracks that were being pointed out. "I think that we are right on course," he said. "We should arrive in Glendale in the next 15 to 20 minutes."

They were able to spot the airport without very much difficulty. They had passed over the Coachella Valley where Palm Springs was located, seen the San Gabriel Mountains, and were heading for the San Gabriel Valley, the eastern part of the Los Angeles basin. They were told to expect 90-100 degree weather at this time of the year but after their experience in the Mojave Desert, those temperatures did not seem too bad. Unlike the situation in the East, the desert heat was very dry rather than humid and was therefore more bearable. Moreover, they had also been told that unlike the Midwest and the East, the desert cools off significantly at night so that a comfortable night's sleep in the summer was not going to be the problem that it often was back home.

They had chosen to land at Grand Central Airport on Sonora Street in Glendale, just northeast of Los Angeles. As they descended, they saw that a large crowd had gathered. It was later estimated to number 2,000—a large number for an occasion such as this. They had made the trip in two and one-half days with a flying time of 33 hours and 15 minutes, significantly faster than the flying time of 41 hours and 21 minutes that Banning and Allen had required over a period of three weeks.

The crowd that greeted them included Lt. William J. Powell who gave the welcoming address and represented Black Wings, Clarence Muse, a colored actor who was master of ceremonies and later interviewed them on his radio show, Floyd C. Covington who represented the Urban League, Percy Buck, a representative of the Negro Elks Club of Los Angeles that would later entertain them, Clarence Johnson, a representative of labor, Dr. Howard of the *California Eagle*, Harry Levette, a reporter for the Associated Negro Press, and radio reporters from several stations.

After a series of speeches of welcome, they were taken to the Y.M.C.A. on 28th Street and enjoyed a well-deserved break. In the evening the Eastside News Shopper gave them a reception. One hour of the next morning, Thursday, was spent with Clarence Muse doing a broadcast over a two-station hook-up, KD and KWB, Warner Brothers, and two broadcasts over KMX, Paramount. During the two-station hook-up, the fliers gave Los Angeles Mayor Frank Shaw the letter that Atlantic City Mayor Bacharach had sent to him. He in turn extended the greetings of the city and gave them a letter for Mayor Bacharach. Soon after, they flew their plane over a march given by the American legion in Huntington Park and followed this with an address to that group. That night, they attended a presentation of the play "Ethiopia Spreads Her Wings", a production that echoed their theme of advancing the colored race.

At the banquet after the reception, the fliers were naturally asked to address the group. As Bert approached the battery of microphones that had been assembled for him, he became anxious. 'Strange', he thought. 'I survived the fog, the gale, the electrical storm, and the desert heat with only a slight anxiety. Why is it that I feel twice as nervous now as I did then?' Despite his fears, he stood outwardly calm in front of everyone. The speech was not recorded but the sentiments were the following.

"There can be many reasons for taking a trip such as this. It's nice to be the first to do anything. Al and I are the first coloreds to be flying across country round trip. Even if we weren't the first, a flight such as this is a wonderful experience in itself. America is a beautiful country with so much variety that it is hard to imagine it unless you see it from the air as we have done. One can also take a trip such as this for personal fame or financial reward or to just prove to yourself that you could do it. Our trip was for none of those reasons."

"We undertook this trip for a purpose. There are still a lot of limitations on people of colored ancestry even when they have exceptional qualifications. Al for example is a natural born pilot who had the skills that were needed to overcome some of the tough situations that we experienced on this trip. Although he was naturally skilled and had a burning desire to fly, he found it extremely difficult to get flying lessons, difficult to get a license, and difficult to make a living through flying. By making this trip we have proven that coloreds are capable of performing complex jobs such as flying and should no longer be excluded from aviation. We should have coloreds who are pilots and mechanics and not just coloreds who are porters in the airports."

There was a tremendous ovation from the assembled group at hearing sentiments that so closely mirrored their own. Had these words been spoken before a white audience, there would have been the change in the atmosphere that occurs when a speaker's words touch on an uncomfortable subject or express sentiments that are at odds with the feelings of most of those present. The oxygen content does not change; the electrical charge is the same; yet there is a difference that everyone can feel. Some of the difference can be attributed to the sound level as a room that previously was characterized by a shuffling of feet, the occasional cough, and low-grade whispers suddenly becomes eerily quiet. But Bert was wise enough to address different aspects of his trip to different audiences.

His diplomatic skills were evident in a telegram that he sent to Mayor Bacharach as he departed Los Angeles on Friday, July 21, 1933. "Have letter from Mayor Shaw for you. We are guests of Legionnaires at Huntington Park. Flew over earthquake area. Starting eastward. Left 11:13 and continuing service to the Playground of the World. Forsythe and Anderson, pilots 'Pride of Atlantic City.'" The mayor was not burdened by references to Negroes in aviation, he was only given references to "The Playground of the World" and the "Pride of Atlantic City," phrases that would be picked up by the white press thereby insuring that the trip, and by association their cause, would receive publicity.

They had been scheduled to leave Glendale at 10 A.M. but were delayed when the excited crowd came onto the field and broke the gasoline gauge on the left wing. A temporary repair was made that allowed them to take off close to their appointed time. Their flight plan called for returning by a more northerly route that followed Route 80.

After leaving the Glendale airport they flew north to Oakland, passing over the large aqueduct that carried the water that made the growth of Los Angeles possible and sustained the vineyards and produce farms that dotted the landscape along their way. As they approached Oakland, they saw the famous San Francisco Bay and the early stages of the bridge that would span it. The amount that they had seen in less than one week was truly astounding.

After a short reception and speech, plus refueling, they turned away from the west coast of the continent and directed their plane towards Reno, Nevada and then towards the Great Salt Lake. But just as the Gods had subjected Hercules to serial encounters with the destructive forces of nature on land and sea, the two adventurers, lulled into complacency with the excellent weather that had prevailed since the heat of the Mojave Desert, found themselves in conflict with yet another of the potentially lethal products of the skies.

As they passed south of Idaho and approached Salt Lake City, in a brief period of time that seemed like seconds, the snowy white cloud cover became dark, the sky ahead became obscured, and a sudden sense of dread enveloped them as they instinctively recalled the circumstances that had preceded the electrical storm. Quickly they found themselves in the midst of a dense cascade of pebbles of condensed water. Visibility fell to a few feet as the cabin of the plane reverberated with a staccato that grew in volume as thousands of these pellets had the force of their impact magnified in intensity because of the speed of the plane.

The hailstones seemed relatively small and unlikely to do any harm but they knew that at any moment they might encounter some that could shatter their windshield and wreak havoc in the cabin. Moreover the cloud cover, the darkness, and the stones combined to reduce their visibility to zero. Up ahead were the mountains that adjoined Salt Lake City— mountains that they could crash into if they were forced to veer off course while the lack of visibility persisted. There was of course no radar, they had no radio contact, and they had no idea what direction the hailstorm might take or how long it might last. Once again fear stimulated the adrenalin to flow. Their senses became more acute, their reflexes seemed faster. Should they try to fly above the storm? Should they turn to one side? If so, which side would be the safest?

The pilot slowed the plane slightly in order to reduce the impact of the hail on their windscreen while the co-pilot carefully checked the compass and the altimeter to ensure that they were on a route that would not take them crashing into a mountain and peered out of the window in the vain hope that some landmark might be visible. Minutes crept by during which their pupils widened as they attempted to penetrate the surrounding gloom and their body muscles tensed in preparation for any potential emergency. Meanwhile the steady patter of stones discouraged them from making any attempt to communicate and made it difficult for them to sustain any train of thought.

Fortunately, as such storms usually do, it ended within a few minutes, the skies cleared, and it was almost as if it had never happened. Without saying a word to each other, they resumed a more relaxed posture and prepared for their next landing. There had not been the fear that they had experienced in the electrical storm, only a concern that had quickly dissipated after the episode was over.

Soon they saw the Great Salt Lake off to their left and prepared to descend for their landing. On arrival they were pleasantly surprised to see that the size of the crowd that greeted them was larger than they had expected in this town known primarily as the headquarters of the Mormons, the members of the Church of Jesus Christ of Latter-day Saints.

Bert knew very little of this group but had heard that like coloreds, its members had been subject to persecution.

The early church had a very troubled history. It was founded by Joseph Smith in 1830, was first headquartered in Kirtland, Ohio in 1831, and then moved to Missouri in 1838 because of conflicts with neighbors. That same year, after an attack that resulted in many deaths, the church members left for Illinois. However, when their leader Joseph Smith was murdered, the remaining members were forced out of Illinois.

Their new leader, Brigham Young, moved the group to the Great Salt Lake valley. The area became a territory in 1850 with Young as governor but his governorship ended after a war in 1857 when Young was forced to accept a different governor. One of the sources of friction between the Mormons and the general population had been their acceptance of polygamy. This irritant was removed in 1890 when the church outlawed the practice.

A member of the reception committee told Bert and Al that although they had so often been the victims of discrimination, the Mormons practiced discrimination themselves. However their level of discrimination seemed to be based on religious interpretations, was not aimed at perpetuating economic suppression, and was nothing like that practiced in the South. Nevertheless, it never ceased to amaze Bert that those who had been subject to discrimination could practice any form of discrimination against others. Certainly the segregation, prejudice, discrimination, and economic injustice that he had experienced had caused him to think differently about the relationships that he had had with the servants as a child, the attitude he had to the working man in Jamaica, and the attitudes that he saw in middle class Jamaicans.

Bert had thought about such dilemmas often enough to know that they were insoluble. The best that an individual could do was to make an effort to recognize the tendencies to prejudice in himself, modify them as much as possible, and work to minimize those tendencies in society. He hoped that the accounts of their trip in the Salt Lake City newspapers would begin the process of changing the attitudes there and elsewhere.

There followed a series of routine flights, landings, speeches, and take offs. Fortunately the speeches became a little easier to give with each stop, the flight routine became more automatic. The plane took them across the Great Plains once again. After an overnight in Cheyenne, Wyoming, they went on to Des Moines, Iowa and then landed in Chicago where the Urban League was very influential and the colored population was very large. The turnout was second only to that which they had experienced in Glendale, the destination of their trip.

Bert had frequently come into Chicago while he was working on the railroad. Chicago was a hub city where many railroad lines converged. It was also a city that exhibited marked segregation and prejudice. If you were first generation Polish or Irish or Italian or Catholic or Jewish, or if you were a colored who could trace your heritage back for many, many generations, you were likely to experience discrimination. That had always seemed ironic to Bert inasmuch as the city had grown up from a trading post that had been established by a Negro fur trader, Jean Baptiste Point du Sable.

The very large colored population that migrated to Chicago after World War I found itself highly segregated and confined to the South Side of the city where the quality of the housing was not very good and the inadequacy in the number of available units led to overcrowding. One plus was that the size of the colored population was so great that it facilitated the development of a large professional and entrepreneurial class. The many colored schools provided employment for colored teachers. There were trade schools that taught occupations that would provide a better life for the next generation. A large colored newspaper, *The Chicago Defender*, chronicled the problems of the colored community and agitated for change. As an aviator, Bert appreciated the efforts made by Abbott, the publisher of the *Defender,* on the behalf of Bessie Coleman a decade earlier.

The circumstances in Chicago represented a marked change from the situation that had previously prevailed in the South where the colored population received an inferior education, could only obtain low paying jobs, and had to spend their money in stores owned by whites who never put anything back into the colored community. Without labeling their actions, the Chicago community was following the pathway advocated by Booker T. Washington and advancing themselves by relying on education and entrepreneurship rather than simply on an insistence on social equality.

Despite its northern location and its having been founded by a colored man, race relations in Chicago were never very good. They deteriorated severely after four days of riots precipitated by the death of a colored youth on July 27, 1919. His crime was that while out for a swim in Lake Michigan, he drifted past the boundaries of the colored beach and was forced to try to come ashore on the white beach. Angered by this terrible 'affront', those on the white beach threw stones at him. He was forced to retreat far into the lake where he drowned. The lesson for the colored community was that the villainy perpetuated by prejudice was not confined to the South.

Even after the riots, the colored migration to Chicago from the South continued as desperate people searched for some of the many jobs that became available as the city grew to become the second largest in the United States. The large stocks yards, the Board of Trade that was the center for commerce in grain, the many museums, professional sports teams, and universities were the source of many jobs. Additionally, at the time of Bert's arrival, the city was enjoying a very successful exhibition entitled the "Century of Progress" that created even more jobs that paid well. The new colored immigrants however worked primarily as domestics, janitors, porters, or in other similarly low paying positions. The downtown area known as 'The Loop' because it was contained in a loop made by the elevated train, sustained many unskilled colored men who worked as busboys, bellhops, shoeshine 'boys' and washroom attendants. Colored females worked as maids in the downtown hotels and in private apartments along the expensive waterfront stretch on the North Side of the city that was known as the Gold Coast.

The city was also famous for its nightlife in both the colored and the white communities. Famous entertainers moved from New Orleans to work in the speakeasies and clubs that flourished on the South Side during Prohibition. Whites often considered it chic to frequent these clubs where they expected to receive priority service while the regular colored clientele waited.

The city was infamous for its criminal element. The newspapers and the movies made it seem as if gangsters regularly roamed the streets while dueling with submachine guns. Notorious episodes such as the St. Valentines Day massacre in 1929 contributed to the mystique. Chicago was a vibrant city that held a special attraction for many people.

After they landed, they were met by Colonel J. C. Robinson, an instructor at the Aeronautical University in Chicago and President of the Challenger Air Pilots Association located in Robbins, Illinois, an all Negro town that was 15 miles from Chicago. Later, they were entertained by the Elks Lodge.

When Bert had been in Chicago before, he had observed that, as in Atlantic City, the colored neighborhoods were not as well kept as the white ones. Trash collected on empty lots, streets that did not receive routine maintenance were littered with paper. To add to the problem, the heat of the summertime combined with the humidity from Lake Michigan to create an atmosphere that was so stifling that it sent people out into the streets. Everywhere there were unemployed and underemployed young men who preferred to be out on the streets rather in their apartments. Groups gathered in front of pool halls and liquor stores often smoking marijuana under the name of 'reefers'. The scenes that he encountered often seemed chaotic. When asked if the police were keeping things in control, the response would be that the police were only interested in receiving bribes.

The problems that he had encountered in Atlantic City seemed magnified in Chicago. The opportunities should have been more in Chicago because of its size; instead the only thing that was demonstrably bigger was the area that was labeled as colored, an area that was referred to as slums. In places like this, the cause of civil rights seemed almost hopeless.

The scale of the problem in Chicago was daunting but not completely disheartening. There were many, such as the educator Mary McLeod Bethune, who would make a concerted effort to improve the situation. The civil rights organizations were very active and constantly pushing the political establishment for improvements. The Chicago politicians were adept at doling out just enough patronage to keep the various ethnic constituencies under control. The unused area around the city was so large that opportunities often arose for colored business. Some local colored aviators had established a school of aviation on the west side of the city. Despite these positives, Bert felt a sense of discouragement and was anxious to leave Chicago and proceed to a very special stop, Toledo, Ohio where they would spend the night.

After living in Toledo for so many years, Bert was looking forward to seeing it from the air. It did not have the raw beauty of Jamaica or any of the spectacles he had seen in the last ten days such as the multicolored deserts and rock formations of the West or the wide bay area of San Francisco. But it did evoke nostalgia. As he approached, he tried to pick out the areas where he had gone canoeing, the Zoo, and other sites that he had frequented during the years that he lived there. Although he was very modest by nature, Bert felt some satisfaction in that after working in so many menial jobs in Toledo, he was returning under entirely different circumstances.

As an industrial town with a large colored population, Toledo had an active chapter of the Urban League. The chapter did its job well and saw to it that there was a substantial group there to welcome him. In addition to the crowd that was attracted by the publicity and the efforts of the Urban League, many of his old acquaintances were on hand to wish him well. After the ceremonies were completed, they went to the house of one of Bert's old friends for a dinner that was more memorable for its conversation than for its food. That night they went to bed a little later than usual and Bert drifted off feeling a bit more satisfaction than usual.

The 23rd of July was to have been the last day of their trip. However the type of fog that had briefly delayed them when they left on the 17th was again in evidence that day and they were unable to resume their journey. Finally, on Friday, July 28th, 1933, they were able to depart. They descended towards Atlantic City from their cruising altitude of 4,000 feet, circled the airport, flew over the city and the boardwalk then landed at 6:55 P.M., after a total flying time of 67 hours. Twelve days and 5,000 miles after their departure they were back in the Garden State where they received a hero's welcome from colored and white alike.

Their feat was so significant that Mayor Bacharach greeted them personally and did not delegate the task to a lesser official. He congratulated them on a remarkable achievement and recognized the fact that this was the first transcontinental round trip made by any aviators from Atlantic City. He then said, "Flying in a small plane with the limited equipment that you men used called for a high type of courage and skill and the citizens of Atlantic City are indeed very, very proud of you." Then he gave each a medal with their name inscribed on one side. Bert's read "To Dr. Albert E. Forsythe the first colored aviator to make a Round Trip Transcontinental Flight. From the citizens of Atlantic City, Harry Bacharach, Mayor." The other side read "Freedom of the City of Atlantic City" and had an engraving showing the emblem of the city and a key with the name Harry Bacharach, mayor underneath.

Director of Public Safety Cuthbert praised the flyers for their vision and ability and said that in supporting this flight the colored people were making a worthwhile contribution to progress.

Bert's speech stressed the point that, without the support of the colored race, especially those of Atlantic City, Ardmore, and Bryn Mawr, the flight would not have been possible.

When Al spoke, he commented that all along the route of the flight great interest had been shown in the project and a better interracial understanding had been brought about as well as greatly increased self-confidence and self-esteem among the members of the race, especially among the Negro youth.

A parade of 35 cars plus a number of pedestrians then took them to the All Wars Memorial Building. The parade included two colored police officers, a fire engine company that was wholly colored, Dr. Stanley L. Lucas of the Atlantic City board of education and the board of health, many representatives of social organizations, with the two aviators in an open car. After speeches at their destination, they went to a reception at the home of Dr. and Mrs. Lucas. Finally, at 10:30 P.M. a dance was held at Fitzgerald's auditorium when Bert and Al gave an account of their trip.

The trip received press coverage all over the world. Page 29 of the August 7, 1933 edition of Time magazine contained a reference to the flight. However, while the main Atlantic City paper gave the event significant coverage, the Newark newspaper relegated their article to a small report at the rear of the paper. Not unexpectedly, the greatest coverage was in the colored newspapers.

An additional reception that had been scheduled in Newark for September 1st had to be postponed to September 23rd. The duo flew from Atlantic City to Newark, arriving at 4:30 P.M. As usual, they circled twice in salute to those who awaited them below. After landing, a police motorcycle escort took them to Lincoln Park where there was a parade of 15,000 people that took them down Broad Street to the Sussex Avenue Armory. The parade was so large that business was disrupted causing many of the stores to have to close. Afterward the parade they met with New Jersey Governor A. Harry Moore for one hour and received his well wishes and expressions of appreciation for the publicity and pride that they had brought to New Jersey. The day ended with an evening reception and ball at the Armory with mayor Ellenstein of Newark in attendance.

A few days after his return in July, Bert had returned to his practice. He was by no means wealthy inasmuch as he had only recently started practice, was practicing with a low income population in a time of depression, and had spent a great deal of money on acquiring his plane and maintaining it. Had it not been for the assistance that he had obtained from the monies that had been collected through small donations and the help of the Urban League with logistics, meals, and lodging, he would not have been able to manage the expenses of the trip. He began to devote himself to replenishing his finances through his practice.

While seeing patients, he contemplated his next move. He had always felt that one trip alone would not accomplish his goal. In order to change long established public patterns, one had to reinforce the need for change in the public memory. He shared his thoughts with his co-pilot.

"Remember Al, we talked about the need to make some follow up flights? The round trip coast-to-coast flight was a success but we need something different to get continued attention. Think back. Lindberg received a lot more publicity on his transatlantic flight than he did on his coast-to-coast flight. A transatlantic flight is out of the question with my small plane but we could do a more limited international flight. Right now I suggest that we think small and make a trip to Canada in November of this year. The Urban League can't help us there but I have been in touch with friends in Montreal and they have written back agreeing to help us."

A faint crease developed across Al's forehead thereby revealing that he felt some doubt about Bert's latest suggestion. "Canada is not that far away Bert. Do you think that the newspapers and the public will accept that as being something worthy of note?"

Bert, like his mentor Booker T. Washington many years ago, was ready with a reply to an expected challenge. "They would not have had we made that flight first but now that we have the publicity of the round trip flight to our credit, they will pay some attention. The idea is to keep the issue before them. Our main goal will be a Caribbean goodwill tour in 1934 but for the time being we will concentrate on the Canadian trip."

"My friends in Montreal have written the Canadian government and obtained the necessary permission for us to cross the border," Bert continued. They will also take care of notifying the local politicians, the newspapers, and the colored community in Montreal. Food and lodging will not be a problem. I'm checking now on how to cover us for re-entry into the United States. We should not expect as much publicity as the last trip created but some publicity is better than none."

September quickly became October as the leaves changed from green to shades of red, orange, and yellow and then disappeared leaving behind the skeletal limbs of branches that raised their crooked digits to the sky. The daily crowds on the Boardwalk had dwindled and been replaced by a modest weekend flow as the heat of summer gave way, first to the chill of fall, and then to the promise of wintry cold. In November, before the snows of winter could make their appearance, the two pioneers set out for Montreal.

The trip to Montreal was, for a change, straightforward. Once again Bert had the opportunity to see a city that he had lived in from the air. The island nature of the city was more apparent when one was high above; the famous mountain looked more impressive from above than from below. Because the airport was quite a distance away from the city, the size of the crowd that was there to greet them was not very large. Nevertheless, a speech was given and some publicity did ensue.

Afterwards Bert had a chance to visit with friends that he had not seen for over four years and savor the taste of the excellent French cuisine that could be found in so many bistros. Because prohibition had ended in the United States the previous year, Canadian cities had lost one of their attractions for Americans. Montreal however still exuded a palpable charm.

All too quickly their trip was over and they began their return flight. On the trip back to Atlantic City they reversed their initial flight plan and followed the Hudson River. As usual, they always felt more secure if they did not rely solely on their compass but had the backup of a landmark such as a river, railroad track, or a major road. The pair alternated at the controls so that neither man would become overly fatigued and make a careless error that could be fatal.

As had happened so frequently before in this light plane, the weather caused some anxious moments. Half way home a head wind came up that slowed their speed significantly. When they looked at the road below, the cars that were heading in their direction were achieving a speed that was greater than theirs. This created the feeling that their plane was going backwards. They were never in any real danger because of this, but this anomaly did provide some humor on an otherwise routine flight.

On their return they received some moderate publicity, about what they had expected. While the major newspapers did not give it much attention, it was a subject of great interest in the colored community. That was very important because they needed community involvement in order to raise the money that would be needed for their most challenging trip.

Al had established a flying school and a charter flying service in Norristown, Pennsylvania near Philadelphia using Bert's plane. Their efforts were beginning to pay off-- a flying school would train more coloreds and create more pressures for change, the charter service would show that there was an income potential. The two aviators felt a great deal of satisfaction with the progress that was being made as a result of their flights.

Atlantic City to Los Angeles and Return - 67 Hours - July, 1933

PILOTS

9

THE GOODWILL FLIGHT

Bert resumed his practice but devoted a great deal of time to his next project. Over the winter, he continued to crystallize his plans in conversations with the members of the National Negro Aeronautical Society. That group felt that it had served its purpose and should be replaced by a new entity that would widen the involvement of the community and facilitate fund raising. The title chosen was "The Interracial Goodwill Aviation Committee."

This committee was staffed primarily by local school principals and teachers. The chair was Julia Goens while a key participant was Mary J. Washington, a teacher who was the publicity director and very adept at getting their story into the papers. On March 11th the *Philadelphia Independent* reported that Bert and Al met with Philadelphia leaders about their upcoming trip. On April 5th, the *Tribune* reported that Bert and Al soared one-half mile above the boardwalk as part of a celebration.

One of the first decisions of the committee was to establish a 'Flight Advisory Board' composed of famous people that could bring publicity to the venture and aid in fund raising. On April 23, 1934 a letter accepting a position as advisor was received from Oscar De Priest, a colored congressman from Illinois. Others who accepted the position included Eugene Kinckle Jones from the Urban League, and

W.T. Coleman. The committee, with advice from the council, embarked on several fundraising projects.

One large project was the Flight Boosters Club. By buying a button that supported the tour, one became a booster. A contest was set up with captains who were to enroll boosters. The captain who enrolled the most boosters was given a prize. The result was an enrollment of 400.

Personal appearances were important. On July 10th there was a lantern travelogue by Dr. Lucas and Bert at the St. Augustine Parish Hall where Julia Goens reported that 6 people had each given $5 towards the flight. She then announced the various schools, churches, and other organizations that had enthusiastically supported the avowed goal: "to bring about better interracial and international relations and to gain prestige for the colored race." Groups continued to join for months afterwards, including the West Indian Federation of America and, on August 9th, the Caribbean Union.

The committee lobbied local government to lend their support. They were successful in getting the director of the New Jersey Department of Aviation to send a letter on July 31st to the director of the U.S. Bureau of Aeronautics attesting to the capabilities and character of Bert and Al.

While these activities were taking place Bert decided that a new plane was necessary because the current Fairchild plane would not provide the fuel efficiency that was needed to fly over large expanses of water where landing and refueling was impossible. The Fairchild had been preferable when they had needed extra horsepower to provide them with the altitude necessary to fly over the Rocky Mountains but for this flight Bert wanted a Lambert monocoupe, a plane with two seats instead of three, a more streamlined shape, a lighter weight, and 90 horsepower instead of 95. These features were expected to provide them with a longer flying range than the Fairchild had and consequently a higher margin of safety in the flight over water.

Even with the longer range of the aircraft there were some segments of the flight when fuel capacity might not provide an adequate margin of safety. For that reason they also decided that it would be prudent to attach an auxiliary gas tank under each wing of the plane to increase their fuel capacity to 43 gallons in case of above average fuel consumption due to unexpected headwinds or a detour caused by weather conditions. Their previous confrontations with the weather had blunted the feeling of invincibility that had existed at the onset of their coast-to-coast flight the year before.

The plane had to be picked up at its manufacturing site in the city of Robinson, Missouri, just outside of St. Louis with the old plane used as part of the purchase price. They therefore flew the Fairchild to St. Louis with fundraising stops in Pittsburgh and Columbus then an overnight stop in Indianapolis with Dr. Theodore Cable for a third fundraiser.

On August 23, 1934 Bert and Al arrived in St. Louis. While they were in the second floor office at the plant awaiting final delivery, they talked with the manager about their plans to fly to the Caribbean and then to the Panama Canal and Mexico. "Just a moment," said the manager, "there is some-one I think you should meet".

The manager went downstairs then came back up a few minutes later with a handsome man in his early thirties who had a decided air of assurance. "I'd like to introduce you two to Charles Lindberg," said the manager as he deferentially ushered in his companion. "He is here supervising the construction of his newest plane, one with 200 horsepower, a lot more than yours has. He will need the extra horsepower because the plane is going to have a lot more equipment on board. Mr. Lindberg has been over some of the same territory that you will be covering. When I told him about you, he wanted to talk with you."

For a moment, the two were at a loss for words. Charles Lindberg was of course the most famous flyer in the world. It was his solo flight across the Atlantic seven years ago that had led to the dramatic increase in aviation. Without his flights, they probably would not have been standing there today. Here they were, two fellows who had trouble getting a license less than three years ago, getting advice from Charles Lindberg!

The three men had a conversation that went on for almost one hour. ˊ Lindberg was quite agreeable in his demeanor. The two men of color might have had problems getting into the rank of licensed pilots, but now that they were there, they shared with all pilots the bond that arose from their mutual love of the air and their exposure to the same risks, the same thrills, and the same problems. As an aviator, Lindberg knew of the dangers that they would face on this trip and wanted to help wherever possible. When they recounted the problems that they had faced on their cross-country trip, he cautioned that there would be new problems on their overseas flight.

"I've landed at most of the places you plan to visit," Lindberg counseled. "Your worst stop will be in St. Thomas. That is considered to be one of the six worst airports that there is. The edge of the airfield is very close to the water so if you overshoot on your landing, you will sink in the ocean. If you are off to the side when you land or if you try to turn, you will run into a hill. Since you know what you are getting into, you shouldn't have a problem."

With the confidence of a professor lecturing his students, Lindberg continued. "Then there is always the risk that you will have to crash land in the ocean if you run out of fuel because of headwinds or straying off course or getting lost. You need to have the right equipment. Besides your radio and your altimeter, you need an instrument to measure wind direction and speed. Plus you will need to carry parachutes and a canvas lifeboat on board in case you go down over the water. Those are the things that I took along when I made a similar trip a couple of years ago to help Pan Am plan a route to South America."

After an hour they had asked all of the questions that they could think of and Lindberg seemed to have offered all of the advice that he could. He wished them well and went back downstairs. After his departure, Bert and Al commented on what had just transpired.

"I appreciate his trying to help, but a lot of that advice can never apply to us," Al observed, impressed but not overawed by the opportunity to speak with this most famous aviator. "He had a 200 horsepower plane. That meant more fuel capacity, higher payload capability. Our 90 horsepower plane could never carry all that equipment, even if we could afford it. And where would we put a lifeboat? The only place that it could fit would be in my seat."

That's for sure," Bert responded as his head nodded perceptibly in agreement. "We would need twice as much money to do things the way that he suggests. I must admit that there were a lot of times that a radio would have come in handy on our cross-country trip but we managed without it. That tip about the St. Thomas airport was really useful however. Landing and takeoff will probably present our biggest problems. I've written letters to everyone I could to get information on our landing sites."

When the purchase of the plane was complete, they took off for Atlantic City with fundraising stops in Detroit, Toledo, Cleveland, Pittsburgh, Buffalo, New York City, Richmond, Washington, and Baltimore. Once they were back Bert redoubled his efforts to increase the publicity for the trip and raise funds to help defray the expenses. The donations were important not just for the money that they raised but because they developed a sense of community involvement in the project. It became a matter of ethnic pride to contribute to the cause of proving the capabilities of coloreds and helping to open up new job opportunities.

Meanwhile Miss Goens used the endorsements that she had received from local officials in a letter that she wrote to President Roosevelt on September 7th on Bert's behalf, explaining that their aim was "to cement the friendly understanding and goodwill between the peoples of the Western Hemisphere." On September 19th Thomas Wells wrote back on behalf of the President giving encouragement to the flight.

This response from the Office of the president of the United States made all members of the group ecstatic. They could now expect to get excellent cooperation from government. In fact, on October 15th they received a letter from the Department of Commerce, Bureau of Air Commerce reporting that a telegram stating that permission had been granted for entrance to the English ruled islands of the Caribbean had been received from the American Embassy in Paris. With the endorsement of the President, The State Department was now taking an active role.

One cannot overstate the degree of skill and foresight that went into this undertaking. The planning and execution were brilliant. First, local business leaders then local government were brought in to plan a national trip. Then, after establishing bona fides with a national trip, national leaders were willing to join in promoting an international trip. The presence of national leaders brought in national government and the support of the national government opened the door to international governments. This universality encouraged the participation of the overall population.

The stepwise cooperative approach that Bert had set in motion was in keeping with the philosophy of Booker T. Washington rather than the more confrontational approach advocated by W.E.B. DuBois and adopted by some of the other black aviators. Any success that they had would be the result of well thought out efforts and not sheer luck.

The growing publicity caused Bert to be invited to the annual meeting of the Federation Aeronautique Internationale Congress which was being held at the Mayflower Hotel in Washington. This was an international body headed by Prince George Valintin Bibesco that had been set up to promote aviation. At the meeting, Sir Sidney Veit the chairman of their foreign relations committee said,

"No medium can bring the people of the world together more quickly than the aeroplane. In the air there are no frontiers and no bitter nationalism and stupid animosity."

..... "This flight will have a telling effect on both interracial goodwill and mutual understanding between the peoples of North and South America. Moreover, the federation looks upon this unprecedented Negro aviation venture with the keenest interest because of its possibilities for the future of Negro Aviation." He called Bert the "Wilbur Wright of Negro aviation."

Bert also wrote asking Dr. Robert Moton, the successor to Booker T. Washington as principal of Tuskegee Institute, for permission to honor Bert's mentor Booker T. Washington by naming the plane after him. This commemoration would recognize the influence that Washington had had on Bert's life and on the cause of civil rights in general. Bert realized that what he was undertaking was exactly what Washington had advocated--utilizing a demonstration of the capabilities of educated coloreds to advance the cause of civil rights.

Bert also knew that naming the plane after Washington would increase the level of publicity for the trip. More than a decade after his death, Booker T. Washington was still held in esteem in both the white and the colored communities because of the efforts that he had made to provide an education to as many coloreds as possible. Just as his decision to name his first plane 'The Pride of Atlantic City' after his home city had increased the local level of interest, he expected that naming the new plane after Tuskegee's most famous educator would generate national publicity that would be good for both the school and for the trip.

When he received Bert's letter Dr. Moton was enthusiastic about the project. He wrote back that he concurred with Bert's conclusion that Washington would have supported this type of undertaking and agreed both to having the plane brought to Tuskegee to be christened as 'The Booker T. Washington' and to helping in fund raising.

On Friday afternoon September 15th the plane landed on a field and was towed to the parade grounds of Chambliss Children's House where the band, a guard of honor, the faculty and students, and hundreds of visitors including Washington's granddaughter Nettle, witnessed the christening ceremonies. The Tuskegee Messenger stated that no event "is more significant of (Tuskegee's) forward look than the christening".

Dr. Moton presented them with a replica of the Hampton-Tuskegee medal commemorating the fiftieth anniversary of the founding of the Institute and gave them a letter commending their "courage, vision, and self-sacrifice" and their "efforts to show the world the black man's courage, stability, and progress".

When asked to speak, Al, with his usual shyness, stated that he was an aviator and not a speaker and said very little. Bert then spoke at length about their plans.

"We are anxious to establish friendly relations between the various peoples of the earth with the hope of gaining favorable worldwide attitudes towards the darker races. We are desirous of increasing race pride and confidence and especially of inspiring our youth and awakening in our people generally a realization of new possibilities for advancement."

"{Our} committee already has in hand $800 which is approximately the amount necessary for the operation and maintenance for the proposed flight. For blind flying and special navigation instruments $2,400 is still needed. Two parachutes which will cost $600 would add considerable to the peace of mind of the flyers but are yet to be supplied. But whether or not we get this added equipment, we hope to take off for the West Indies and Central America on November 8th."

After his speech the State Federation of Colored Women's Clubs presented them with a contribution of $50. The idea that they might have to undertake the trip without parachutes caused an anonymous donor to contribute another $10. Dr. Moton then announced the formation of a committee to collect further funds and later agreed to join the Advisory Council of the Goodwill Committee.

During this time Bert was also quite busy corresponding with friends and friends of friends in the countries he planned to visit. In the Bahamas he contacted Etienne Dupuch, the current publisher of the Nassau Tribune and the son of the witness at his father's wedding, Leon Dupuch. His contacts in several of these countries wrote that an open field or a straight stretch of road were the only sites available for a plane to land but offered to make sure that any ditches or telephone lines or other obstructions that might interfere with the landing path of the plane were removed. By the time that he was ready to leave, he had received assurances from every country except Trinidad that all would be in readiness and had been given maps and/or written directions as to how to find the landing sites.

They were in a quandary about what to do about the landing authorization from Trinidad but anticipated that the problem would be resolved. Trinidad, like all of the countries involved, seemed interested in using the flights to generate interest in their islands among tourists and to promote the future of aviation in their countries. At this point in time, plane travel to these islands was very limited although Pan American had begun a seaplane service to several islands including Trinidad in 1929. These flights could only accommodate a limited number of passengers so most tourists continued to arrive by boat.

After prolonged reflection on their options, they decided that they could not delay their flight by waiting until they had permission. They wired the government of Trinidad that they had a schedule to keep, would be leaving on their scheduled departure date, and asked that any reply be sent to Bert's father in Port Antonio who would then relay the information to Bert.

Meanwhile they continued their fundraising efforts. Pan American Airways agreed to assume the fuel costs in those countries where they had a presence because it was very interested in developing commercial aviation in the Caribbean. The 'Mainline Branch of the Interracial Goodwill Aviation Committee' raised funds by holding a viewing of the newly christened "Booker T. Washington" on Monday September 24th at 6 P.M. at the Practice Golf Course that was located at Argile and Haverford Roads in Ardmore, Pennsylvania. The chairman of the committee was Reverend James Scott and the speaker was attorney H.H. Robb.

Every contingency was considered. On October 1st, Mary Washington came up with a list of the major newspapers on the islands that would be visited and a list of many in America to use for press releases. The quality of her work was so good that she was later accorded the status of a journalist so that she might obtain a professional discount on the use of the wire services. Mary also compiled a list of two ham radio operators for each island. Their job would be to notify the islands of time of departure from the previous island and expected time of arrival at the next. They would also see to it that the aviators would have information on weather and other important items forwarded as necessary.

On Thursday, November 8, 1934, at 7:58 A.M., the flight departed from Atlantic City. A large crowd, both white and colored, gathered to see them off and wish them well. The spectators included politicians, reporters, and the curious. More than one spectator, of both races, wondered about the sanity of these men who planned to fly over open water in their small plane on a trip that would take over one month. Some came expecting to see a disaster.

The event made an indelible impression on those who were there that day and changed their way of thinking. Whites realized that coloreds could be courageous, self-confident, and capable of significant undertakings. Coloreds realized that discrimination was not an absolute block to participating in activities that had been previously considered to be restricted to whites.

It was a perfect morning for flying when they took off from Atlantic City on the first leg of their flight. For several hours they flew through clear skies without incident. From their previous experiences they should have realized that this circumstance would never prevail for an extended period.

When the plane was just below Norfolk, Virginia a fog arose to threaten their flight plans. The moisture laden white banks that looked so attractive when they floated high in an open and sunny sky in the form of clouds, became potential deathtraps when they descended close to the ground and blocked the aviators ability to see other planes that might crash into them or judge the height of mountain ranges that were totally unfamiliar. On two prior occasions, they had landed and waited for the fog to disappear. The wait had been less than an hour at Camden, New Jersey, but lasted 5 days in Toledo, Ohio. On this occasion, rather than risk a wait of unknown duration, they decided to detour around the fog, a decision that caused them to have to travel 100 miles out of their way.

Then, over Charleston, South Carolina, in the region of the Four Hill swamp, the natural barrier that nature placed in their way changed as they encountered a severe air turbulence that buffeted their small plane. The experience could be compared to riding at high rate of speed in a boat that was traversing a very choppy sea. For a fraction of a second all seemed effortless as you enjoyed the tranquility of free falling through the air. Inevitably you were rudely brought back to reality as the body of your vessel was slammed against a usually pliable medium. Air that normally melted out of the way in a gentlemanly fashion so that you could pass, became an unforgiving bully that shoved you forcefully and repeatedly.

The two pilots worked together in an effort to counteract the stress that the plane was experiencing. Had this been an elderly vessel such as those that some impoverished fliers relied on, it is doubtful that it could have survived. As the ordeal continued, they found themselves tensing during each lull in preparation for the inevitable vibrations that threatened to separate the plane rivet by rivet and leave them to plummet through the sky towards an unforgiving earth that waited below, ready to reclaim each modern Icarus. The minutes passed and the pair began to perspire. It was not the fine cool mist that covers the skin at a time of fear but the flood that cascades from the forehead and armpits as straining muscles overheat, metabolic wastes build up, and the body attempts to cool itself.

They struggled against the tendency of the plane to pitch and yaw for approximately ten minutes before the ordeal came to an end and both aviators were able to relax and begin to check their instruments and the cabin to see if any problems had developed. To their dismay they quickly realized that they had a problem with the auxiliary fuel tanks that they had attached under the wings of the plane just before their departure.

Al made no effort to minimize his concern as he yelled out what he had discovered and realized the ramifications. "Bert, look at the fuel gauge! The level in the auxiliary tank is falling rapidly. I think that the turbulence that we just went through must have loosened the line to the auxiliary tank and caused the tubing to leak!"

They watched the fuel gauge for seconds that were painfully long in order to confirm their suspicions. Then Bert, the timber of his voice subtly altered by excitement, made another observation. "It's not just the auxiliary tank that is leaking. The gauge on the main tank is falling also. At this rate we will be out of fuel in only a few minutes. We have a major problem!"

Once again, the gnawing sensation in the lower abdomen announced the presence of the aviator's frequent companion, fear. Those who had the audacity to defy gravity recognized and respected fear but were not awed by it. Fear was not simply an irritant; it was not evidence of a defect in character; fear was a fact of life that could paralyze but could also mobilize. Like a scavenger of the Serengeti it was not pretty but it did serve a purpose. Now, as they began to feel their old enemy invade their bodies, their senses were heightened and their thought processes became much more acute as they considered their options. There was never a sense of panic but a clear recognition that there was a problem to be solved and a determination to discover a successful solution.

It was actually fortunate that this type of situation had arisen at this time. Had it happened later in their flight, while they were over the sea, they might have been forced to ditch in the ocean where their chances for survival would have been minimal. Lindberg's admonition that they should carry a collapsible boat had foreseen the possibility of that occurrence. However, in their small plane, they had not had the space that would have permitted the luxury of protecting against that contingency. Instead, they relied on their confidence in their ability to avoid those problems that could be avoided and solve those which arose.

Even though they were over land and not over water, their options were limited. Below was a dangerous swamp, totally unsuitable for landing. There were no airports that they knew of ahead of them and no evident potential landing sites that they could see nearby. A crash landing, even in a lightly populated area, would put those on the ground at risk. With their fuel rapidly disappearing, a decision had to be made quickly. "Lets head for the ocean," Al suggested. "With all of the beaches in this area, the chances are pretty good that we can find a clear stretch to land on without endangering anyone. At worst we can ditch in shallow water where we could make it to shore."

Once again their luck held. Just as the fuel gauge registered empty they came upon an airstrip at Beaufort, South Carolina. Out of gas, the plane went into a long glide as Al tried to coax a few extra meters of flight time by carefully controlling the attitude of the nose. With the skill that he had developed over their many hours of flying, he was able to achieve a perfect dead stick landing on the airstrip. Once again they had been confronted with a potential disaster and shown an ability to survive.

When they landed they discovered that the copper line to the left auxiliary tank had ruptured. They spent the night in Beaufort, made a temporary repair the next morning, then refueled and flew to Miami where they were able to make a permanent repair that made a reoccurrence unlikely. While awaiting the repairs, they kept a prearranged appointment and spoke to a group of students at Booker T. Washington High School about their trip and about the future of aviation for colored youngsters.

It was after 3:00 P.M. before they were ready to leave. When notified that they were about to proceed, the manager of the Miami airport approached the pair to express several concerns. "I would strongly recommend against starting out for Nassau at this time of day" he told them. The small furrow that crossed his forehead added physical confirmation to his oral disapproval of this course of action.

"You will be the first land plane to land in Nassau and you won't be landing at a real airfield but at a makeshift landing site that would be questionable in the daytime but is an impossibility if you arrive after dark since there will not be any landing lights to guide you. Moreover headwinds have been reported between here and Nassau that will further delay your arrival and increase your risk. These winds will also increase your fuel consumption and limit your options if you decide to turn back. I suggest that you stay in Miami tonight and wait until tomorrow morning to make your flight."

The pair listened attentively then discussed the situation in depth. They had had a similar dilemma when their plane overheated in the desert and they had been forced to decide between the risk of proceeding and the disruption that a delay would cause with regard to the plans of the people who were expecting them. In that instance however it had not been a life or death decision. If they were too aggressive on this occasion, they might find themselves forced to attempt the almost impossible task of landing at a dangerous location in the dark.

Before making a decision, they carefully calculated the normal flying time to Nassau and added a safety factor for the headwinds. Their analysis showed that they could complete the journey with approximately a half of an hour to spare before darkness fell. This information allowed their desire to maintain their schedule and not disrupt the plans made by the Bahamians to overcome their apprehension over the very real risks that they would face with a late arrival. They presented their figures on the projected arrival time to the manager for his confirmation and were relieved when he ratified them.

Had the calculations not been in order, they would not have received permission to depart. Even then, the manager was evidently concerned. "I tell you what, normally we shut down at dusk but I'll leave the airport lights on for you tonight. If you think you can't make Nassau before dark, turn around and come back. Don't cut it too close; if it looks like you will have to double back, don't wait until the last minute to decide but turn around while you still have more than a half a tank of gas left. I have been asked by Washington to extend every cooperation that I can, but no one will thank me if you crash. It would be better to disappoint one island the first day because you were late than to disappoint every island because you crashed. Good luck, you are going to need it to complete such an ambitious undertaking."

With that admonition, they took off at 3:30 P.M. for Nassau, the capital city of the 700-island group known as the Bahamas. The city was located on the island of New Providence, a relatively small island that, with the distant and larger island of Grand Bahama, contained most of the people who lived on the islands. Their destination was approximately 270 miles in an easterly direction from Miami, and one hundred miles to the north of the Tropic of Cancer, the northern border of the equatorial zone of the earth. Bert was looking forward to returning to the island where he was born even though his memories of his three years there were almost non existent and his ties to the relatives who had remained there were not strong.

During the first twenty minutes of the flight they checked the fuel gauges every few minutes to be sure that there was not a repetition of the leak that had forced them to land in South Carolina. As each reading proved normal, their confidence grew and the checks became less frequent. The predicted headwinds made their presence known but there was not enough turbulence to threaten the integrity of their fuel lines or enough force to increase fuel consumption above the calculated level. Still, they were slowed by the winds and realized that the margin of safety between their time of arrival and the onset of darkness was minimal.

After they had passed the Bimini Islands, a minor area of concern was the lack of any landmarks while they were flying over miles of an ocean that lacked any of the topography of their flights over land. They had been accustomed to supplementing their main navigation aid, the compass, with visual confirmations such as rivers, railroad tracks, towns, or mountains. When over water, they had to place total reliance on the accuracy of their compass. These readings, always accurate in the past, were equally reliable on this journey so that as dusk neared, they were elated to see the large island of Andros on their right, followed by the tiny Berry Islands on their left, and then New Providence, arising on schedule, straight ahead.

Horatio had seen to it that friends in Nassau had sent Bert a map of the landing site that was being prepared along with some written instructions about the area. These friends wrote that although there was not an airstrip for the plane to land on, the brush had been cut down and the ditches had been filled in along a road to the west of the town and near to Fort Charlotte in order to create a landing site. They assured him that the night before his arrival linemen would take down the telephone poles and the wires that lined the roads in order to make sure that they did not obstruct his approach.

To reach this landing spot, the directions stated that he should fly to the most visible landmark, an old lighthouse that had guided mariners to the harbor for centuries, turn right at the small dirt road that passed nearby, but be careful not to hit the old windmill. Brush, ditches, telephone poles and wires, turn at the dirt road, watch out for the old windmill. That was the primitive nature of the landing site, the sketchy nature of the directions that they were given, and the multiplicity of the risks that they faced. The pair accepted these risks as a fact of life; they were neither intimidated nor frightened by them. The risks were there to be acknowledged so that they could be planned for and surmounted. They were not an excuse to quit.

The headwinds, added to the delay in departure due to the ruptured fuel line, had used up their margin for error and caused them to arrive at the island with only a few minutes to spare before darkness set in and the risk of landing increased. As expected, the lighthouse was the most prominent feature in the area and guided these travelers from the skies as efficiently as it had guided those from the sea. As they drew near, they had no trouble seeing the road next to the lighthouse and then portion where the adjacent land had been cleared to form a rough landing site just days before. Pleased by the ease with which they found their target and confident that their first objective would soon be attained, they circled and came in for a landing.

As they did so, the crowd of people that had gathered to greet them became highly excited and surged onto the road that they were about to land on. With their runway clogged with people, they were forced to abort the landing, climb and circle, and repeat their approach. Meanwhile the sun continued its relentless descent to the horizon; the closer it got, the faster it seemed to descend. The bright blue tropical skies faded with increasing rapidity to a mellow orange hue that became progressively dimmer as time became their mortal enemy.

They circled the site once and began a new descent in the rapidly receding light. Once again the eager crowd, anxious to welcome the visitors, ran onto the landing site and unwittingly forced them to abort the landing and ascend back into a sky that was now showing traces of purple. Now the situation was becoming dangerous and the pilots were truly worried. Fuel was not a problem, but the fading light was. The sunset that had been such a delight to behold from the shore in Port Antonio was now a creature to be dreaded by the pilots and, unknowingly, by the people below who would be at risk if they had to attempt a landing in the dark.

Fortunately for both those in the air and those on the ground, someone in the crowd realized what was happening and took some action. On the aviators' third approach, Bert and Al saw that the crowd was no longer clogging the road.

Moreover the headlights of the cars that were parked at the beginning of their landing strip had been turned on in an effort to light their way. This time they were able to complete their approach and land without any incident. With Al at the controls, at 5:30 P.M. on Friday November 9th, they touched down on the road in Nassau, braked to a stop, and turned off their engine, safely arrived at their first major stop. After they disembarked from the plane, a very large crowd that included several dignitaries greeted them. The crowd cheered and rushed forward in an effort to touch the men who were instant national heroes.

Among the greeters was a man who made his way to Bert and said, "I'm Buster Bosfield, a relative on your mother's side." That became the extent of their conversation as the surging crowd swallowed Bert and moved him away. Nevertheless, Bert was happy to know that a relative had made contact and expected that future contacts would follow.

Their arrival touched off a citywide celebration in which 5,000 people participated. The two fliers were bedecked with garlands of flowers and taken into town where his Excellency Sir Bede Hugh Clifford, the Governor of Nassau, received them at Government house. Bert presented the governor with a copy of the scroll that he would give to the head of government in each country. The scroll gave the reasons for the flight and had the signatures of those who had sponsored the flight. It read, in part:

""Whereas it is the desire of the people of the United States of America to effectuate more cordial relationships, establish firmer bonds of friendship and bring about a truer and deeper understanding between the various races and peoples of the western hemisphere, therefore be it remembered that we, the undersigned, do hereby cause our names to be fixed to these greeting as having subscribed to the noble purpose of this worthy undertaking."

The governor in turn gave Bert a letter to deliver to the Governor of Jamaica when he arrived on that island.

This meeting was followed by several receptions, then a giant street party. It seemed like the entire population of Nassau was out dancing in the streets that night as the celebration went on until the early hours of the morning. The next morning a parade was held in their honor.

There was tremendous pride exhibited by the crowd because Bert was a Bahamian, because he was colored, and because their island was receiving recognition. The story was front-page news throughout the Caribbean, but especially in the Nassau *Tribune*, the paper founded by Leon Dupuch, the witness at his fathers wedding.

As best he could tell from what Bert saw in his short visit to the Bahamas, the social structure was very similar to that which had developed in Jamaica. He felt quite at home on this visit to a place where he was an honored member of the majority and not subject to a high level of discrimination and prejudice.

The time of departure was set for 12:30 after a light lunch. With reluctance the Bahamians said goodbye to the aviators and asked for assurances that they would return to the island in the future. There was no doubt in Bert's mind that he would. Most of his early years were spent in Jamaica, he was now an American citizen, but there is an attraction from the land of your birth than never disappears. Just as a salmon is drawn to the stream where it was born by invisible forces whose origin is uncertain, so also is man drawn to his roots by unknown forces.

Another large crowd was on hand when they climbed into the "Booker T. Washington" and taxied down the makeshift runway. Hundreds of hands continued to wave at the two who were considered to be heroes and continued to wave long after there was any possibility of their being seen by the pair on the plane. On a typically warm tropical day they followed a southwesterly flight path that would take them to Havana, the capital of Cuba.

They crossed over dozens of miles of ocean without incident as their Lambert monocoupe performed flawlessly. Soon however they ran into an intense tropical storm. It was as if they had flown into a waterfall. Sheets of water poured over their aircraft driven by forceful winds. When they looked out of the window of their plane, there was no ocean below, no sky above, and no clouds to be seen—only a torrent of water. While the absence of visibility was not the danger that it would have been in mountainous territory or in an area where other planes might be flying, it was disconcerting. After several minutes of flying under these conditions, the combination of the roar of the rain, the absence of visual stimuli, and the physical battering that they were taking became a matter of concern. So much so that anxiety, the precursor of fear, began to insidiously invade their psyches.

There is a tendency to assume that the weather nearby is identical to the weather that is being experienced locally. That is seldom true at ground level and is definitely not true in the sky. Air currents can create significant differences in the weather that prevails at different altitudes. Knowing this, the flyers decided to descend closer to sea level to see if their situation would improve. The plane was put into a gradual descent; after a drop of 1,000 feet, there was no change so the descent was continued for another 1,000 then another. Bert alternated between watching the altimeter and looking out the window to make sure that they did not crash into the ocean. Finally, the strength of the wind lessened and the force of the water diminished so that their visibility increased, the ocean came into view, and their sense of well-being was enhanced. The ferocity of the rain that they had passed through was confirmed later when they had landed by the finding that some of the paint had been peeled from the struts of their plane.

Bert had been looking forward to visiting Cuba, one of Jamaica's nearest neighbors, the largest island in the

Caribbean, and a part of a chain known as the Greater Antilles that is situated in the equatorial zone below the Tropic of Cancer. Unlike the Bahamas, Jamaica, and the majority of the West Indian Islands, Cuba's colonial influence had been almost entirely Spanish. Its population was 75% of primarily Spanish/Indian origin and 25% of primarily African origin.

The record of slavery in Cuba had not been good. The cruelty of the Spanish towards their slaves intensified their natural discontent. One revolt was foiled in the planning stage in 1812, an actual revolt failed in 1826, and there was a full pledged slave uprising in 1844. In 1868 a ten-year long war with Spain began but it was not until 1886, some time after all of the other islands had ended slavery, that slavery was abolished in Cuba.

The Cubans attained their freedom from Spain in 1898 with the help of the United States—The Spanish American War. This led to rule by a U.S. military government until pressure by the Cubans for self-rule caused the U.S. to leave in 1902. In addition, there were U.S. interventions in Cuba on several subsequent occasions, including a 1912 rebellion by the colored population. This uprising was the culmination of decades of dissatisfaction with the treatment that the dark skinned Cuban minority of primarily African descent was receiving from the light skinned Cuban majority of primarily Spanish descent. There was racism in Cuba, albeit not as severe a form as that practiced in the United States.

By 1934, the year of Bert's flight, a dictator named Batista had seized control of the government. Like other Latin American dictators, he used the power gained by his coup to continue the exploitation of the people of his country rather than to improve their circumstances. Because of a fear that his coup might precipitate the re-intervention of the United States, he had signed a treaty that year that left a Cuban port called Guantanamo Bay under a long-term lease to the United States. His desire to attain the favor of the United States at that time may have contributed to the success that Bert had in gaining authorization to include the island on his tour and then being welcomed by a dictatorship that had very little in common with the desire of the other islands of the Caribbean to promote goodwill between people.

They arrived in Havana, Cuba at 4:00 P.M., the first land plane to travel between Nassau and Cuba. "I'm glad the weather cleared," said Al in his quiet manner. "Landing would have been quite difficult in a driving rain:

"No question," Bert responded offhandedly. "We were quite fortunate that the storm occurred at sea."

The plane circled the airport once, and then headed for the landing strip. A few hundred yards before landing, Al noticed some unusual activity on the field. As they landed, the calm disappeared from his voice and he cried out excitedly, "Look Bert, those are soldiers with guns running towards us! What is going on?"

"I have no idea," Bert replied with evident concern. "Let's sit still until someone tells us what to do."

They did not have long to wait. One of the soldiers gestured at them with his gun to indicate that they should leave the plane. However just then an officer came running up and got the soldiers to lower their weapons. As Bert and Al disembarked, he apologized in halting English.

"I am sorry señores. You have landed in the military part of the airport. The soldiers were not expecting you and became concerned. Por favor, come with me."

They were then directed to the civilian airport where they found that the surroundings seemed almost military. The circumstances were nothing like they were accustomed to in the United States. Scattered throughout the airport were soldiers who kept their hands resting on large guns that were maintained in an upright position as if to be used at the slightest provocation. Signs prohibited the use of any cameras and warned the visitor not to stray from assigned areas. There was an area set aside for body and luggage search but they were spared this aspect of Cuban welcome because they were being received as if they were diplomats. The usual customs formalities were waived for these goodwill fliers. However their initial reception had none of the warmth that they had experienced in Nassau.

The stultifying effect that a military dictatorship exerts on its people is felt in many ways. As they drove down the streets from the airport the people that he saw walking along seemed less animated than those one saw in the northern United States or Montreal or the Bahamas. Instead he recalled the demeanor of Paddyfoot when he had met him at the railroad station in Tuskegee twenty years before. Another obvious difference between a totalitarian state and a free country was the military vehicles that roamed the city, a sight that he was unaccustomed to.

The reception that they received was more formal than spontaneous but it was very courteous and was covered prominently in the local newspapers. This was not unexpected since he had heard that the government carefully controlled the Cuban newspapers. Bert noted that the number of dark skins that he saw at the reception was less than he had seen in the streets. This led him to question the level of equality between the different ethnic groups in Cuba.

Bert's speech on arrival stressed the goodwill aspects of the tour rather than the effort to reduce prejudice against coloreds. From what he knew of Cuba, the social history was not comparable with that in the United States. Cuba had many famous writers, poets, and artists but the government did not tolerant any political dissent by these groups.

As occurred throughout this trip, their hosts gave them a short history of the island and took them on a brief tour of the city. Havana was by far the largest city in Cuba. It was located on the northwest coast of the island, about 100 miles from Key West, Florida. Their tour took them through the narrow streets of Old Havana, past old houses that were topped with tile, and by the grand Havana Cathedral. In the distance they saw Morro Castle, the fort that had guarded the harbor for almost four hundred years.

Havana was a very popular vacation center for Americans in search of relaxation because it had beautiful beaches, proximity to the mainland, and a nightlife that was notorious. Unfortunately the prosperity that the tourists brought to the island was not equally distributed among the inhabitants of that beautiful country. The city contained some of the largest mansions that Bert had ever seen; the accommodations of the very wealthy in Cuba seemed much more ostentatious than those he had elsewhere in the Caribbean. On the other hand, although his hosts did not take him to the poorer areas, he could see signs of poverty everywhere. The quality of the clothing that ordinary people wore, the condition of their shoes, and the shacks in the distance, all indicated that Cuba, like the other Caribbean nations, had its problems.

They were taken to Military Headquarters where they met the dictator, Colonel Fulgencio Batista. Batista wanted to be sure that there was no recurrence of the episode at the airport earlier in the day so he assigned a captain to be in charge of their visit and gave him the responsibility to notify all military stations of the arrival of these distinguished visitors.

After the greeting by Batista, the captain suggested that they enjoy one of the main attractions for tourists that came to the island--the gambling that was available at nightclubs where the men smoked Cuban cigars that were acknowledged to be the best in the world and drank an excellent rum that challenged Jamaica's rum in the quest to be proclaimed preeminent. They went to a nightclub where they enjoyed an extravagant floorshow that surpassed any that he had seen before and also had an opportunity to observe the activities of the local inhabitants.

The Cuban bands played a rhythmic type of music that was very popular in the United States. The best-known Cuban music was called the rumba. Its beat was different from the ones that were popular in Jamaica yet very similar in its intensity and in its ability to express a willingness to abandon your inhibitions and to release your passions. While there were tables with Cuban couples that spent most of their time in close contact on the dance floor, there were also tables composed of middle-aged men who seemed to be enjoying a culturally acceptable stag night. In these groups there always seemed to be an alpha male that the others deferred to. Bert allowed himself to create a few sociological hypotheses on these observations, sipped from a small glass of rum and coca cola while he watched the floorshow, then retired early.

The next morning they had a breakfast that was decidedly different from those they had had in Nassau. As in the rest of the Caribbean, plantain was popular and other fruits were available. He was unaccustomed to being offered rice or beans at that time of day however. Nevertheless, the food was excellent and an interesting change of pace.

Then it was time to leave Havana and proceed to Santiago, Cuba. The captain had done his job so their second landing in Cuba did not create any confusion. They were feted at ceremonies that were attended by both the mayor of the city and the governor of the province. After a nights rest, they were anxious to leave for the country in which Bert had been raised, Jamaica. While they had been treated well in Cuba, their departure, unlike that from the Bahamas, did not invoke feelings of regret.

In Jamaica, as in the Bahamas, excitement had been running high prior to their arrival. The countries leading newspaper, the *Daily Gleaner,* notified the population of their expected arrival in a front-page article. While Bert was a Bahamian by birth, he had grown up in Jamaica and had a large family, including a prominent father, living on the island. These facts led to a feverish level of involvement throughout the island. Anyone who had ever met him, if even for the briefest of moments, referred to him as a close friend. His actual friends and relatives were extremely proud, especially his father.

Once Bert's plan had been announced, Horatio had been inundated with compliments about his eldest son. The *Daily Gleaner* had interviewed him and gotten a lot of background information on Bert, his struggle with diabetes, and the reasons for his trip. While all Jamaicans understood the importance of advancing the cause of people of color; some did not truly understand the complexity of race relations in the United States and the influences that had led Bert to this undertaking.

Arrangements had been made in advance for the plane to land on the polo grounds at Up Park Camp, a site that could easily accommodate the large crowd that was expected. A telegram had erroneously stated that they would arrive at 8:30 A.M. causing a crowd to gather prematurely. It fell to their ham radio network to inform Kingston that the flight had not left Santiago until 11:30 A.M

In Port Antonio large crowds gathered at different locations with heads tilted towards the northern sky in order to catch sight of the plane that was expected to pass over Port Antonio on its way to Kingston. Even Baa, now almost ninety, joined in the cries at 12:42 P.M. "There they are!! I see them!! Isn't it wonderful!"

Bert was of course at the controls for this triumphant return. He circled Port Antonio, dipped his wings to the crowd, then headed towards St. Margaret's Bay with the intention of crossing over the Blue Mountains. There was however a bank of rain clouds such as those he had routinely encountered in Port Antonio on most fall afternoons in his childhood. Now however the clouds did not seem so routine to him.

"Al, because of these clouds I'm going to change our flight plan and enter Kingston from the east instead of going over the Blue Mountains."

"The clouds and the storm don't look half as bad as those we had going into Cuba," said Al, as a quizzical look crossed over his face. Why lengthen our trip?"

"The Blue Mountains go as high as 7,000 feet in some places Al," was Bert's reply. "It might not seem dangerous, but take my word for it. You don't want to be caught in a down draft over those mountains with poor visibility. We go around and not over."

Around 1:30 P.M., the crowd assembled in Kingston saw the faint speck coming over Kingston Harbor. As was the pair's usual practice, they circled the landing site twice to express their appreciation for those below before descending for their landing. Bert made such a perfect three-point landing that the representative of Pan American Airways who was on hand to oversee Pan Am's commitment to servicing the plane called it the best landing he had ever seen.

A huge crowd, including many of the cities officials, was on hand to greet the pair who stepped out of the plane wearing dark suits, ties, and straw hats. They were not dressed like Lindberg or Amelia Earhart but they were perfectly dressed for the image they wanted to set—that of colored gentlemen on a diplomatic mission. The compliments that they would later be paid confirmed the wisdom of taking the small matter of dress into account.

The first person to greet Bert was Horatio who unashamedly embraced and kissed his son. Also on hand was his brother Roger who had only recently returned to the island, his sister Irma, and May's son Owen who was attending school in Kingston. Among the politicians was Marcus Garvey, a Jamaican who had initiated a huge back to Africa movement in the United States in the 1920's. His old headmaster, Major Plant, was also in attendance. The large pictures that were published in the *Gleaner* showed a group of about forty dignitaries. After the customs formalities, Bert and Al left for a visit with friends and relatives in Kingston.

The next morning they returned to Up Park Camp to a plane that had been fully serviced. On a typical tropical morning of sunshine and cloudless skies they took off in the Booker T. Washington for Port Antonio where two functions had been scheduled. When they approached the site that had been prepared for them, Bert looked down at the harbor, the city, and the area where he thought his home was situated. A deep feeling of nostalgia permeated his very essence. He thought not of the time that he had first left, an untested boy of fourteen, but of the months that he had spent as an adult who had to live at home, almost helpless at first, as he recuperated from the ravages of diabetes. He thought of the effort that his family and friends had made on his behalf, and was anxious to land and express his thanks for all that they had done for him when he had been at death's door.

After descending towards Carder Park, the intended landing site, they concluded that the field was too short to permit a landing. They therefore flew back to Kingston then drove to Port Antonio. The sight of workers in threadbare clothes, and huts on small plots of land that grew a few stands of bananas, reminded him of the island's problems. These were quickly put aside that night when, as in Nassau, there was dancing in the streets, parties, speeches, and a general celebration in the city. What was most special for Bert however was the time that he spent with his family.

The pride that his father had in his accomplishment was obvious. He clearly appreciated having been included in the center of attention at the landing in Kingston and his invitation to the upcoming meeting with the Governor. His siblings were equally proud of the accomplishments of their brother and the opportunity to visit with him. Since his last visit, his sister May had had a fourth child, George, now a

BANANA HARVEST
COLLECTION OF RUTH FORSYTH

rascally six-year old who delighted in creating mischief among the large contingent of relatives who had gathered for the occasion. The other sisters, except young Carmen, had all married fairly recently and did not yet have any children. The eldest of his younger brothers, Lorenzo, had just gotten married and had come to live with his bride in his father's home along with his youngest brothers, Harvey and John. His brother Roger was now also living in Port Antonio with his family. He had gotten married in Toledo in 1928 and now had two daughters with a third child due within a week.

Roger had completed his studies and had graduated cum laude with degrees in pharmacy and chemistry. Although he graduated cum laude, this had not been mentioned at his graduation. He was later sent a letter of apology, but harbored the suspicion that the failure to recognize him was due to his color. Was this conviction a reflection of the instinctive paranoia with which people who are constantly subjected to prejudice react? Given the climate in the United States, both Bert and Roger suspected that the action was deliberate.

After his graduation from Toledo University Roger had written Bert and Horatio that he was unable to find a job in either of his fields and was continuing to work on the railroad where he supervised a group of dining car waiters. The Depression had made it difficult for any 1932 graduate to find a professional position but everyone knew that because of the prevailing discrimination, color was an impediment to finding a professional position in the United States in the best of times. A colored pharmacist would have to rely on the colored community for patronage since very few in the white community could be expected to have the confidence that a colored could be competent. Roger's experiences personified the type of prejudice that Bert was fighting.

Early in 1934 Horatio had made a trip to Decatur, Illinois where Roger was living with his wife Ruth and his two girls, June and Mary Ann and requested that he return to Port Antonio. Horatio's second wife Juanita had died, and Horatio missed having an adult female available to supervise the house. Consequently Roger and Ruth were asked to bring their family to Port Antonio and live in the unoccupied portion of his six-bedroom house. He also offered to help Roger financially so that he could open a pharmacy in Port Antonio. With no immediate prospect of practicing his profession in the United States, Roger agreed and moved to Jamaica.

Roger's plan to live at the family home in Port Antonio had fallen through with the marriage of his brother Lorenzo in the interval between Horatio's offer and Roger's arrival in Jamaica. The house now had a mistress and did not need, and probably could not have survived, the presence of a second adult female in a supervisory position. With the offer of free lodgings in Port Antonio withdrawn, Roger no longer felt restricted to opening a pharmacy in Port Antonio.

He applied for a position as a chemist with the Soap and Edible Products Company in Kingston. That company dealt with coconuts and coconut products. Normally such a job with a foreign owned company was considered to be 'a white man's job'—not so much because prejudice precluded the hiring of a colored person but primarily because most professional skills had to be imported. In America he was totally shut out but here in Jamaica there was some opportunity. However, instead of opening a pharmacy in Port Antonio, the city of his birth, Roger would be working at a factory in Kingston.

In time Roger would prove that intelligence was not inextricably linked to the color of ones skin. While previous chemists at the company had contented themselves with simply repeating routine tests on the quality of their established products, Roger was able to innovate and develop processes that found new uses for the oil of the coconut. With his direction, the company began to manufacture margarine from coconut oil. Roger independently began to market an imitation form of vanilla and a soap that he named Lady June after his daughter.

Bert was delighted that the brother with whom he had shared the years of financial deprivations, the cold winters of Ohio, and the parties and picnics, was present at his return. In private moments they spoke of their childhood in Port Antonio and their shared memories of the hardships they had endured in the 1920's. When they finally had finished reminiscing and caught up with all that had happened since their last visit, Roger told Bert that he wanted to do something to recognize all the help that his brother had given him over the years.

On a pleasantly warm tropical night, under a sky iridescent with unpolluted starlight, seated on the veranda where they had spent so many years, Roger expressed his admiration for his older brother. "Bert, as you know Ruth is over eight months pregnant. We are hoping that it is a boy since we already have two girls. If it is a boy, Ruth and I have decided to name him Roger Albert to recognize your trip and what you are trying to accomplish. Everyone is really proud of what you are doing. I must confess however that I'm a bit nervous about your flying. Promise that you will be careful."

A sense of warmth suddenly appeared across Bert's back as a pleasurable sensation spread over his entire body then quickly disappeared. The affinity that these two had was more like that of identical twins than siblings who were separated in age by three years. "I'm flattered that you want to use my name as your son's middle name," said Bert, his deep smile leaving no doubt about his reaction to the offer. "With two girls you're due for a boy. For both of us, I hope that it will be a boy. The way I am going it looks as if there won't be an Albert Jr. so Roger Albert would be the next best thing. Who knows, maybe he will be a physician or a pilot when he grows up. Hopefully it will be easier for people of color to enter every profession by then."

Bert sat back in his chair and continued with a more somber air. "As far as the danger, don't worry. We are of course very careful. If I told you about all of our near misses, you would probably have a heart attack. Takeoffs and landings present the most danger so we try to anticipate the problems and correct for them. For example we wrote ahead everywhere and asked that landing sites be smoothed and potential obstructions such as telephone wires be removed. We didn't think to tell the Bahamians that they should not run onto the landing site. As a result, we almost had a catastrophe there."

"Then on our way to Havana we ran into a rainstorm that you wouldn't take a car into much less an aeroplane. That <u>was</u> scary. We also had a problem landing in Havana. By mistake we landed at the military part of the airport among lots of heavily armed men. Take it from me, you don't want to make men with guns nervous, especially in a country that has a military dictatorship. Yesterday we were careful to go around the Blue Mountains instead of over them when we saw them covered in clouds and today we drove to port Antonio instead of risking a landing on the short field at Carder Park. Al and I are not risk takers who are trying to generate publicity for ourselves. What we want is to create goodwill and further the cause of the colored man in a white man's world."

Now his face took on a different countenance, his posture changed ever so slightly. He expressed a mixture of emotions and philosophy that gave his brother a fresh view of his character. "Flying an airplane is the most thrilling thing that I have ever done or will ever do. You must always expect the unexpected. You are like a bird that can go in any direction at any time; the whole world is spread out below you and it is beautiful. I can't begin to describe to you the fantastic things that I have seen. Mountains, oceans, rivers, cities, deserts, swamps all look different from the sky."

"While there is the danger of death, the danger makes you feel alive. When you are up there you have to worry about lightning, wind, hail, heat, fog, rain, and turbulence. And you feel fear; you come to know that fear comes dressed in many different clothes. There is the immediate fear of death at times but there is also the fear caused by anticipation. The anticipation that you might fail and disappoint those who supported you is perhaps the greatest fear of all. Yet fear is not necessarily bad because fear can stimulate you to act quickly or motivate you to do things that you did not realize that you could do."

Then Bert concluded their conversation with a bit of prophesy such as older brothers are wont to pass on to their younger siblings, siblings whose own opinions will always be somewhat suspect simply because they will be espoused by someone who is younger. "Aviation is going to make the train and automobile seem like the horse and buggy. There is no doubt that it will change the future in ways that we cannot begin to imagine. It is growing so fast that soon every city will have a decent airfield and the danger from faulty landing strips will be eliminated. And the colored man will participate fully in the future."

The flood of memories that developed whenever Bert departed seemed to be less pronounced with each departure. As he prepared to leave for Kingston the next morning, a flash of memories caused him to visualize his past—the multicolored kites, the bullas, the patties, and grater cakes that he ate, the Champaign Colas that he drank, and the nude swims in the warm ocean. His mind shut out the agonies that he experienced while recovering from the diabetes and dwelled instead on the trips to Kingston that he made during that year and the parties that he had attended. Then they said their goodbyes and his mind was emptied of these thoughts as they drove through the lush tropical countryside on their way back to Kingston.

In the island's capital, Bert and Al, with Horatio in attendance, were received at 11:30 A.M. at Government House by His Excellency, Sir Edward Denham for a period of one hour. The U.S. Consul Calvin Oakes was present as was Marcus Garvey. Bert presented Sir Denham with a copy of the scroll from the Goodwill Committee and with the letter from the Bahamas that Sir Clifford had sent. Then, at 2:30 P.M., the Ward Theater, resplendent with decoration provided by the welcoming committee, was opened to the public so that they could participate in the occasion. At 8 P.M., there was a large dinner at South Camp Road Hotel.

At the dinner many, many speeches were given. Noteworthy was that of the Rev. Mr. Jacobs who said, "..in the modern world today the aeroplane is an instrument of warfare and it has been left to two coloured gentlemen to employ that instrument.....to decide to outbid Lindbergh and all other aviators by using the aeroplane to bind the peoples of the races of the earth. Dr. Forsythe and Mr. Anderson have outbid all the aviators of all nations of the world, not for any trophy, not for any 10,000 pounds, not on behalf of any commercial transatlantic aeroplane organization, but in order to bring God's glory."

Bert and Al, with the customary humility that endeared them to all those that they met, spent their speaking time giving credit to the Goodwill committee and many of those in the United States and locally who had participated in the planning and execution. Speakers who had attended school in the United States spoke affectionately of the education that they had received there and the capabilities of colored Americans. On the other hand, Major Plant, the long retired headmaster from Titchfield secondary school in Port Antonio, could not resist endorsing the superiority of an English education over an American one by recalling how

15-year old Bert had outshone the 25-year old students at Tuskegee.

Around noon on the next day a crowd of hundreds gathered to see them off. Marcus Garvey came with a case of rum for the fliers but Bert declined inasmuch as every extra pound affected their mileage. When they had been offered baskets of food in the past, Bert's refusal to accept them had led Al to say, "If Bert has a fault, it is that when he is into something, eating is completely unimportant to him."

The next leg of their goodwill flight would cover 288 miles and take them due east to Port-au-Prince, Haiti. The contacts that Roger and his father had in Haiti and with Haitian organizations in the United States had provided Bert with assurances that a proper landing site would be available. However the day before the maid at his father's house had been concerned about something besides landing sites. When the opportunity had arisen for her to speak to him privately she spoke in the hushed tones reserved for important confidences and in a patois accent that he now found difficult to decipher.

"Them have a lot of duppies in Haiti, Mr. Bert. Them have powerful obeah and voodoo there. Yu be careful them don't turn yu into a zombie!"

Bert had thanked her for her concern and smiled inwardly. He had forgotten about some of the superstitions and religions that prevailed in the West Indies. In Jamaica, a duppie referred to the spirit of a dead person that at times could be found residing in a silk cotton tree. Its existence was usually invoked in an effort to frighten small children who were not behaving themselves. Obeah referred to a white magic whose practitioners could be called on to cast spells or remove them. If you were having a problem with your love live, a practitioner of obeah, for a small fee, could cast a spell and solve your problem.

Haitians had their own versions of strange creatures and unusual religions. Zombies were people who had been drugged into a stupor, buried, then resurrected in an enslaved state where they had no will of their own and could be called on to do terrible things. Voodoo was a native form of religion that was hard to describe because there were so many versions. During voodoo rites, participants often engaged in frenetic dances that seemed physically intolerable to an outsider. It permeated even the recognized religions in Haiti and was greatly feared in other countries where the origins and aims of voodoo were generally misunderstood.

With the warnings of the maid just barely in his conscious thoughts, Bert took off for Haiti. He never failed to marvel at the beauty that lay below him in Jamaica. It was not just that it was located in the tropics—Havana was also in a tropical setting but the topography was not as magnificent. No, he concluded, his admiration was not parochial but realistic. He watched the island fade from view and mentally prepared for his next stop in Haiti.

The landing site for airplanes was outside of the city of Port-au-Prince. As a result, the size of the crowd that was present when they landed was not as impressive as it had been in Nassau and Kingston. That changed once they made their way into the city where their arrival had been eagerly awaited. The Haitians were clearly excited to have these visitors who represented a welcome change of pace from the monotony of their daily lives. They took full advantage of the opportunity to engage in a general celebration that included some very uninhibited street dancing to a rhythmic movement that could easily have been part of a voodoo ritual.

The poverty that Roger had described in his letters almost twenty years before was clearly in evidence. There were fewer sidewalks and paved roads than existed in Jamaica and street cleaning did not seem to be a high priority. The attire of the common man in Haiti was not impressive; they wore tattered shirts and patched trousers that ended above feet that often had never worn a shoe.

Women on the other hand caught your eye with a cornucopia of color created by the multicolored scarves that they wore on their heads and the solid bright colored blouses and skirts that swirled, whether they were dancing or simply walking, over buttocks that were quite ample by western standards.

For the people of a country with an illiteracy rate of over 90%, the sociological significance of a flight that was intended to promote the cause of blacks in aviation or goodwill between Caribbean countries was not their primary concern. They did not have the irritant of a significant white power structure that was promoting suppression on racial grounds. Instead there was a very small ruling elite, often very dark-complexioned, whose sartorial elegance was in marked contrast to the attire of the masses, and whose dominance was based on military force and class rather than on race.

The President, Stenio Vicente, received the aviators at the Presidential Palace. He praised them profusely, decorated them with an order of distinction termed the "Honor of Merit", and made them honorary citizens of Haiti. The next day they were guests at a reception given by the newspapermen of Haiti. To honor their arrival, a troop of boy scouts marched by their hotel. Their days and evenings were filled with parades, speeches, and heartfelt appreciation.

While in Haiti they met with some of the influential members of the society as well as the American consul. The United States had played a major role in Haitian affairs over the years. Bert recalled that it was the United States intervention in 1915 that had encouraged his brother Roger to go there to seek his first job. U.S. control of Haiti had lasted from 1915 until earlier in 1934 when control was turned over to the Haitian government that had been elected in 1930.

The Goodwill Flight fit perfectly into Roosevelt's efforts to improve the reputation of the United States in the region. The interventions of the United States into the affairs of Haiti, Cuba, the Dominican Republic, and Puerto Rico had created a marked ambivalence in their interrelations. American intervention, even when it had eliminated a repressive rule and provided economic benefits, created resentment. The invader and the invaded both wanted to improve their relations.

Bert also met with acquaintances of his brother Roger and his father. Communication was not a problem as most educated Haitians spoke English with the beautiful slur characteristic of French-speaking people. In these conversations he confirmed that the elite had very little respect for the common man and very little concern for their future.

While he was in Haiti he found that the fatigue that develops after a full day of tours and other activities was accompanied by a desire to stay awake for a while after retiring in order to reflect on the different problems of different societies. These ruminations never seemed to result in any conclusions. Americans in both the North and the South, Mormons, French Canadians, Bahamians, Cubans, Jamaicans, and now Haitians. Segments of the population in each society seemed to be repressed in ways that were different yet similar. Eventually other thoughts would interrupt that train of thought, he would sense that his level of consciousness was declining, and a deep sleep would ensue.

Three days passed and it was time for another flight. Today they would only fly over land inasmuch as Haiti shared the island originally named Hispaniola with their next stop, the Dominican Republic. On their flight from Port-au-Prince they planned to follow a valley called the Cul-de-Sac past the sub sea level Lake Enriquillo and then along the southern coastline towards the major city of the country, Santo Domingo.

On December 6, 1492, during his first voyage to the new world, Christopher Columbus landed on the island. On January 1, 1494 he established a 1,200-man outpost on the northern shore to search for gold. In 1496, La Nueva Isabella, now called Santo Domingo, was established on the southern shore. This city is the oldest in the Western Hemisphere to be founded by Europeans.

People of purely African descent were in a minority in the Dominican Republic. The population was 15% white, 20% black, and 65% of a Spanish-African mixture. The country had a chaotic political history. A gold rush there in the first half of the sixteenth century had led to the decimation of the native Indian population and the importation of African slaves. This was followed by a period of neglect then an era of competition between Spain and France as the Spanish decision to consolidate their settlers near Santo Domingo allowed settlers from other countries to occupy parts of the island. In 1697 Spain ceded the western one-third of the island, the area now know as Haiti, to France.

The two countries developed independently; after the French Revolution, the Haitian slaves revolted against the French and took over the whole island briefly in 1801. The Haitians again gained control from 1821 to 1844. Mismanagement by the Dominicans led the United States to take over the collection of customs duties in 1905 in order to pay outstanding European debts. The U.S. also assumed military control from 1915 to 1924 when the country became chaotic. In 1930, four years before Bert's arrival, a dictator named Trujillo assumed control.

Bert was mentally reviewing this history of the country when the ennui of flight was again interrupted by the terror of the unexpected. While flying at 2,000 feet over Lake Enriquillo in the Nayce valley of the province of Barahona, without any warning, a cylinder cracked and the plane began to lose power. "We're going to have to land almost immediately," cautioned Al as his usually confident demeanor barely managed to mask the gravity of the situation. "I saw a dry lake bed behind us, to the west of Lake Enriquillo. I want to put down there."

The bed of a dry lake is hardly the optimal place to attempt to land an airplane. There are rocks, depressions, elevations, and often the remains of trees or other detritus that create potentially lethal obstacles. Somewhat desperately their eyes scanned the vicinity in search of a site that seemed relatively clear and smooth.

Meanwhile the welcoming committee in Santo Domingo waited. The expected time of arrival came and went with no sign of the plane. Fifteen minutes passed then thirty. The ham radio operators in Haiti were contacted. "Had the fliers left on time?"

"Yes," came the reply. "They should be there by now."

Now the level of concern among those assembled was palpable. One of the officials present contacted the Dominican military and asked that a plane be dispatched to search for survivors to the presumed crash. After several hours the would-be rescuers radioed back that they had been unsuccessful in finding any sign of the plane or the fliers.

The landing of the Booker T. Washington had required skill, but more than that it had required luck, a commodity that had been generously supplied up until that point. Fortunately luck was still their patron and as Al skillfully found a relatively clear area before descending the last few feet, luck decreed that there would be no hidden objects that would cause a crash. They landed with a minimum of damage to the plane and considered their options.

"I saw some buildings about a half dozen miles up ahead," said Bert as he hopped out of the monocoupe. "I'm sure they will come looking for us but we shouldn't count on that. First of all, they might not find us right away. Second, even if they find us, they would have a problem landing."

"Agreed," said Al. "The sooner we get started, the sooner we can see to the repairs."

It was a seven-mile hike to the buildings that they had seen. It turned out that they were part of a military outpost with a rudimentary landing field and a radio that had been in contact with Santo Domingo. When the adventurers arrived, a radio message was sent out and a military plane was dispatched from Santo Domingo to pick them up.

Messages that told of the planes failure to arrive in Santo Domingo had been sent out to Atlantic City, Nassau, Kingston, and other sites shortly after the ham radio operators had confirmed that the plane was overdue. When the news arrived that the fliers were unharmed, the apprehension that had been felt was replaced with rejoicing.

With aviation in its infancy, there was no expectation that parts such as a cylinder for a Lambert would be available in a small country like the Dominican Republic. After diagnosing the problem they wired to St. Louis and received a reply that told them to expect the part in approximately one week. These unexpected events interfered with the timetable for their reception, but eventually the planned activities were carried out.

Once again the two fliers received a reception worthy of a head of state and were asked to attend dinners and speak of their experiences. The government offered to assume all of their expenses during their prolonged stay. With time on their hands, they had much more time for sightseeing that on their previous stopovers. They particularly enjoyed the opportunity to ride about on horseback and enjoy their own company without the restraints of a cramped cockpit or the presence of an official delegation.

On several occasions they decided to simply wander about the city. During one of these strolls, while relaxing in a park, two Jamaicans in their early twenties spoke to them.

LAYOVER IN SANTO DOMINGO

"We want you to know that you have the deep felt appreciation of all West Indians, mon," said one. "It is a marvelous ting that you are doing. Now everyone will know that blacks are a people who can do anyting."

Bert and Al thanked their well-wishers, little realizing that they would ever hear from them again, and continued their walk through the city, the capital of the Dominican Republic as well as the largest city in the country. The son of Christopher Columbus, Diego, became governor in 1509 and built a residence along the front of the Ozama River, the Alcázar de Colón. The site contains the oldest university, monastery, and hospital in the Western Hemisphere. A major attraction for the sightseers was the Cathedral of Santo Domingo, completed in 1540 by Diego Columbus. Christopher Columbus had been interred in Seville in 1505, exhumed and reinterred at this cathedral in 1542, and supposedly returned to Seville in 1796. The Santo Dominicans insisted to their visitors that the wrong bones had been sent to Spain and that the remains of Christopher Columbus were still in Santo Domingo.

Although most of the city had been destroyed by a hurricane that hit the island four years before their visit, the dictator Rafael Trujillo had done an excellent job of reconstructing the city. They were particularly impressed by the reconstruction done in the old walled area of town known as the Zona Colonial. They also were offered a visit to witness a popular national pastime, cock fighting, but they declined. They did enjoy going to clubs where they could listen to the sounds of drums that were accompanied by maracas, dried gourds that contain seeds, while watching the rhythmic dancing of the local population.

In the countryside, the majority of people were farmers who either owned their own farm or worked as sharecroppers. Living standards were not high; many farmers lived in thatched roofed two-room shacks with dirt floors. Tobacco was a major crop, especially near the north shore town of Puerto Plata where German tobacco traders made fortunes and built large mansions. In other areas the main crop was sugar cane.

Because many Dominicans either owned their land or were self-employed, the problems of discrimination and prejudice were not as severe as they were in other Caribbean countries where coloreds, although in the majority numerically, were in the minority economically. The major problem for coloreds here was not the lack of an opportunity to make money but the fact that the money that was made was siphoned off by the dictatorship.

Their welcoming ceremonies did not seem to be as impressive as those that they had received in Nassau, Haiti, and Jamaica. In those countries the majority of the population was of primarily African descent and their welcome was given in English. Was the difference in reception due to color? Or could it have been the language barrier, the disruption in scheduling created by the plane's malfunction, or the effect of the dictatorship? They could not be sure. Having lived in a society where color was all-important, there was always a suspicion that any untoward circumstance might be color related.

While they wondered about the difference, they had no complaints. The signs of dictatorship, so evident in Cuba, were somewhat muted in Santo Domingo. The presence of the military was evident, much more so than in the Bahamas or Jamaica where they were rarely seen, but not as oppressively evident as in Cuba. Meanwhile Mary Washington continued to generate publicity for the flight. On November 27th Louis Howe, Secretary to the President, sent a letter acknowledging receipt of copies of the scrolls being delivered to the islands.

The delay initially estimated at one week stretched to three weeks but eventually the part for their airplane arrived and was installed, and on a Saturday, the 8th of December, they departed from Santo Domingo and flew slightly northeast to San Juan, Puerto Rico. Like Cuba, Puerto Rico had been chafing under Spanish control prior to 1900. Ironically, just as the Spanish granted greater local rule to the Puerto Ricans, the Spanish American War of 1898 occurred and Spain surrendered control of the island to the United States. Soon thereafter Puerto Rico became an American territory and benefited from extensive U.S. construction of infrastructure, especially schools. Spanish was the native language of Puerto Ricans but many also learned English in school. As in other Spanish speaking countries, most of the population was Catholic.

In 1917 Puerto Ricans were granted American citizenship but were exempted from the payment of United States taxes as long as they remained on the island. With citizenship came the freedom to migrate to the United States at will, a freedom that many utilized.

Based on what he had read, Bert realized that Puerto Rico had had a much different ethnic development than any of the countries they had visited to date. Their slave population had not been as large, they had not had multiple slave revolts, and the friction level seemed palpably lower. There was a small colored population, approximately 10 per cent, the majority of whom lived along the coast.

He was told that the major concern on the island was not race but a debate about the status that should exist between the island and the mainland. Puerto Ricans had benefited from the investments made on their island by the United States; they appreciated the combination of citizenship without taxation; but they were divided about the fact that their country was not completely independent. Some wanted total separation from the United States; others favored various forms of association. At times these factions could be violent.

After their arrival, their hosts insisted that they take a short tour of the city. The most striking area was known as Viejo San Juan. In old San Juan the narrow cobblestone streets meandered by pastel-colored buildings with balconies that fronted filigreed wrought iron windows similar to those he had encountered in Haiti. There were plazas adorned with weatherworn statues, mosaic-tiled churches, and gardens filled with hibiscus, bougainvillea, and fountains. A short distance away were the forts that had been erected centuries before in order to protect the city from pirates and from other great powers.

El Morro, the older of the two forts, had 20-foorthick walls and six levels of canons that protected the city from the sea. The fort successfully repelled Sir Francis Drake in 1595 while sinking ten of his ships. It also survived a bombardment by the United States Navy in the 1898 Spanish-American War. The structure was truly impressive.

The other fort, San Cristobal, was completed in the 1780's to protect the sides of the city. It contained a moat and so many rows of fortifications that had it ever been tested, it probably would have been impregnable. The final element of the compound was Ballaja Barracks that had housed the Spanish who defended the city.

That night they were guests at a huge reception that included Governor Winthrop. The presence of a large contingent of Tuskegee graduates on the island was evident from the program of the reception where the names of 42 graduates of Tuskegee were listed and the words of the Tuskegee school song were written in Spanish. The San Juan newspapers, *El Imparcial* and *El Mundo, and El Dia,* the newspaper established at Ponce on the south coast of the island in 1909, carried excerpts of the speeches.

While in San Juan they received a telegram from the mayor Bernier in Banos de Coamo inviting them to visit his city the next day. First they visited the rain forest of Puerto Rico, familiarly known as El Yunque. Bert had always bragged about the lushness of the Jamaican countryside but not that day. When they entered the rainforest, a steady mist punctuated by bursts of showers created waterfalls and streams that nourished giant ferns, wild orchids, sierra palms, and a multitude of flowers. The forest seemed to sing as thousands of tiny "coquies" or tree frogs traded serenades with uncatalogued varieties of birds. The sight and sounds were impressive.

After lunch at the Hotel Melia there was a reception at Casa Ayuntamento. Two bands played for them and the assembled crowd in the Plaza Munoz Rivera. That night there was a reception in the club Juan Morell Campos.

Much later they would receive a rambling letter from a Puerto Rican who urged Bert not to believe what he had been told about comity of race relations in Puerto Rico. The validity of the letter could not be verified so Bert never paid any attention to it but it was a reminder that race could be a problem anywhere.

Shortly before their scheduled departure on the third day, they received a wire from Bert's father in Port Antonio. Trinidad had finally wired the necessary authorization for them to land; they were in fact very enthusiastic about the visit. With that good news, the pair got ready to say goodbye to Puerto Rico and take up the next leg of their trip, to the airport that Lindberg had called one of the six worst in the hemisphere, on St. Thomas in the Virgin Islands.

The Virgin Islands were divided into two groups, one under British control that was usually referred to as the British Virgin Islands, the other group of three small islands and many tiny islets were under American control and usually referred to simply as the Virgin Islands. The American islands were only forty miles from the easternmost portion of Puerto Rico in the chain of islands known as the Lesser Antilles.

The history of the Virgin Islands reflected the power struggles that went on between the European powers in the seventeenth to nineteenth century, and the emergence of American influence. Columbus claimed the islands for Spain in 1493; Dutch and English settled St. Croix in 1625 but were driven out by Spaniards from Puerto Rico in 1650 who in turn were driven out by the French in 1670 who in turn sold the islands to Denmark in 1733. Denmark established a settlement on St. Thomas in 1666, and then claimed St. John in 1717. The British occupied the Danish islands in the 1790's and again from 1807 to 1815. Finally the Danes sold their islands to America in 1917 and the islanders became American citizens in 1927.

There was a slave uprising on St. Johns in 1733 and another on St. Croix in 1848 that led to the immediate abolition of slavery as the Danes realized that the islands were too small and too hilly to be profitable. The checkered history of the island combined with its proximity to Puerto Rico and affiliation with the U.S. led to a population that was about 60 per cent black, 20 per cent white, and 20 per cent mixed with over 10 per cent of the inhabitants being born in Puerto Rico and almost 10 per cent being born in the U.S.

St. Thomas had only one city, Charlotte Amalie, where 10,000 people resided and the painter Camille Pissarro had been born. This, the capitol of the Virgin Islands and also the largest city, was situated by an excellent harbor that served the entire chain of islands. The landing site for the plane was a golf course that ran in a north south direction to the west of the city. They had been advised however that if the winds necessitated an east west landing, they were to use the field and addition that was north of the broken windmill. For Nassau they had used a lighthouse for orientation, in St. Thomas it would be a windmill.

With Lindberg's warning heightening the normal apprehension that occurred each time that they prepared to land, the pair exercised extra caution as they performed their customary circle before landing. The field they were to land on was a very short one that was flanked by a low hill that limited the room that they had to maneuver. Fortunately the local population had enough respect for the danger posed by the landing site that they did not invade the airstrip as the Bahamians had done. After circling and determining that everything was in order, Al was able to execute another perfect landing.

The arrival of a plane was a major event that brought out every inhabitant of the city that was physically able to attend. The Governor, Mr. Pearson, was their host. The celebration was not as boisterous as in Nassau or Haiti, but it was obvious that the people were quite appreciative of their inclusion in this tour. As recently proclaimed citizens of the United States, they welcomed the arrival of two men of color and their message that all was possible for all Americans. Bert and Al were pleased to be asked to address many schoolchildren and several gatherings.

Their sightseeing was limited on this small island. They drove up the steep Crystal Gade to see the St. Thomas Synagogue that had been built in 1833 by Sephardic Jews. Then they went to the Grand Hotel for lunch. Later they were taken to Magens Bay where they had a drink and enjoyed the quiet beauty.

After an overnight stay, it was time for their departure to the island of Grenada, located in the group termed the Windward Islands. Once again they tensed as they prepared to navigate their limited pathway. Departure was not as dangerous as landing inasmuch as they did not have to worry about unexpected ditches or errant pedestrians. Still the uncertainties of flying were great. A sudden gust of wind might force them into the water or into the hill. However takeoff was uneventful and they were relaxed as they flew over St. Croix and St. Christopher on route to their next destination.

Grenada was a dependency of Great Britain with a population that was 95 per cent African or mixed. A large proportion of the remaining people were descended from East Indians who came there after the abolition of slavery in 1834. The others consisted of various Europeans. Again, the whites were generally in positions of influence, the blacks, because of their numbers, did not have much social discrimination but did feel an economic discrimination. The East Indians also felt some discriminatory pressure. The ignominy of slavery had left its residual effect on all populations.

The country produced nutmeg and a spice called mace in addition to bananas, sugar cane, and coconuts. This led some to call it the Spice Island although that name is generally associated with an island group in the Pacific. At 4:35, Bert and Al were welcomed at Queens Park in the capital city of St. George, a town of less than 10,000 on the southwest coast of the island. Once again they were the beneficiaries of dinners and speeches. The pride that the inhabitants felt about their historic trip and the publicity that two colored men were receiving was quite evident.

The first stop of the city tour that they were given was at Fort George, built in 1705 by the French. Next they were taken to the half-moon-shaped harbor of the city and the lovely Anse beach. They had no time to visit the interior of the island, the site of many waterfalls and the groves of the nutmeg trees that had made the island famous.

The departure from Grenada on Thursday was not routine. On one attempt they developed a flat tire and had to abort. They also experienced gusts of headwinds that were estimated at 30-35 miles per hour—enough to impede their takeoff. All in all they made three attempts at departure before they were successful at 10:30 A.M. and were able to fly 90 miles south over a period of one hour and five minutes to Trinidad, an island that had been united with the smaller island of Tobago in 1898.

This was another country with a ping-pong history due to the machinations of the great European powers. Spaniards settled Trinidad in the late sixteenth century, many French settlers came throughout the eighteenth century, and Britain captured it in 1797. Tobago was colonized by the Dutch in the early seventeenth century and was fought over by the Dutch, French, and English until Great Britain won control in 1814.

The population of the island was quite dense and consisted mainly of those of African descent and East Indians. There was also the usual cadre of financially influential whites. The large East Indian contingent enjoyed some commercial success and this success at times led to some resentment by the blacks towards the East Indians. In addition to these groups, there remained pockets of people who spoke French or Spanish as their ancestors had done. The French influence accounts for the extremely popular pre-Lenten festival known as Carnival that featured days of dancing by people in highly colorful costumes.

Trinidadians had a reputation of being a fun-loving people. Their music had a distinctive beat that had been given the name of Calypso and adopted by other islands in the West Indies including Jamaica. Although the island was only seven miles away from the mainland of South America, to which it had been linked in pre-historic times, the temperament of its peoples was much more like that in Jamaica and the other islands of the Caribbean that had developed under British influence than like the temperament of the Spanish speaking countries of South America.

Their flight plan called for a landing from the direction of Tucker Valley at Mucuropo in the capital city of Port-of-Spain. Pan American had been servicing the city by sea since 1929 but theirs was the first land plane. As they exited the clouds they saw that they were dealing with another short runway, one that was close to a populated area. They dipped low to acknowledge the crowd below, and flew over the city briefly. From the air the city was well laid out and appeared to be very clean. After circling, they swung over the harbor, banked, and then descended. Despite the potential obstacles, they were able to land without any difficulty and alight from their plane to a wildly cheering crowd.

In spite of the efforts of the constables provided to maintain order, the large crowd that had assembled almost crushed the pair in their attempt to touch them and give congratulations. When a semblance of order was restored, they were received by a large group of dignitaries including the American Vice Consul, Mr. C. Christiani and the mayor, whose full title was His Worship the Mayor, Captain the Honorable A. A. Cipriano. The plane was turned over to a representative of Pan American, Mr. Bearden, for refueling and servicing. Then it was on to Government House where they were welcomed by the Governor. Later they proceeded to Town Hall, had lunch at the Hotel de Paris, attended receptions in the afternoon, and were guests for dinner at the Sands Hotel.

In an interview with the Port-of-Spain Gazette, Bert said, "The flight is a goodwill flight in every sense of the word. It is being made to bring about better feelings between races and peoples of the Western Hemisphere and it is unique from the fact that this is the first enterprise of its kind to be attempted by members of the coloured race. But it is not supported only by members of the coloured race. By using the air plane we focus attention on our mission in a way that nothing else can do, and by our receptions, our addresses, the scroll that we carry, the contacts that we make, we hope to establish those firmer bonds of friendship that are our objective."

Later, in a speech at the reception held in their honor, Bert thanked those assembled and those in the United States then said, "We are trying to foster through this programe the idea of democracy, meaning an equal opportunity for all people everywhere regardless of race, creed, colour, or religion, or anything. When we go if we can leave behind the thought and idea that we would like, that our people of America would like the people of this country to think a little more about our country, do a little more towards friendship between the people, to do a little more in all ways towards

**THE GOVERNOR, HIS FAMILY
AND OFFICIALS**

creating friendships and towards giving every man and woman a better opportunity to live and be men and women, we shall feel that our trip has been well worth while."

The message was clear to all those of color. While the goodwill aspects of the trip were stressed in the scrolls that they brought and the speeches that they made, equal opportunity for people of color was of paramount importance.

Al, as usual, was brief but well spoken. "Your Worship, Councilors, and friends, I should like to say that this flight that we are making is not a stunt flight, we are not trying to break any records or promote aviation, we are simply making a flight to try and improve our relations and get a better understanding between all people."

After the reception they were taken to the balcony of the Town Hall where the mayor introduced them to the waiting crowd in Woodford Square. They gave short addresses to the crowd and were rewarded with resounding cheers in appreciation of their efforts and their demeanor.

On Friday December 14th it was time to leave the friends that they had made. Shortly before their departure they sent a telegram to British Guiana to let them know the expected time of their arrival. As the hour of their departure drew close, a fairly large crowd gathered to see them off on a day that seemed warm despite a moderate breeze. They said their goodbyes, climbed aboard the plane, warmed up the engine, taxied to the end of the field, and accelerated down the runway.

The plane quickly reached takeoff velocity. The pilot pulled back on the controls and began the ascent. Without warning, the breeze that had been moderate became gusty as it traversed the mountain ahead of them and created a strong downdraft. As is usual in such conditions, there was a lot of confusion as to the exact sequence of events that followed.

Some reports state that the plane brushed against a strand of bamboo and headed for a row of houses. Bert and

Al believed that the problem had been the downdraft. In any event, Al was at the controls, a fortunate circumstance given his great skill as a pilot. To the onlookers, it seemed as if he considered a forced landing on a city street then thought better of it when he saw the amount of traffic. Straight ahead of the plane was the row of bungalows that had to be avoided at all costs. Decisions had to be made in nanoseconds. There was no opportunity to discuss or to equivocate—one had to rely on instinct and judgment and act immediately. Al was superbly qualified for a situation such as this. With great skill he managed to turn the plane towards a fifty-foot wide backyard, away from the car-strewn street, away from the houses filled with people. Then, with a sickening shattering of wood, the plane tore through a fence and came to rest in some bushes between two houses.

The crowd surged forward in alarm, expecting the worst. Instead, they saw Bert step out, completely unscathed, while Al had a minor scratch. Miraculously, no one on the ground was injured. The skill that Al had used in landing the plane was unbelievable. However the plane had had major damage. The sound that all had heard was the smashing of the front of the plane beyond repair. A battered and defeated Booker T. Washington had come to an end, a victim of a downdraft, one of the many forces of Nature.

After making sure that no one had been injured and gathering their thoughts, Bert and Al proceeded to survey the situation. Fortunately there was no sign of a fire. Nevertheless their first action was to check the attachments on the auxiliary tank for signs of a fuel leak. After assuring that there were not any leaks, they turned their attention to the plane. The extensive nature of the damage to the propeller, the front of the plane, and the wing was self-evident. The dream was over. The rude awakening was here.

Whereas they had been totally fearless during the emergency, now that it was over, they felt a weakness in their legs and a sinking sensation in their abdomens, as they

CRASH OF THE BOOKER T. WASHINGTON

understood just how close they had come to death. The adrenalin that had primed their bodies to act in the emergency had drained away and they were left with a vague sensation of emptiness. Despite the warmth of the day, they felt a chill envelop them

At the start of every day, at the start of every flight, they had been filled with a sense of purpose. They had always been confident of their success and had never consciously contemplated the possibility that they might fail. Now the subliminal fear that had lurked in the recesses of their minds had become a reality. They had failed. Their journey was over.

Once they determined that there was nothing more to be done at the airfield, they returned to town. Their first action was to send another telegram to Guiana in order to inform them of the accident and give their regrets at not being able to see them. Then telegrams were sent to Atlantic City and to the countries ahead on their itinerary. After this was accomplished, they prepared to make arrangements to travel back to the United States.

Before these plans could be completed, a reply came back from Guiana telling them that they fully supported what they were doing and wanted them to come to Guiana anyway at government expense. They were to travel to Georgetown where a large welcome had been planned. Thanks to the generosity of the Guianese, arrangements were quickly made that placed them on a Pan Am 'flying boat'. The crew of the plane, like everyone in the region, had heard of the exploits of these two passengers, fully appreciated the risks that they had taken, and showed them special consideration. For Bert and Al it was a pleasant contrast to be a passenger in a large plane that could fly over and around inclement weather at any time of day rather than being sandwiched into a small plane, hostage to sunrise, sunset, and the weather.

Two days after their crash landing in Trinidad, they flew to Georgetown, a city that arose from the South

American continent where the Demerara River emptied into the Atlantic Ocean. The majority of the inhabitants lived along a narrow costal plain that was approximately four feet below sea level at high tide. To protect the homes and crops from the sea, a system of sea walls, dikes, and drainage canals had been built. Besides sugar cane and other crops, the country exported many different timbers, the most important o which was the greenheart tree, often used to build wharves.

Bert knew that Guiana had a population mix that was unique in the West Indies. Moreover, even though it was quite a large country, it had a small population since large areas were undeveloped. A small portion of the population was comprised of American Indians who mainly lived in the southwest where there were treeless plains known as savannas. There was also a small population of Europeans and Chinese who were usually independent businessmen.

Somewhat less than one-half of the overall population were blacks whose ancestors had been brought to the country as slaves three to four hundred years ago. When slavery was abolished in 1838, many blacks refused to continue to work on the sugar plantations and moved to the cities where they became a majority of the urban population. This urban migration resulted in blacks achieving a higher level of education, a greater penetration into the civil service and the professions, and a dominance that exceeded their numerical representation in the population.

A slight majority of the population consisted of the descendants of indentured workers brought from India in the mid 1800's by planters to counteract the loss of their labor force after the abolition of slavery. These workers tended to remain on the plantations or to start small farms of their own rather than to move to the cities. These historical factors created an urban-rural racial division of the society that created the potential for problems.

The two aviators received a triumphant welcome in Georgetown. The crash landing that they had survived served to remind everyone of the risks that they had undertaken in order to make this flight. The man on the street in Guiana wanted an opportunity to express the admiration that they felt for the two heroes. The parade that had been scheduled in their honor was held, they were received by the Governor, His Excellency Sir Crawford Douglas Jones, had pictures taken, were the guests at several receptions, attended a grand concert and ball at the largest municipal hall, and then an open air fete in the park.

In his last speech of his aborted Goodwill Tour, Bert, as usual, took time to give his thanks to those who had helped to make their flights possible and summarize the goals that they had started out with and the accomplishments that they had been able to achieve despite the abortion of their expedition. He thanked the people of Guiana for their generosity in bringing them to the island after the crash.

The population was elated to have been included in this historic flight. By ancestry, by language, and by political history they were closer to the countries of the Caribbean than to their immediate geographical neighbors in South America whose racial origins were primarily a combination of American Indian and Spanish rather than primarily African, spoke Spanish rather than English, and were governed by dictatorships rather than the British parliamentary system.

The concept of a goodwill flight had provided them with an opportunity to participate in the activities of their cultural cousins. For a month the people had followed the progress of the flights in the newspaper and through word of mouth. They knew of the fuel leak over North Carolina, the problems caused by the anxious crowd in Nassau, the near crash in Port Antonio, the cracked cylinder and the lake bed landing in the Dominican Republic, and finally the crash landing in Port-au-Spain. The fliers were looked on as authentic heroes who had risked their lives to promote a cause that was important to the people that they had visited.

Just how much Bert and Al had risked became apparent to them when they were taken on a tour of Georgetown after the parade. As they drove along having the sights pointed out to them, their host pointed out the field that had been prepared for their landing. When they saw the condition of the field that they were supposed to land on, the two fliers felt a sense of astonishment followed by apprehension as they realized what might have been.

"My God Bert," exclaimed Al in a voice that simultaneously expressed astonishment and anxiety. "Look at that depression running across the middle of the field! It would not have been a problem for a horse and buggy or a car but if we had ever landed there we would have flipped over for sure! There is no way that we could have survived if we had hit that ditch at the speed we would have been going."

"No question about it," Bert replied, his jaw slightly agape with disbelief as he surveyed the landscape. "Up until this moment I was very disappointed that we had to cancel our tour. Now that I see this field, I am thankful that we were unable to fly to Guiana. Somebody was really watching over us in Trinidad. I think it must be a message that we have done enough. Its time to stop tempting fate and go home."

After two days they returned to Trinidad. They were received as warmly as they had been on their first arrival. With ample time as they awaited arrangements for their return to the United States, they were able to participate in extensive sightseeing and attend many functions. For example, on one occasion they went to a local school and handed out the class certificates. On Boxing Day they went to the races with the mayor. Activities such as these kept them fully occupied until December 29th when they boarded the Munson liner "Western World' for the United States.

The Booker T. Washington was disassembled, put on board and never seen again.

Over a period of 51 days they had traveled 3,689 miles out of the 12,000 intended and had visited ten countries instead of the 25 envisioned. While they had not accomplished all that they had sent out to do, they felt confidant that the publicity that had been generated would further their cause. Years later when he no longer had to be diplomatic, Bert would state that the primary goal had been to "demonstrate to all concerned that blacks were able to navigate and fly aeroplanes under the most hazardous situations and thus demonstrate that the myths about blacks, myths held up by the U.S. military and others, were irresponsible and a threat to racial harmony in the United States."

With the cataclysmic fatigue that envelopes one after a challenge is completed and the bodies adrenalin stores are depleted, they went into a somewhat vegetative state for their journey to New York. As they had expected, only a moderate number of friends and supporters were on hand for their return. The mayors of the cities of Newark and Atlantic City were not as involved as they had been for the coast-to-coast flight when the sole focus of the trip had been the United States. Moreover, unlike the cross-country flight, the outcome was not successful and therefore not newsworthy. Still, there were articles that detailed their accomplishments in the local papers and in the international press. On January 9, 1934 Congressman Bacharach sent a letter to the President in an effort to have him meet the two fliers but that did not occur.

The news of their crash had reached the two young Jamaicans that they had met in the park in Santo Domingo. They sent a letter extending their condolences and expressed the suspicion that the Booker T. Washington might have been sabotaged by those forces in the white community who did not want to see a black man succeed. While there was no evidence of this, and it is commonplace for a conspiracy theory to arise when a project fails, it is instructive to recognize that they were expressing a commonly held belief—i.e., there were many who did not want Bert to succeed.

While the general press was restrained in their coverage, the colored community was quite appreciative of the effort that they had expended on the tour. Bert and Al received many requests to appear at different functions. Over a period of months Bert returned to the churches and civic organizations that had contributed to the funding of their flight and gave speeches that described what had occurred—the parades, the awards, the dinners, and the disasters. The interest displayed by the young people in the audiences validated his flights. It was clear to him that the next generation would not accept anything less than full participation by coloreds in the coming aviation age

In time the initial flurry of speeches died away and his medical practice became the focus of his attention. However, other benefits were to ensue as a result of their efforts, and multiple honors were yet to be bestowed.

10

CHANGES

After their return, Al continued to be very involved in his primary love, aviation. By 1939 he was operating a comercial seaplane service from a site on the Potomac River in Washington, D.C., and a land service from an airfield in Virginia. This represented some progress in the ability of coloreds to participate in aviation. However such a comercial undertaking by a colored was, unfortunately, still very unusual even though six years had passed since they had made their transcontinental flight. The grand total of pilot's licenses held by coloreds in the United States at that time consisted of only four full commercial pilots licenses, four limited commercial licenses, twenty-three private licenses, and ninety-four amateur licenses.

Then the door to the cockpit was opened slightly, not because of an increase in the enlightenment of the population or the government, but because of external events. In early 1939, because of the threat posed by Adolph Hitler, President Roosevelt authorized a Civilian Pilot Training Program (CPTP) to provide flight training for twenty thousand college students each year. In this program, the cadets were to receive five weeks of preflight processing and training, then a ten-week course of ground and flight training. Schools had an incentive to sign up inasmuch as the government offered a stipend of $175 per student.

At first, like aviation in general, the program ignored the colored students. However, West Virginia State, a colored college that was active in aviation, applied for inclusion and was approved because of pressures that were constantly being applied by the leaders in the colored community. Soon after five other colored colleges including Tuskegee Institute were accepted. Since Tuskegee did not even have an airfield that was suitable for training within ten miles of its campus, it was not a likely candidate. Its decision to apply may well have been stimulated by the christening ceremony that Bert had arranged for his Goodwill flight at Tuskegee five years before. That event had raised the level of awareness at the Institute about the importance of aviation.

At first the training was done at Montgomery Airport, an eighty-mile round trip. Then a very basic airport, Kennedy Field, was built near the Institute thereby eliminating the many hours of wasted time that the students had to spend on the road. Funding came from a $1,000 donation from the Institute, labor was provided by the students.

The quality of the students and the training that they received was evident after the first examinations in the program in May 1940. One hundred percent of the first CPTP class at Tuskegee passed the Civil Aeronautics Authority exam, many with excellent marks, and received their private pilots license. Their exemplary results were a clear indication of the fallacy of believing that coloreds did not have the mental capability to fly an airplane and helped to promote a rethinking of the predominant social attitudes towards the role of coloreds in aviation.

After the curriculum and the facilities for the primary training program were in place Tuskegee needed a skilled aviator to be in charge of the secondary training. Not surprisingly the president, Fred Patterson, thought of Al Anderson, one of the two aviators who had distinguished themselves by making the first cross country round-trip by coloreds, had come to Tuskegee in 1934 and recognized the

Institute by christening their plane the Booker T. Washington, and had made a Goodwill Tour to the Caribbean.

This was one concrete result of the efforts of Bert and Al to promote aviation--an invitation to Al Anderson to be in charge of the secondary flight-training program at Tuskegee for the graduates of the CPTP course. Al accepted the invitation, and on July 29, 1940, displaying the flair that was typical for aviators, he buzzed the Institute as he delivered Tuskegee's new plane for secondary training, a Waco, to Kennedy Field.

Earlier that year the Air Corps had been mandated by Public Law 18 to contract with civilian schools of aviation to provide elementary and primary training for military aviation cadets. The Air Corps, like all of the armed services at that time, had been resisting the inclusion of coloreds in the military and continued to do so until it was forced to do so on September 16, 1940. In January of 1941 an all-black pursuit squadron was approved and the contract for pilot preflight and primary training was awarded to Tuskegee. Other colored schools had applied but Tuskegee, possibly because of the presence of a hospital on site, was chosen.

At that point, the Institute did not even have an airfield that was suitable for the secondary training of its students. They had been granted the contract on the assumption that any school that bid would have the necessary facilities. The Institute now needed a more acceptable airfield in order to proceed with its training but it did not have the finances necessary to complete the job. After several applications for funds were turned down, the decision was made to apply to a fund that was due to have its annual meeting for 1941 at Tuskegee Institute, the Rosenwald Fund of Chicago. Among the members of its board was the wife of the President of the United States, Eleanor Roosevelt.

Eleanor Roosevelt had a long record of solid support for the cause of civil rights. She had met regularly with colored educators, including the presidents of Tuskegee, to promote the improvement of colored education. She was also involved in providing improved housing for coloreds and could generally be counted on to be sympathetic to the causes of minorities. On her arrival for the board meeting, she was approached about the need for an airstrip at Tuskegee.

Mrs. Roosevelt was very enthusiastic when she was told about the project and even requested that she be taken for a flight in one of the Institute's Cub planes so that she could have a first hand experience in flying in a training plane. The only appropriate person for such an honor was the chief pilot, Al Anderson, a pilot who had proven his skills many times over.

Her bodyguards however had no confidence in a colored flier, regardless of his qualifications. They tried vigorously to deter Mrs. Roosevelt from this course of action. In trying to dissuade her, they stressed the danger of flying in a small aircraft. In fact, while the quality of the aircraft was a factor, their primary concern was that this plane was maintained by colored mechanics and would be flown by was a colored pilot! The agents, like most whites of their day except for some members of the intelligentsia, readily adopted the prevailing stereotype and assumed that coloreds were inferior and were not to be trusted with the lives of ordinary people--much less the life of the wife of the President.

Mrs. Roosevelt however was a woman of great intellect and exceptional political instincts. She knew of the prejudices of her agents and was determined that their biases would not affect her decisions. A short flight in a trainer would do very little to improve her understanding of the needs of the program or the skills of the instructors; the flight would however be very symbolic—it would demonstrate that the wife of the president had confidence in the ability of coloreds in all areas of endeavor and help to convince others that they should have the same confidence.

From past experience, the agents knew that Mrs. Roosevelt was not a woman to be denied once she had made up her mind. After the futility of their attempts to dissuade her became evident, they acceded to her request and turned their attention to Al. "Remember that you have the wife of the President with you, "said one agent, his facial muscles molded into a template that made his displeasure evident and his voice pitched into a warning tone. "If you have any doubts about your plane, tell me now. If anything goes wrong, Tuskegee is through. Don't do anything fancy on this flight, keep it short. If the slightest thing doesn't seem right, don't attempt to complete the flight, land immediately. "

Al was of course extremely careful on that flight. He gave the plane an extra inspection, went over his pre-flight checklist a second time, and warmed the plane up a bit longer than usual before taxiing onto the runway. After explaining to Mrs. Roosevelt what they would be seeing, he took off, made a 40-minute flight around the area of the Institute, and brought the plane in for a perfect landing. What an honor!

With the skill that comes from years of political activism, Mrs. Roosevelt made sure that a picture was taken of her in the plane with Al to provide visual proof of her confidence. She expressed confidence in the program that had been explained to her and stressed the potential for the Institute to contribute to the war effort. She also promised Patterson that she would convey her impressions to the President and help in any way that she could both now and in the future. When she returned to the board meeting, she reported to the other board members about the enthusiasm of those that she had met, the confidence she had in the staff, and the fact that she felt that this would be a worthy program to support.

With the backing of Mrs. Roosevelt, a loan for $175,00 was made to the Institute by the Rosenwald Fund. In September of 1941 the new airfield was completed, again with the help of students who volunteered their labor. The airfield was named Moton Field to honor the previous president of the Institute, the man who had succeeded Booker T. Washington and had presided over the christening of the Booker T. Washington airplane at the gravesite of the school's founder in 1934.

Al Anderson went on to participate in the training of all of the aviators who went through Tuskegee. Like Bert's father, he was generally called by his title, "Chief". One of his most notable students was Benjamin Davis who, with his father General Davis, constituted the only colored field officers in the armed services at the onset of World War II.

All who learned flying under the tutelage of the "Chief" were appreciative of his skills as an aviator and grateful for the pioneering flights that he and Bert undertook in order to ease the burden of prejudice on subsequent generations. They themselves were still pioneers in that they experienced a great deal of discrimination as fliers in World War II. However, they realized that without the efforts of those who had preceded them, they might not even have had the opportunity to be involved in aviation. Without a Bert Forsythe to suggest that his plane be christened the Booker T. Washington, would Tuskegee's entire faculty and students have been exposed to aviation? Would Tuskegee have had a program? Without the skills that Al Anderson honed on these flights, would the students have achieved the capabilities that they did? There were other colored schools that could have enrolled them, other colored fliers that might have trained them, but it was the Booker T. Washington that had been triumphantly received in the Caribbean and publicized the capabilities of coloreds to the world and it was Al Anderson who had been on that flight.

When the military phase of the training started, the cadets were subject to all of the machinations present in the society, both military and civilian. There were frictions with whites in the town of Tuskegee just as there always had been. Now there were also frictions caused by the reluctance of the armed services to utilize coloreds fully. Some of the students who flunked out of the program felt that their dismissal was for purely racial reasons. Those who graduated the program often sat around for months without receiving an assignment. The stultifying effect of prejudice on its victims and the loss of human potential that society experiences as a result of prejudice were painfully evident for the early graduates at Tuskegee.

The United States was experiencing the loss of other human capital in this time of national emergency because of the inanity of its racial policies. The draft caught up highly trained colored professionals that the army would have had no trouble utilizing—if only they had been the 'right' color. Physicians such as Hackley Woodford would graduate from Howard University and be drafted into non-medical duties because the government would not allow them to treat white soldiers and did not have enough colored soldiers to utilize their talents. On transfer to Tuskegee, they had an opportunity to be involved in the Tuskegee hospital and to help treat the students who suffered burns in the occasional crashes that occurred during training. Hence there were non-aeronautical consequences to Tuskegee's aeronautical breakthrough.

The exigencies of the World War prevailed and colored pilots finally entered the war in a combat role in North Africa on June 18, 1943. Their units, the 99th Fighter Squadron and the 332nd Fighter Group, acquitted themselves well in the war and should have dispelled once and for all the canard that coloreds did not have the intelligence to fly. However the vestiges of prejudice were slow to atrophy.

The colored units returned to the United States between July and October of 1945. On their return they were often given demeaning assignments. As a result, early in 1946 Tuskegee president Fred Patterson asked the War Department to close down the military aspect of the training program at the school. However, while there were many examples of the failure of desegregation, the need to utilize blacks in the war effort had been a major force in the inexorable, but painfully incremental elimination of segregation. It was not until President Truman terminated military segregation on July 26, 1948, against the wishes of a very large number of his generals, that the stage was set for a more rapid rate of progress.

Because of the war and the subsequent development of black squadrons, Tuskegee trained coloreds became involved in all of the aspects of aviation including maintenance and flight control. The role of coloreds in civilian aviation was increasing at the same time but the Tuskegee military graduates were the core of a pool of skilled personnel that was available after the war for an industry that was experiencing a shortage of workers due to its rapid growth. With time coloreds became not just airport porters and washroom attendants but also pilots and mechanics for the commercial airlines in the United States, thereby reaching the goal that Bert and Al had set so many years ago—the ability of coloreds to participate in aviation at all levels.

Bert's accomplishments subsequent to his three flights were unrelated to aviation. In fact, after 1935 he never piloted a plane again. Did his retirement from aviation result from fear, fear that resulted from all of the near misses that they had experienced and the actual crash in Trinidad? Or had he simply accomplished what he had set out to do and was now directing his efforts elsewhere? More than likely, it was the latter since fear was never a limiting force in any of the actions that he took before he discontinued piloting a plane nor afterwards when he continued to fligh as a passenger or pursue various civil rights.

The greatest fear for many men is their fear of change—a fear that often paralyzes them and prevents them from taking any of the steps needed to achieve fervently desired improvements in the status quo. Why is it that some individuals are willing to challenge authority and injustice while most will acquiesce to almost any indignity? How many have the fortitude to switch from a pampered childhood in a country where they enjoyed privilege, to a decade of study and menial work under a system of discrimination? Who might not have decided to desist from their plans after the terror of an electrical storm, the sputtering of an overheated engine, or a forced landing due to a fuel leak or a defective cylinder? Is it luck that one person succeeds where many fail?

Was the fact that this endeavor was initiated by Bert rather than someone else the result of a genetic predis- position to a fighting spirit inherited from his Scottish ancestors, warriors at Culloden in 1746 and in the hills of North Carolina in 1783? To what extent was it due to an inculcation of the leadership traits that were exhibited by his East Indian grandmother in the Bahamas? Or was it perhaps the assimilation of the cultural devotion to freedom dis- played by the African descended Maroons for 80 years in the mountains of Jamaica, or the expectations nourished by the British class system in Jamaica, or the teachings of the American Booker T. Washington, or the reaction that Bert had to the prejudice he experienced in America?

Asking these questions makes the answer self evident—the flights occurred because Bert was a man of character, character that derived not from any one of the factors listed above but from the combination of factors that shaped his life, character that allowed him to recognize an opportunity when it appeared and gave him the fortitude to act on that opportunity.

As is usually true of those with a pioneering spirit and a willingness to change, Bert had multiple areas of interest and many other contributions to make. He continued to be active in many different efforts to eliminate discrimination. One of his actions was the organization of an interracial group that set out to eliminate the practice of segregated seating in movie theaters in Atlantic City. The men on the committee would go to a theater and sit in the 'whites only' section. At first it was an interracial group then later this approach was used without the assistance of any whites. If an usher came and told them to move or leave, they would refuse. Bert never experienced any violence but on one occasion an usher severely sprained their arm in a futile attempt to force Bert from his seat.

That tactic predated the publicized sit-in activities of Martin Luther King and others in the South by over fifteen years. It was applicable in the North but had it been used in the South at that point in time, it would have resulted in harsh countermeasures and failure. Since the colored population in Atlantic City was not subject to the same level of violence as were the coloreds of the South, the tactic was eventually successful.

When Bert happened to mention this activity in a letter to his brother Roger, he learned that his brother had independently adopted this approach in the city to which he had moved in 1942, Sandusky Ohio, where he had further challenged prejudice by renting a house in the 'white' section of town. He however was unable to find anyone else who was willing to 'sit-in' and risk the wrath of the authorities and had had to wage a solo battle. The two brothers had demonstrated their closeness by independently choosing the same approach to a situation.

The beneficial effect of the war effort on increasing the number of occupations available to coloreds was evident in the job that Roger now had. He had returned to the United States because Jamaica, a relatively unprotected island, seemed vulnerable to possible enemy activity with the involvement of the British in World War II and a declaration of war by President Roosevelt in 1941. On returning he was quickly hired at a war plant as a chemist, an occupation that had been closed to him ten years before. The genie was out of the bottle. No longer would color be an automatic disqualification for a position of competence.

Civil rights were only a small part of Bert's contributions to his community. The majority of his time was devoted to his medical practice. The practice was not a lucrative one due to the severity of the effect of the depression on the most disadvantaged members of the community, the colored population that Bert treated. He did not however need a large income because the years spent working to both support himself and pay his way through school had taught him to be very frugal. Although he could have afforded his own home or apartment, he continued to rent a room in the house of Dr. Lucas so that he could minimize expenses. Moreover, he spent very little on luxuries.

In fact his practice cost him money at times because of his generosity. Most physicians had a sliding fee scale based on what the patients could afford but Bert took this standard one step further. On several occasions during the winter months he would make a house call to someone suffering from a severe respiratory infection and find that the apartment or house was unheated. He would then advise that his patients turn the heat on only to hear that they could not afford to do so. The next day the coal truck would pull up with a load of coal ordered and paid for by Bert. Because of his modesty, he would never mention what he had done unless asked by the patient.

He found another way to be charitable. The crowding and malnutrition in the colored community in the 1930's was associated with a high rate of tuberculosis that was having a devastating effect. In an effort to be of help,

Bert began to volunteer on weekends at either the Glen Gardener Sanitarium or the Seaview Sanitarium on Staten Island. After a few months as a volunteer, he realized that he needed to increase his expertise in the field and decided to get a degree in Public Health.

He might have applied to one of the eastern schools but decided to take the opportunity to return to McGill for his studies. At one level of thought he dreaded the idea of resuming the drudgery of studying after eight years away from academics. On the other hand, he looked forward to increasing his skills and to being in Montreal again where he could visit with those friends who still remained. It took a little time and convincing, but he finally arranged for Dr. Lucas and another physician to provide coverage for his patients so that he could take time from his practice and travel to Canada.

As he expected, the city of Montreal had grown in the time that he had been away. Fortunately it had the same exotic ambience that it had previously exhibited. Moreover, his ability to enjoy the opportunities that the city presented had multiplied since he was last there. Now that he had a profession, a reasonable income, and some savings, he could afford to spend an evening at a sidewalk café on a more frequent basis. There he would engage in discussions of medicine, politics, and life in general.

His Sunday routine was unchanged. He still enjoyed the inexpensive pleasure of a stroll through the Parc Mont-Royal or a trip to one of the museums. The time that he spent in Montreal was a pleasant change of pace from the daily grind of a medical practice. Of course this was not as exciting as the experiences that he had had when he was flying from country-to-country and participating in parades and speeches with the local dignitaries, but he had long ago realized that he did not need an adrenalin rush and in fact craved a more peaceful existence. Time tempers the primal drives that impel us in our youth towards physical activities that involve some degree of danger.

A pleasant realization slowly made its way into his consciousness. The pressure that he had felt in medical school did not exist during the months that he was studying public health. He came to realize that this change in his perception was due to the fact that his instructors were treating him as a colleague and not as a student. This was post-graduate work whose sole purpose was to increase the participant's level of knowledge rather than doctoral drudgery that was designed to determine whether or not one had the ability to absorb a large volume of knowledge. It felt entirely different to be building on a foundation than it had felt when he was laying that foundation.

The available treatments for tuberculosis were limited in number and limited in value at the time of Bert's studies. Whether a patient lived or died depended more on their innate ability to fend off the infection than the efficacy of the treatments that their physician applied. Overcrowding such as regularly occurred in the colored communities magnified the risk of contracting the disease. Alcoholics or those malnourished due to poverty were at even higher risk. Once again he instinctively wanted to help those who were discriminated against by society.

Bert went to Montreal intent on learning the new treatments. However his instructors soon pointed out that tuberculosis had to be approached the way that all medical problems were approached. The first step in the care of a tubercular patient was a good history, the second was a complete physical examination, the third was treatment, and the fourth and perhaps the most important given the limited efficacy of treatment, was the follow up of contacts so that the spread of the disease could be minimized.

Because of the tuberculosis epidemic, he had many opportunities to learn how to take a respiratory history and to receive advanced instruction on the use of the stethoscope as part of the physical examination. In 1939 the primary tool used in diagnosis and follow up, other than the x-ray, was the physician's skill in using their stethoscope. A physician's medical reputation was often established by his ability to listen to a chest then make a diagnosis and recommend a treatment based on what he heard rather than what he had learned from an x-ray or a laboratory test. For example, an experienced examiner such as Bert could quickly tell with his stethoscope whether fluid was present in the lungs, whether a lung was collapsed, or whether adhesions had formed between the lungs and the lining of the lungs.

Often the first sign of tuberculosis in an individual was the presence of blood in their sputum. A mild amount indicated that only small blood vessels were involved and that there was hope. A large outpouring signified the involvement of a larger vessel and a diminished hope for recovery. In severe cases one treatment for bleeding was the creation of an opening in the chest wall so that the external air pressure would collapse the lung and clamp down on the bleeding artery.

Other methods were tried to help the patient survive an acute episode of bleeding in the hope that the body would recover and heal the ruptured vessel. One approach was to pile sandbags on the chest of the unfortunate patient in the hope that the pressure on the chest would filter down to the bleeding artery and close it off. Another approach involved packing the chest with ice with the expectation that the lowered temperature would constrict the blood vessels and stem the flow of blood. Bert's studies gave him the skill to perform these procedures.

Since the treatments were not very effective, his professors stressed the importance of preventing the disease by checking contacts for the early signs of disease. If tuberculosis was caught early, improved nutrition often allowed the body to fight off the infection and heal itself. If nothing else, early detection allowed the public health physician to isolate cases before other family members and contacts could be affected.

A persistent cough often preceded the suspicion that an individual could be tubercular. However, a recent cough could be due to a simple infection such as a virus, a bacterial infection such as pneumonia or bronchitis, as well as to tuberculosis, the disease that was often called consumption. At McGill, Bert learned how to make these differentiations so that he could apply the appropriate treatments.

On May 25, 1939 he was granted a diploma in Public Health. He returned to Atlantic City and resumed his practice and his volunteer work at the sanitaria. The discrimination that hospitals practiced still prevented him from hospitalizing patients in Atlantic City, but he gained a reputation for expertise in Public Health and in the treatment of tuberculosis that expanded the scope of his practice.

Bert became the first colored physician in his area to have his own x-ray unit in his office. This provided him with the means to achieve earlier diagnoses of tuberculosis and follow cases more carefully. He taught his patients how to avoid exposure to tuberculosis and helped to reduce the spread of the disease. His reputation, already formidable because of his flights, grew even more. The medical establishment now paid attention to the fact that he had received special training in public health and had skills as a physician. In 1941 he was asked by the city to provide public health teaching for the twelve visiting nurses who went to the homes of housebound patients in the area.

There were three colored nurses among the twelve that he taught. Among them was Frances Chew Turner, an attractive lady who caught his eye. They did not see each other again for over a year, but eventually they came into contact again and began to date. On April 27, 1945 they were married in Allentown, Pennsylvania. The areas most eligible colored bachelor had finally succumbed.

By the time that Bert and Francis had married, the efforts that he and others had engaged in, combined with a new sense of empowerment due to the expanded opportunities brought on by World War II, had been successful in reducing the level of discrimination in Atlantic City. For example, whenever they went to a movie on the boardwalk, they were able to sit in any seat without harassment from the ushers. The beaches were open to anyone. Housing continued to be segregated but slowly prejudice was responding to the pressure that was being placed on it.

Bert affected the cause of civil right is less obvious ways also. The interracial flight board, the interracial group to desegregate theaters, and his activities in tuberculosis expanded his contacts in the community. One white became his patient then others followed. By the quality of his medical practice he helped to eliminate the prejudice against accepting professional advice from someone of a different color.

There was one white patient in particular with whom Bert developed a rapport that grew into respect and friendship. As part of that friendship, Bert and Francis were offered the unlimited use of a cabin cruiser called the "Queenie". The boat reunited him with his favorite recreational area, the sea. Until their departure from Atlantic City in 1951, Bert and Francis spent many weekends using the cruiser to go crabbing or fishing.

Bert and Francis did not have an extended honeymoon until late in 1945 when the friends that Bert had made on his Goodwill Flight finally prevailed in convincing him to return to the islands and celebrate his accomplishments of 1934. With the end of World War II making travel easier and his marriage to Francis giving him a reason to travel, he decided to make an abbreviated version of his Goodwill Tour that would include the Bahamas, Cuba, Haiti, Santo Domingo, St. Thomas, Puerto Rico, and Jamaica.

The trip was delayed because Al's wife Gert was expecting a baby in November and insisted that the baby had to be delivered by Bert and no one else. Gert went into labor very close to the expected date with Bert in attendance and a healthy baby boy was delivered without any problems. After the delivery Al and Gert announced that boys middle name would be Forsythe and asked that Bert and Francis agree to be his godparents—a request that they happily honored.

In December of 1945 Bert and Francis were finally able to take their delayed honeymoon. The flight to the Bahamas was uneventful as were all of the flights he took in commercial planes. The technology that guided aviation had progressed and eliminated many of the dangers that he had faced. Commercial planes had two-way radios, lifeboats, and radar control. A lot of the advances, especially radar, had been perfected because of the stimulus of World War II.

When they reached Nassau, those who had been there for his flight years ago spoke of the event as if it had just occurred. Several now admitted that they had wondered about his sanity in participating in such a risky undertaking. However they also told him of their appreciation of the role that he had in publicizing the islands and stimulating the politicians to look into the future of aviation in the Caribbean.

The circumstances of this visit differed in many ways: there was not the wild celebration that there had been, plane flights into the island were now commonplace, and although all commercial pilots still were white, flights in small planes by coloreds was no longer unusual. A modern airfield had increased tourism and improved the standard of living for working class Bahamians. For the new generation, the current rights and privileges were to be taken for granted. Blatant discrimination was ancient history, a history that in their limited perspective had evolved spontaneously and was not attributable to the sacrifices of others. They knew however that most major hotels were still segregated

His arrival on the island was again front-page news. Many of the people he had met before were on hand to welcome him and arrange for dinners to be held in his honor. The discrimination in hotels caused him to initially stay at the home of an acquaintance. However his relative, Buster Bosfield, soon insisted that they stay with him. In private conversations relatives informed him that the influence of the whites from England had receded as a result of the limitations that World War II had placed on movement from England to the islands. It was no longer automatic that some jobs were reserved for whites. Change seemed to be in the air.

After leaving Nassau he went to Cuba where he found that the situation had not changed very much. He was welcomed, but as before the warmth of the reception did not compare to what he had received in the Bahamas. When one landed at the airport on an island such as Jamaica, you were greeted with steel bands and offered a rum punch. As in 1934, when you landed in Cuba, you were greeted with warnings that photography was not permitted and surrounded by men with submachine guns. The contrast was sobering.

The country had elected a new president in 1944, Grau San Martin, but there was still a high level of discontent due to the pervasive level of poverty and a constant concern that Batista might overthrow the government and resume his dictatorship. It was said that many of the dark skinned Cubans felt that they were being oppressed by the light skinned ones. As a visitor, Bert could not be sure as to the accuracy of what he heard, but it was disquieting. He accepted the hospitality that was offered, but was anxious to continue to this next stop.

His trips to Haiti, Santo Domingo, and St. Thomas followed the pattern of his trip to Cuba—warm welcomes, renewals of friendships, tours of the islands. When they reached Puerto Rico, he was pleased to find that a large dinner had been set up in his honor. At the dinner he surprised the attendees who did not know him by giving part of his speech in Spanish when he thanked the country for the hospitality that they had shown in 1934 and again on that day. After the dinner he had an opportunity to inquire about the social conditions on the island and was told that their problems were mainly a result of the population density and poverty, not the result of any prejudice that was racially motivated. The letter that he had received about race relations years ago did not seem credible.

After the official functions Bert and Francis were able to take an extended tour of the city and then to travel to the rain forest. For Francis the scenery was all brand new and fascinating. Bert was surprised that although he had seen these sights eleven years before, they had not been fully appreciated because of the hectic schedule that he had had. The current leisurely pace was perfect for the magnificent scenery that they passed through.

He vaguely realized that he was seeing things in an entirely different light now that he was in the company of his wife than he had when he had been in the company of his good friend Al. It was hard to describe, but there was much more satisfaction in sharing travel with your life partner than there was in sharing that travel with a friend. At the end of every day, as they relived what they had said, seen, and done, they were adding to the life-long bonding that occurs between spouses as they share experiences.

As he looked around the plane that they had boarded to leave Puerto Rico, Bert marveled at the contrast between it and the seaplane he had first flown in to leave Port Antonio or the Lambert that he flew on his Goodwill Flight. The current planes were huge and could carry dozens of people comfortably in contrast to the earlier planes that accommodated less than twenty. Speed had more than doubled now that there were two engines instead of one and would increase even more in the near future when jet engines became available for civilian flight. Commercial planes landed on the ground, never on the water. Passengers did not have to curl up into a pretzel position in order to obtain enough room for their legs and hips. The meals seemed like culinary masterpieces from a French chef when he compared them to what passengers were given on those early flights. However he once again noticed that the pilots and the stewards or stewardesses were all white. Since he had left Miami, the only coloreds that he had seen were the porters and the janitors. Aviation still had a long way to go before it would throw off the prejudice that he had fought to eliminate.

The Pan Am flight from Puerto Rico touched down in the city of Montego Bay on the north side of the island before proceeding to its final destination in Kingston. Port Antonio's hopes of using its excellent harbor to become a major site for tourism would be eclipsed by the construction of an airport in the more spacious Montego Bay and the subsequent primacy of the northwest shore of the island. With Cuba being in a perpetual state of unrest and air travel increasing its accessibility, Jamaica was developing a reputation as a good alternative to Cuba for American tourists.

Bert's arrival in Kingston was once again on the front page of every newspaper. He had been to the island in the period that followed his flight and preceded the war because of the death of his father in 1939. After being notified of his father's illness he had returned to the island to find that no one had recognized that Horatio's problems with his vision and hearing were the result of a stroke. His father was now at a stage where he felt that he no longer wanted to fight to stay alive and instead wanted the release that death brings. He grasped Bert's hand and squeezed it in appreciation of the presence of his oldest son, a famous aviator.

In 1939 there was very little that could be done for the victim of a stroke and Horatio soon passed away. When a leading citizen dies in a small town such as Port Antonio, business grinds to a halt as even those who knew him by reputation only took the time to pay their respects. At the funeral there had been a large outpouring of appreciation for "Chief" with many testimonials to his integrity.

Outwardly Bert had been very calm at the time of his father's death. In western culture, a man is expected to keep his emotions restrained at such a time. This custom obscures the fact that this major event in our lives triggers a universal internal dynamic that cannot be suppressed. There is always some guilt for the things left unsaid and the promises not carried out. Why did I delay when he asked me to visit last year? Perhaps I should have acceded to his wishes and completed architecture before entering pre-med. Why? Perhaps.

The man engages in this silent monologue knowing fully well that given the circumstances that existed at the time of his decisions, the same actions would be taken again. Still, the facts have to be revisited and the decisions have to be re-justified before the guilt can be assuaged and the mourner can be at peace internally.

The death of a parent is a seminal moment for other reasons. The child in us sees the parent as eternal. They were there before the dawn of our history. In our minds they were always there and should always exist. Our parents are our foundation and when that foundation is shaken, we become very introspective. We know intellectually that neither they nor we nor anyone that we know will endure. We have seen other relatives and friends pass on but a parent is different.

When a parent dies, we are forced to confront the realization that our own existence is tenuous. Their death precipitates one of the periodic occasions in our lives when we feel compelled to question the entire meaning of life and rethink the explanations that we have adopted for the relationship between man and the universe. Then, as we must, we go on. Perhaps we take solace in our confidence that the soul is eternal, perhaps we are ambivalent about an afterlife and rely on a sublimation of our ignorance and fears to get us through the discomfort. We adapt.

Bert had long since accepted the loss of his father and was now concentrating his thoughts on strengthening the connections that he had with his siblings and reminiscing with his friends Danny, Osmond, and Leslie, the ones who had helped him triumph in his struggle against diabetes. Most of the people that he had grown up with in Port Antonio had followed the postwar migrations that were reallocating the population of the planet from rural or semi-rural areas to large cities. In the case of Jamaicans who remained on the island and did not migrate to England, Canada, or America, the urban area of choice was Kingston. Danny now managed a plantation close to the nearby city of Spanish Town while Leslie was a supervisor at a wharf in Kingston and Osmond had a white-collar job.

One purpose of the trip was to introduce his wife to those who had not yet met her. All of his siblings were now married and had children of their own. His brothers had all achieved the success that their father had expected of them. John was still in school, Lorenzo was a ships pilot, and Harvey had fulfilled the aspiration that Horatio had had for Bert and become an architect. Roger was the only sibling that Bert did not see while he was in Jamaica inasmuch as he was now living in Chicago where he planned to purchase a pharmacy on the South Side of the city. At mid life the Forsyth family and its close friends were quite comfortable.

On this visit he briefly reflected on the philosophical contradictions he had struggled with during the year that he had spent recuperating from diabetes and pondering the differences between the class system in Jamaica and the system of segregation and discrimination in the United States. His family had achieved the successes that middle class families the world over take for granted. Meanwhile, the poor children that were his age when he left Port

Antonio, children whose names and faces he could not recall, were just as static economically as the poor colored children who had grown up at the same time in the United States. Once again he resolved his moral dilemma in the manner that he had done previously and concluded that the presence of blatant prejudice in the United States made that country the proper battleground in the struggle for civil rights.

Such deep thoughts did not linger since this trip was primarily a vacation. He took special pleasure in getting to know his many nieces and nephews, particularly the younger ones. Throughout his life Bert had exhibited a droll sense of humor that had captivated everyone that he met but was especially well received by children. He could make any child seem very, very special by admiring some feature or their clothing or a toy. Then he would tease them in a pleasant way or offer to draw their picture. At times he would demonstrate his artistic talent by drawing a remarkable likeness. At other times he would capture the child's attention by drawing a caricature that never failed to provoke a giggle. His personality naturally drew children to him but the respect that the children recognized in the conversations of the adults around them made them realize that in addition to his ability to relate to them, their Uncle Bert was someone very special.

When Bert and Francis finished their visit to Kingston, May's son George volunteered to drive them over the Junction to Port Antonio. The drive was as beautiful as he remembered, but scarier because of the way that the 18–year old George drove and the vast increase in the number of cars that were on the road. Cars were much more common than when he had lived in Jamaica but donkey-drawn carts seemed no less frequent than they had been in the past. The combination of cars and carts made Bert and Francis very apprehensive.

Although George never knew what obstacle might await him, he flew around the hairpin curves in his small

English car, a Morris Minor, with abandon. His only concession to the danger was a vigorous toot of the horn as he approached the more dangerous curves. When he did find an unexpected blockage as he rounded a curve, he would utter a curse in the local dialect then complain to Bert about the temerity exhibited by those who dared to place themselves in his path.

"*Rahtid*, man. Why yu no keep off the road with that cart," George would angrily shout to the driver of the cart as he leaned out the window of the car to make sure that his words were clearly heard. "Yu no know that cars come down de road? Uncle Bert, the country is going to hell you see! People don't have any respect for the cars. They need to put a warning up when they stop like that! "

To the uninitiated foreigner, George was brimming with anger. To a fellow Jamaican, he was simply letting off steam in a culturally acceptable fashion. He was a very skillful driver, but when Bert silently compared the tension that he felt on that drive with the tensions that he felt during all of the emergencies that he had experienced from the electrical storm right up to the crash, this two-hour drive across the island was the clear number one on his list of horrors. He preferred a few moments of terror fighting a situation over which he usually had some control, to two hours of constant tension under circumstances that made him feel helpless.

A mild sense of sadness enshrouded Bert as he realized that another generation had taken over. When he had flown, he had recognized the *possibility* that the outcome could be disastrous and consequently planned ahead in an effort to minimize the possibilities. However the self-confidence of youth was such that he *knew* internally that the *probability* of adversity was almost non-existent. That certainty allowed him to take the risks that he did.

As George tore down the country roads, he had Bert's prior ability to sublimate the probabilities while anticipating the possibilities. Bert on the other hand now was concerned about both possibilities and probabilities. Nature had implanted a self-preservation mechanism that diminished his daring as his reflexes slowed and his mental dexterity atrophied, albeit ever so slightly.

In contrast, George, with movie star good looks, free flowing testosterone, and an ability to charm any female, was entering the peak of his self-confidence. He would later dismay his mother by leaving a coveted white-collar job at an export-import company to become an apprentice ship's pilot. As a ship's pilot, he would gain a reputation for going out in weather where no one else would in order to guide ships into one of Jamaica's many harbors. As the pilot's boat suddenly rose and fell in swells of 6 feet or more, he would cavalierly balance on the deck of the pilot boat with a one-hand grip, time the rise of the swell, confidently grasp the ladder to the incoming ship, and swing through the blinding salt water spray in order to climb onto the ship's deck. Such an activity was inconceivable to Bert at this stage of his life.

The Morris Minor emerged from the mountainous phase of its cross-island journey unscathed, crossed the plains made green by the fronds of thousands of banana plants, and hurtled towards the ocean road that led to Port Antonio. While Kingston had grown dramatically since Bert had first left, Port Antonio had stayed the same or perhaps even shrank. Competition in the banana business had stunted its commercial appeal so that new businesses were not moving in and construction was at a standstill. Three married sisters had remained in the city but all of his brothers had moved away. He visited with his sisters Dottie and Erma who had married plantation managers before proceeding to the house of his sister May.

A day seemed to last much more than 24 hours when you were a guest on a plantation. Daytime conversations were few and far between on weekdays since there were no visitors and the host and hostess were preoccupied with their regular duties. As yet there was no television broadcast to help to fill the time. There were very few sounds heard around the house except for the reports from the BBC that were listened to with almost religious regularity on arising in the morning and again at 6 P.M. just before dinner.

Before the war the greatest contribution of the BBC was the broadcast of the test matches in cricket. Everyone was looking forward to their resumption. During the war the BBC served to maintain the link between the islands and the rest of the empire. It was easy to see why the ex-patriates from England relished the broadcasts, but after thirty-five years in the United States, Bert could not appreciate the fascination that the middle class Jamaicans had with the programs.

The plantation routine was very predictable. First there was a morning shower in water so cold that every hair follicle on your torso snapped to attention. Then a leisurely breakfast was followed by a morning spent rocking quietly on the front veranda and looking out over the green foliage of the plantation to the nearby blue of the Caribbean. Next a small lunch, an afternoon nap, the 4 P.M. tea, and then the evening shower in anticipation of the evening meal and an hour or two of reminiscences and complaints about local politics and local gossip. Life was as it had been when he was a child without a care.

Then it was on to Port Antonio proper to visit May. May's life had changed the most. She had been widowed for over five years and had found it necessary to convert her home in Port Antonio into a guesthouse in order to meet her financial obligations. The government's efforts to promote tourism had been the impetus that had led his sister to convert her home into a guesthouse but these efforts at promotion had had limited success. Moreover her earning potential was reduced when their father's widow, his third wife Genie, became a permanent boarder who paid just enough to cover expenses but not enough to provide the profit that May needed.   On many days the other rooms went unfilled while on days when there was an influx of tourists who could pay a profitable rate, one of her rooms was unavailable because of Genie's presence. Bert tried to pay for the room that May gave him on the pretext that he and Francis were keeping May from renting out their room. As he had expected, May refused the offer, too proud to admit that her circumstances were less than they had been in the past.

Every day May saw to it that the maid prepared his favorite Jamaican dishes for the different meals.   He delighted in introducing his wife to green banana porridge, salt fish and ackee, fresh roasted breadfruit with melted butter, and as many exotic fruits as they could find in the markets.   Periodically he would wander into the kitchen where he could experience the odors that had permanently imprinted themselves in his olfactory memory decades before.   He found however that the memories that were evoked did not last as long as they had in the past and were not as prominent as they had been. Was he getting forgetful? No, that was not it. Both his distant and recent memory were excellent.   Those distant memories came and went quickly because they were no longer important to him.

During this time Bert took Francis on short trips around the Port Antonio area and pointed out the major sights.   Titchfield Hotel was to be bought by the American actor Errol Flynn as a luxury hotel for the rich and famous. Portlanders hoped that this would increase the cachet of the city and attract more tourists. After a brief stop at Tichfield they continued on to the Bonnie View Guest House for tea and an opportunity to admire the unparalleled view of the harbor.

On another day, amid copious assurances to Francis that she would not be poisoned, he dragged her into a nondescript Chinese owned grocery store where he bought patties, bullas, greta cake, and Champaign Cola. Then, buttressed with a lunch that had been packed by May's maid, they went to the beach that he had loved when he was a boy. In a short period of time he tried to resurrect every experience that he had ever had and share them with his wife.

One sight was quite displeasing. When his father had become ill, he changed his will and left most of his assets to Genie. As a result, his boyhood home on the hill had left family control, was not well maintained, and was now in a state of disrepair that brought a hint of moisture to his eyes whenever he passed by. Somehow he had thought that the home he had grown up in would always be waiting for him in case he decided to return.

He soon realized that the combination of people and places that had created the spirit that he associated with the word 'home' was no more and that he could never permanently return to Jamaica. His outlook on life had changed. He was a naturalized American, his wife was American, he lived in America and he thought like an American in that he had discarded the British class system and embraced the ideal of equality that was so imperfectly achieved in America. It was time to finish this journey and return home.

Once again they were racing across the countryside in the Morris Minor with George—this time on the way to the airport in Kingston. George thought nothing of taking them from Kingston to Port Antonio then driving back to Kingston in one day. On this occasion he would drive from Kingston to Port Antonio to pick them up, then drive them to Kingston to catch their plane. These two hundred or so miles would have not taken much time in America but on Jamaican roads this was a real test of endurance. A test of ones endurance had seemed a minor matter to Bert on his coast-to-coast trip. Now it seemed foolhardy. However he never equated the two actions; he never realized how much his perspective had changed.

That night they ate at the beautiful Blue Mountain Inn in the hills above Kingston, enjoyed a Planters Punch, and listened to the sounds of the evening. The next day they had lunch downtown at the majestic Myrtle Bank Hotel, listened to the melodic beat of a steel drum band, and then walked down to look at the gentle swells in the harbor one last time. Later they boarded a Pan Am flight to New York City where they then took a bus into Atlantic City and resumed their daily routine.

Every few years the couple returned to Jamaica and some of the other islands. Bert never developed a need to see Europe or the Orient or any of the other popular tourist attractions. After his groundbreaking flights, most of his travel involved visits to friends and family.

On one Caribbean trip they included Port-au-Spain, the site of his crash. Francis was aghast when she saw the location. "Bert I can't believe that you fellows were crazy enough to even think about landing or taking off from this little field!" said Francis in disbelief. "No wonder you crashed. I can't see how any plane other than a helicopter could use that field!"

Bert responded as reassuringly as he could when he realized how concerned his wife was. He put his arms around her shoulder in an effort to absorb some of her discomfort. "It wasn't as bad as it seems now Francis. Remember the planes were smaller and lighter than the ones people fly today. They didn't need as much room as the current planes for their takeoffs and landings. Today the bush pilots in Alaska take off from much shorter fields. Of course, they have much more powerful engines that allow them to do that. In any event, we were confident that we could do it and would have succeeded if the gust hadn't forced us down. Our problem would have been the landing site in Guiana. That is one airfield that you never want to see. It was a death trap."

Meanwhile Atlantic City had become a city in decline and the boardwalk was no longer the attraction that it had been. Tourists were taking advantage of air travel to go to other destinations and merchants did not have enough income to properly maintain the area. In 1951, after many years of sharing a common waiting room with Dr. Lucas, Bert decided to move his practice from Atlantic City to Newark and move his residence to Montclair.

Without intending to do so, Bert created controversy when it came time to choose an office site because, as always, he did not think in terms of what is it permissible for a colored man to do but instead he thought, 'What is it I want to do,' or, 'what is it I can afford to do?' In this respect he differed from the majority of his friends. Perhaps it was because his Jamaican background gave him a different perspective, perhaps it was what he learned from Booker T. Washington, perhaps it was his individual personality. In any event, where others only talked or complained or were only willing to act in groups, Bert was willing to act on his own.

In Newark an excellent medical office was available on Clinton Street, an area populated solely by white physicians. When one of these physicians died, his daughter advertised the offices for rent and then accepted Bert's application. Segregation was still a strong force however and for years afterwards, the white physicians would not speak to the 'traitor' who had rented to a colored. For Bert it was not so much an effort to desegregate, but a manifestation of his determination receive what was rightfully his.

Now Bert began to spend more time on an interest that he had had for many years, painting. He enrolled at the local museum where he took art lessons evenings and Saturdays in order to recieve some formal training and improve his natural talent. This was strictly for his own enjoyment in that he never made any attempt to sell his paintings. Some of these paintings were excellent copies of old masterpieces, some were portraits of family and friends that he frequently gave away, and some were original landscapes. He continued in that activity for many years. He also remained interested in the quest for civil rights and the organizations that were pursuing civil rights both in the Caribbean and in the United States. During the 1950's many changes were taking place in the battle for social justice.

World War II had been responsible for many of the changes. In the Caribbean the war had weakened the involvement of England in the governance of their colonial empire. Moreover the war had impoverished the Empire and made it difficult for the 'mother country' to afford the negative cash flow that was occurring in many of the colonies where populations were growing rapidly. Islands that had been profitable with the combination of a slave economy and an agricultural demand that exceeded the available supply of produce, became a liability when the workers were unionizing and pushing for higher wages at the same time that increased acreage and improved methods of farming were producing a surplus of bananas and sugar.

Had there not been a war, there still would have been the natural tendency of people to resist subjugation even when it was relatively benign. The inhabitants of the colonies wanted to have the ability to totally control their own affairs. Although the country that had been the major imperial power was reluctant to admit that their empire was crumbling, the practicality was that independence for the colonies was in England's best interest also.

In 1958 ten islands including Jamaica were joined into a state within the British Commonwealth of Nations. The federation became independent on May 31, 1962 and Jamaica became independent on August 6, 1962 at which time it left the federation. A major factor in the quest for independence was the feeling among those of African descent that Europeans would continue to have a disproportionate influence in government and a disproportionate share of the top business positions as long as the island was an appendage of the Federation or the Commonwealth.

In the United States momentous changes were occurring with regard to the civil rights movement. World War II had unleashed forces in the Armed Services that led to their desegregation by President Truman in 1948. In 1954, on behalf of the NAACP, Thurgood Marshall challenged the voting laws in the South before the Supreme Court and won. These major victories opened a crack in the doorway to equality, a crack that was to grow exponentially.

Even for those who are in perfect health, the aging process causes us to fatigue a little earlier in the day than we are accustomed to and to a greater extent than we consider acceptable. In our minds we remain teenagers for most of our lives. However our bodies shout out that the mind is deceiving us. In Bert's case the expected fatigability was aggravated by his longstanding diabetes and compounded by the demands of his medical practice. As a consequence, his involvement in civil rights was not as physical as it once had been. He became more of an observer than a participant.

In his analysis, the go-slow approach of Booker T. Washington had been supplanted by the more confrontational approach of W.E.B. DuBois. Stealth techniques such as unpublicized sit-ins in theaters that had been used in an uncoordinated sporadic fashion by Bert and Roger and others in the early 1940's became a highly organized, highly publicized, and largely confrontational mass tactic in the mid-1950's and the 1960's.

The most influential proponent of this tactic was the Reverend Martin Luther King, Jr. King was a Baptist minister who advocated that the nonviolent passive resistance approach used by Mohandas K. Gandhi to achieve India's freedom from British control should be used to further the cause of civil rights in the United States. He began his crusade with a boycott of the buses in Montgomery, Alabama in 1955 in protest of the fact that colored people in that city were forced to sit in the rear of the bus—a clear form of discrimination and humiliation.

King's oratorical and organizational skills quickly made him the leader of the struggle for civil rights. The movement grew as it received the support of students, churches, labor unions, civil rights organizations, and the President of the United States, John. F. Kennedy. People of all races and religions joined in the protests. However, just as the slave masters had resisted the natural desire of their slaves to be free, a large and influential number of white Southerners resisted the aspirations of the descendants of those slaves.

The reasons for white resistance were varied. A large number of Southerners had been inculcated with an almost instinctual certainty that those of a different color were inferior and undeserving of equality. While they had lost the battle to maintain a system of slavery, they had succeeded in maintaining inequality by denying blacks the right to vote and thereby change the system that had supplanted slavery. With non-whites not having any leverage at the ballot box, political influence was exercised only by those who favored discrimination. Politicians resisted change because they feared that the right to vote would eventually lead to their being displaced from office by blacks. Hence every law that the politicians wrote was designed to maintain the inequality that existed. They cloaked their intent in pious references to States Rights, but their motives were in fact selfish.

The general public in the United States allowed this system to be perpetuated for several reasons. Some kept quiet because they feared that they would incur the wrath of the community if they questioned the established traditions. There is a lemming-like quality that is often displayed by humanity despite mankind's superior intelligence. This inheritance from our more primitive ancestors often causes us to unite behind leaders who should not lead or support causes that should not be supported.

Besides the general acquiesce that prevailed, there was a highly vocal opposition to a reduction in segregation that came from poor whites who were themselves subject to prejudice—the societal disapproval that the haves often display against the have-nots, regardless of race. It was said that this group, subject to being derogatorily referred to as white trash, needed to have another group to feel superior to. They were the foot soldiers that defended discrimination without question, just as soldiers everywhere are expected to defend whatever position they are placed in.

Probably the greatest factors in white resistance however were inertia and the presence of a self-fulfilling prophecy. Southern whites grew up in a society in which non-whites lived in worse neighborhoods, dressed poorly, went to inferior schools, were largely uneducated, and were treated with disdain because of these attributes. For most whites, the differences were taken for granted. The poor circumstances of the non-whites confirmed the validity of treating them as inferiors. It did not occur to the whites that better schools and better incomes would lead to better clothing, better housing, and fewer of the differences that caused them to look down on blacks. This entrenched opposition to change made it clear to King and others that it would take a rising level of indignation from the population that resided outside of the South and the imposition of federally mandated governmental changes if basic rights were to be achieved. A strategy of passive resistance evolved, designed to reawaken the outrage that had led to the abolition of slavery almost a century before.

One Sunday in 1963 Bert was with a group of people who were gathered in his apartment and watching television as the police in Birmingham, Alabama used powerful water canons and dogs to intimidate those who were marching in support of civil rights. Peaceful demonstrations degenerated into riots during which demonstrators found themselves being arrested indiscriminately. The group at Bert's house knew and appreciated that the Legal Defense Fund of the NAACP was working tirelessly to extricate the detainees from overcrowded inhumane jails and then defend them in Southern courts that often had no interest in dispensing justice impartially. Expressions of horror at what they were witnessing were interspersed with comments about the need to support those who were on the front lines of America's latest battle against tyranny.

"It's about time that someone did something about the situation in the South," complained one attractive lady whose whitening hair confirmed her long opportunity for exposure to the peculiarities of American culture.

"Thank goodness for the NAACP," was the comment from her spouse who shared the small sofa by the window with her.

"Those policemen are worse than common criminals' said a third person as the group directed most of its attention to the small screen before them and uncharacteristically said very little.

As Bert witnessed these things and listened to the cocktail chatter, his activist inclinations were reawakened. Suddenly he blurted out an idea that had formed spontaneously. He spoke without any of the careful analysis that he had used to tabulate details before letting Al know years ago that he was considering a series of flights.

"Listen folks," said Bert in a quiet but forceful voice that commanded immediate attention, "we have to contribute in some significant way to this effort to end discrimination. At our ages it is not practical to get involved physically. We all give money already, but the amount that each one of us gives is relatively small compared to the needs that the NAACP's Legal Defense Fund has. What we need is some method of raising a lot of money. Most colored people don't have that much money to spare but it occurs to me that we could get them to buy something that they need anyway and let the profits go to civil rights."

"That is a great idea Bert," said one of his guests eagerly. "I would certainly be willing to participate. What would we sell in order to raise the money?"

"I hadn't thought about what to sell," Bert replied then paused for what seemed like almost a minute before continuing. "How about Christmas cards. Everyone uses them. Why spend the money in a store? Who knows if the manufacturer of the card is sympathetic to the cause of civil rights? We can have cards made up that say on the back that the money goes to civil rights. I am sure that people would support us."

Francis was a member of a national group of colored women called Links that had been founded on the boardwalk in Atlantic City in 1949. Through that organization, the concept of selling Christmas cards to raise funds for civil rights was passed on to the local chapter of the NAACP, then the area chapter, then to Roy Wilkins, the national director in New York. The project was enthusiastically accepted and was successful in raising $60,000 for the Legal Defense Fund of the NAACP over a two-year period. Whitney Young from Kentucky who led the Urban League also embraced it. The idea died out, but the program had accomplished its purpose of providing a significant amount of money to the cause of civil rights when the money was most needed.

By 1965 the successes of King's non-violent civil rights movement slowed and it began to be challenged by a much more aggressive faction, one that advocated violent resistance to racism. King had made inroads in providing access to the voting booth and to education, two fundamental building blocks that were vital if equality was to be achieved. The most overt and humiliating aspects of segregation in public accommodations were being overcome. But there was no discernible improvement in concrete factors such as employment and housing, the economic realities that affected the daily physical quality of life. This failure made the radical approach a more viable alternative to a significant segment of the colored population.

To accentuate their radicalism this faction popularized a semantic trend that had previously not been fashionable. Just as the NAACP had found it useful to promote the word colored instead of the word Negro, the new incarnation of radicalism advocated that those descended from slavery now be referred to as being black rather than colored. The concept was incorporated in their general description, the black power movement.

The leaders of this philosophy recognized that words influence thoughts and actions. Historically the word colored had been used to divide those of mixed parentage from those of pure or almost pure African heritage. The black power movement wanted to unite all of the descendants of slavery under one banner and lay to rest the prevailing idea in the white community--that the lightness of an individual's skin was proportional to their intelligence.

By talking in terms of power instead of terms such as rights and equality, these groups fostered an image of self-determination that appealed to a population that was yearning for participation in the fruits of an abundant economy that they had helped to build. Unfortunately their threats and confrontational tactics alienated many of those in the white community who had previously supported change. When several of their leaders met violent deaths and the war in Viet Nam led to a general repudiation of violence as a method of resolving differences, the movement came indiscernibly to an end without producing any notable achievements.

There were others in the minority community who advocated the use of the term African-American as being more descriptive and less controversial. They pointed out that the country had already accepted hyphenated heritages such as Irish-American, German-American, and Italian-American. Neither of these appellations became dominant but gradually the word colored was used less and less and the descendants of slavery in America were referred to either as blacks or African-Americans. This was not a seminal change but it was indicative of the schisms that developed in the community. With time, the civil rights movement was pushed off of the front pages and King began to lose the dominant influence he once had.

Sadly, the violence of that era resulted in the assassination of Martin Luther King Jr. in Memphis in 1968; with his death the civil rights movement lost its most eloquent spokesperson. Although the movement never again achieved the prominence that it had during the early years of his leadership, what he had begun was unstoppable and gradual improvements in civil rights continued in the decades after he died.

With the right to vote, blacks began to be elected as mayors of major cities in both the North and the South. With their election, education improved, housing improved, and employment improved in the black community. Every occupation was now open. Architects, airplane pilots, aviation mechanics, municipal employees, and countless other positions now began to take ability into consideration rather than continue the practice of automatically denying employment on the basis of race. Inequalities continued of course, but their prevalence waned from day to day as programs that were termed 'affirmative action' were put in place in an effort to increase the number of qualified blacks in all professions and jobs.

Perhaps the most evident change was the abolition of the daily indignities that had existed. There were no signs that dictated where one could eat or drink or go to the bathroom. Seats on theaters and busses were equally available to all; beaches were desegregated, as were schools and neighborhoods. Prejudice, discrimination, and segregation were by no means eliminated, but their most odious aspects were now illegal rather than legal and were being curtailed.

These changes were not just due to the efforts of the black politicians. With blacks now having the right to vote, white politicians were forced to compete for their vote by advocating the equal distribution of services for their black constituents. Middle class white citizens in the South who had been afraid to speak out in the past now openly advocated change. A dynamic had been put in place that can end only when full equality is reached.

Bert observed these changes with a keen interest but with minimal involvement. In 1976 he moved to a high-rise building in Newark. Every weekday for the next two years he was a familiar sight as he walked briskly through the lobby of his building and drove to his practice. At the age of 81, he finally retired from the practice of medicine and spent a great deal of time painting.

With the basic dignities of life being restored, the civil rights movement began to be more introspective. Efforts were made to recognize those who had contributed to the movement. February was designated as Black History Month so that the entire population could be made aware of the contributions of black Americans to society. Those white Americans who made the effort to be exposed to black history were amazed to realize how many inventions, how many historical deeds, how many heroic actions could be attributed to black Americans. Slowly the psyche of the country began to accept the fact that capabilities were not linked to color but to opportunity.

With the passage of time recognition began to be extended to Bert and Al. On September 22, 1979 they were given awards at the Smithsonian Institute in Washington D.C. and each was recognized as a 'Pioneer in the Field of Aviation'. Their pictures, along with a model of Bert's plane the Booker T. Washington, was put on display at the Smithsonian Air Museum and they were asked to donate some of their memorabilia to the museum.

Bert's contributions were also recognized in New Jersey. Early in 1984 the Newark Library held a reception and dinner in his honor. 1000 people including the mayor of the city were in attendance. The mayor spoke not only of Bert's pioneering efforts in flying coast-to-coast and throughout the Caribbean, but also of his dedication to the youth of the area and his willingness to speak at schools and churches in an effort to get young people interested in aviation as a career.

Also at that dinner was a representative of the Aviation Hall of Fame of New Jersey. He was fascinated to learn of the risks that had been taken in an effort that was not motivated by prize money or a desire for fame but by a desire to help an underprivileged group. At the dinner he asked Francis if she thought Bert would consent to being inducted into the New Jersey Aviation Hall of Fame. Francis agreed to raise the subject with Bert.

After discussing the suggestion, Bert commented to Francis on a theme he had covered with her before. There was no bitterness in his words but there was a sense of regret "At my age I do not need any recognition Frances. It's too bad that society wasn't willing to give blacks this type of acknowledgement forty or fifty years ago when it would have helped to improve the lives of so many. I can't help but remember that even though Newark gave us a big parade at the time, the local newspapers buried the story deep in the paper, probably because they did not want to give too much credit to blacks. I will agree to the event not because it will benefit me, but because the publicity may attract more young people to aviation and increase their awareness of the contributions of blacks. The more pride that they have, the more that they refuse to let themselves be limited, the sooner we will have true equality."

A meeting was set up for two nights later at which their visitor agreed to submit Bert to the board that decides on who is to be inducted. When they heard of his accomplishments, the board quickly agreed to make him one of the four inductees in 1984, the first black man to be inducted into the Aviation Hall of Fame of New Jersey, a museum located in Teterboro, New Jersey.

There were also less beneficent factors entering into his life. Bert's diabetes had limited his endurance for most of his adult life but the amazing control that he was able to achieve with diet alone spared him from any of the complications. Still, as the body ages, other things begin to go wrong. Cells lose their ability to repair themselves as anomalies develop in the mechanisms that perform those functions. Instead of creating healthy cells to replace the damaged ones, the body can, at times, create an array of unhealthy cells that grow rapidly and overcome the individual.

In 1982 Bert underwent prostate surgery that showed an abnormal growth in his prostate. Added to the frailty of his age and the effect of his diabetes was the burden on a slowly growing tumor. However the gradual effect of this change in his health did not stop him from continuing to speak at churches and schools. In March of 1986 he agreed to speak to the students at a high school in Atlantic City.

Bert and Frances drove to an airport in Caldwell, New Jersey where a friend from Long Island had agreed to meet them so that they could fly to Atlantic City where he would speak. Before landing the plane, the pilot circled the city so that Bert could see the lights from the casinos that had grown up since his departure. The differences between the Atlantic City of 1934, the decaying city that he left in 1951, and the one of 1986 was astounding. Lights of every color blazed from the Boardwalk's casinos. The commercial area that had been in decline when he had left now looked vibrant and healthy.

After landing they went to the Technical Center where he was to talk. While speaking from a podium that included the mayor, Bert felt faint then sat back for several minutes before seeming to know where he was. That night was spent in a hospital where no specific cause for his momentary lapse was found. His body, imperfect as are all human bodies, had entered an accelerated rate of deterioration.

Man is unique in the degree to which he is able to reason. Yet despite that ability, few are rational when it comes to contemplating the end of their conscious existence on earth. Most of us expect to be aware when the end is near. We visualize ourselves expiring comfortably over the course of a relatively brief period, surrounded by friends and family, capable of tying up any remaining loose ends. Then, when all is in order, we will say goodbye and exit peacefully.

In fact, many of us, like Bert, will slip away over a period of weeks, somewhat aware of who we are, where we are, who we are with, but totally unaware that the journey is almost at an end. So it was that although Bert recognized Francis and spoke with her, he was not really aware of what was happening to him. Instead of reminiscing with her, he seemed to put his energies into resisting the invisible enemy that was attacking his body at a molecular level. Often he clenched his teeth and refused to nourish his nemesis even though this act simultaneously denied the healthy portion of his body of its own vital needs.

All that he had put off doing was left undone. Memorabilia that were to be donated to the Smithsonian and to Tuskegee Institute remained unsorted in boxes that might be discarded at some future date by an unthinking friend or relative or, more likely, by an uncaring stranger. He did not relay any last minute instructions nor did he have the self-awareness that would have allowed him to proudly recall his exploits or mentally re-live the bittersweet loves of his life. The memories of his childhood that had been stimulated into a brief re-existence by the desert heat that prevailed while he was on his cross-country flight fifty-two years before had no trigger on this occasion. The dreams and the thoughts of a young boy standing on the dock in Port Antonio could not be conjured into being even though they still existed in the recesses of his consciousness. Then, in the dark hours of the morning, on May 6, 1986 at the age of 89, Bert's spirit soared into the skies that he had loved while his physical being remained in the world that he had striven to change. His dreams and thoughts were lost forever as will be, someday, yours and mine.

On May 10th, Trinity Cathedral on Broad Street in Newark was filled to capacity with those who came to pay their respect to the man who helped to open up aviation to those of color, who promoted inter-island relationships in the Caribbean, who donated his expertise, time, and money to the poor, who encouraged the young not to be restrained by prejudice, and who worked in many ways for the cause of civil rights.

Honors had been bestowed on Bert in the past and new ones were added after his death. The Negro Airmen International, an organization formed to recognize the accomplishments of black pilots, created an Albert E. Forsythe Chapter in New Jersey. That organization later split and the Forsythe Chapter joined the offshoot, the Black Pilots Association.

In 1998 the Black Pilots Association decided to recreate the cross-country flight that Bert and Al had made in order to honor their accomplishments. The Hackensack, New Jersey Postmaster, William Stevens, worked with the United States Post Office to recognize what that trip had meant to black aviation by issuing a commemorative cachet after the completion of the flight.

This flight was not designed to be an exact re-creation. The decision was made to include only thirteen airports on the westbound trip and eight on the eastbound trip. The airports were not identical to those used in 1933 since many that the pair had used then were no longer in existence. The westbound flight began in Atlantic City on November 4, 1998 and ended in Burbank, California on November 7, 1998. The return trip to Atlantic City was concluded on November 17th.

Most segments of this re-creation utilized different pairs of aviators so that a large number of black fliers could be involved in recognizing the efforts of Bert Forsythe and Al Anderson. Their respect was emphasized by including Bert's wife Francis as a passenger on the first leg out of Atlantic City, and on the last leg back in. Had Bert been involved, he would have been extremely proud of the qualifications of those who participated.

For example, Leslie Morris, a retired airline pilot and controller, and Jan Fearance, a college student, completed the last leg of the trip west and began the first leg of the return trip to the east. Their histories typified what Bert had hoped to accomplish with the flights that had been undertaken despite the significant risks that their journey produced on many occasions. Because of their efforts, a black man had applied for, was hired to, and had retired from a well paying position in the air as a pilot for a large airline and on the ground as a controller.

At the other end of the chronological spectrum, a black college student could easily train in the United States to be a pilot. He did not have to travel to Canada like Hubert Julian or to France like Bessie Coleman or to search, like Al, and find a German aviator at a small U.S. airport who would be willing to teach him. He could receive a license without ever suffering the insult of being denied the opportunity merely because he, like a majority of the world's inhabitants, possessed a visible variation in the depth and degree of the pigments that are present in skin of all healthy humans. Neither a dangerous flight nor a demonstration under a gauntlet of dogs, fire hoses, and hostile policemen had been needed in order for them to be granted the simple rights of a citizen.

A large group was on hand to greet the plane as it landed in Burbank. The landing strip, the nearby facilities, and the advanced aircraft that were parked nearby were nothing like what Bert and Al had found on their touchdown 65 years before. The short rough airstrip had been replaced by a long concrete tarmac. Ground control relied on two-way radios that could warn the aviators to avoid any inclement weather, and radar that could guide the plane in flawlessly. The planes parked on the tarmac included sleek, powerful corporate and private jets that contained all of the comforts of home and were vastly superior in technology to the low horsepower, small, Spartan, single engine plane to which Bert and Al had entrusted their lives. Huge airliners passed overhead on their way to the major airport nearby that had replaced the rudimentary one that they had landed on. Changes were everywhere.

The group that had assembled at the airport included several representatives of the Tuskegee Airmen, the Black Pilots Association, local branches of the NAACP and the Urban League, and Glendale Postmaster Andy O'Connell. In addition, there were two of the four children of his brother Roger--his niece Mary Ann Forbes and the nephew who had been given Bert's name, Dr. Roger Albert Forsyth.

The part of the family tree that was Bert never produced a new branch. Nevertheless, his genes live on in the remaining branches--his nieces and nephews and their children and their children's children. The two helices of DNA that had intertwined to create Roderick, Lord and Prince of Denmark in 400 A.D., or perhaps those from Fearsite the Good around the time of Christ, had entered into new combinations over a period of 60 generations or more with helices from Turkestan, Germany, Denmark, France, Scotland, America, Africa, India, and unknown others to produce the current descendants—descendants that were fortunate to live in a time period and a society that was beginning the process of replacing a legal policy of discrimination based on an individuals color, with laws that promoted diversity--a prelude to establishing a general attitude of indifference to color.

Unlike Bert, most of these descendants will not be recorded in history. They can however celebrate the accomplishments of their progenitors and strive to develop the traits, such as Bert's tenacity, that they have inherited. Many of us, if we are lucky, will be exposed to the knowledge of at least five generations within our family. We know ourselves and our siblings, we know our parents and their siblings, we know or have heard of our grandparents, we will come to know our children and our grandchildren. If we are wise, we will respect those who came before, avail ourselves of their knowledge, strive to reach our full potential, and make our knowledge available to those who follow after us.

The time for the arrival of the plane that was participating in the recreation came and went as day slowly turned into dusk and then abruptly became night. With the loss of the weak pre-winter sun, the Southern California landscape that had been artificially converted into a vegetation-filled oasis experienced its customary precipitous twilight drop in temperature as the naturally rocky terrain began to dissipate the heat accumulated throughout the day. The waiting group began to pace back and forth and cast an eye to the terminal where hot coffee was available. A mild unease developed as the minutes passed and everyone wondered if there had been some miscalculation or some mishap that had caused the flight to be cancelled.

Earlier word had reached the airport that the flight would experience a one-hour delay. A delay that stretched into night would have meant an automatic cancellation in the time period that Bert flew in. Now delays were of minimal consequence since the current planes all had landing lights, as did all runways. Even though the revised departure time of the current flight had precluded a daylight arrival, technology permitted the modern aviators to ignore the restrictions that had governed the fliers sixty-five years before.

The concern about the late arrival eventually evaporated as a tiny speck appeared in the sky, descended, touched down, and then taxied along the runway towards the waiting crowd. The single engine plane that was small enough to seem like a toy when compared to those nearby would have seemed like the Concorde had it been compared technologically to the Fairchild that Bert and Al had flown.

When the pilots alighted, they gave an interview to *The Los Angeles Times* in which they expressed deep admiration for the courage of the two fliers who had crossed the country in a plane that was very flimsy, contained minimal equipment, and was not backed up by ground support. Then, as Bert and Al had done sixty-five years before, they attended a dinner in their honor. The flight was not as momentous as it had been in 1933, the reception was less impressive, but the occasion was significant for the changes that it highlighted. The fact that these changes were taken for granted by the participants was significant in and of itself.

With the cultural attitudes that prevailed in the 1930's, very few, if any, females or Hispanics would have been in attendance at that reception. Now, in the late 1990's, they were represented in sex and ethnicity neutral numbers that simply mirrored their prevalence in the population. Moreover, in making the reservation at the restaurant, no thought had to be given as to whether or not the color of the participants would make them acceptable as customers. The green of the currency with which they paid the bill was the only color that counted. These changes would have been considered momentous sixty-five years ago but were invisible in the current society.

The next day the two pilots took off for Oakland on the first leg of a return trip that would take ten days. For the last segment of the flight into Atlantic City, Gary Brooks, a New Jersey State Trooper, and Richard Freeman, a retired fireman, were at the controls. At the time of Bert's flight, blacks in these two occupations would have worked in segregated units and would have found it almost impossible to obtain a pilot's license. The forces that Bert and Al had helped to set into motion had produced the desired results.

A month after the return to Atlantic City, on December 9, 1998, a flight was made from Atlantic City to Tuskegee to commemorate the christening of the Booker T. Washington. Bert was recognized for the years that he had spent there as a student and for the efforts that he had made over the years on behalf of the Institute. Al was recognized for his years of service as chief flying instructor. In their honor the Institute allocated space for their memorabilia at the Daniel (Chappie) James Facility.

Then on February 6, 1999, during Black History Month, The United States Post Office issued a cachet in further honor of Bert and Al. The cachet included a brief monograph about their exploits, the postmarks of the cities that had been visited on the re-creation flight, the signatures of the fliers who participated, a picture of Forsythe and Anderson. Some included a stamp honoring Bessie Coleman, the pioneer black aviatrix who had preceded Amelia Earhart by two years and confirmed, through her death, that the flights of the "Pride of Atlantic City" and the "Booker T. Washington" and been high risk ventures.

The Albert E. Forsythe Chapter of the Black Pilots of America continues to meet regularly. Every year it takes some high school students to Florida and exposes them to aviation so they can see the opportunities that are available to them. They, like students at a commemorative school, are probably only dimly aware of the person for whom the chapter is named. They may know some of the simple facts such as the dates of his exploits, but it will be impossible for them to know the essence of the individual without some knowledge of the times in which he lived, the obstacles he faced, and the experiences that gave him the determination to risk his life for a cause.

By chronicling Albert Ernest Forsythe, we remind ourselves of the way the world was and the risks and the sacrifices that were made in order to improve it. This helps us to realize that each one of us should be willing to continue the process of passing on a better world to the subsequent generation.

ILLUSTRATIONS

ORDER FORMS

Email orders: www.blackflight.org
Postal orders:. AllCourt Publishing
P.O. Box 491122
Los Angeles CA 90049

Name _____
Address _____
City _____ State____Zip_____
Country _____
Telephone (   )_____
Email _____

Enclose check or money order or credit card number
Visa   Master card   Optima Amx Discover
Card # _____
Name on Card _____Exp. Date_____

....

Email orders: www.blackflight.org
Postal orders: AllCourt Publishing
P.O. Box 491122
Los Angeles CA 90049

Name _____
Address _____
City _____ State____Zip_____
Country _____
Telephone (   )_____
Email _____

Enclose check or money order or credit card number
Visa   Master card   Optima Amx Discover
Card # _____
Name on Card _____Exp. Date_____

ORDER BY MAIL

You may use the order form on the page preceding.

Books ordered by mail can be returned for a full refund of
the purchase price if dissatisfied for any reason.

If ordered as a gift, include the name and address of the
recipient if direct shipping is desired.

Visit our website at :   www.blackflight.org
Email: allcourtpublishing@yahoo.com

Add 7.5% sales tax for orders shipped to California
Add $4.00 for shipping and handling for U.S. sales
   or $8.00 for international sales